D1075000

ArtScroll® Series

Rabbi Nosson Scherman / Rabbi Gedaliah Zlotowitz
General Editors
Rabbi Meir Zlotowitz ז״ל, *Founder*

DOVI STEINMETZ EDITION

אֲנִי מַאֲמִין / Ani

Published by

ARTSCROLL
Mesorah Publications, ltd

Maamin

A Mission for Life

UNDERSTANDING
RAMBAM'S 13 IKKARIM
AND BRINGING THEM INTO OUR LIVES

RABBI YECHEZKEL ELIAS

FIRST EDITION
First Impression … May 2022
Second Impression … May 2022

Published and Distributed by
MESORAH PUBLICATIONS, LTD.
313 Regina Avenue / Rahway, N.J. 07065

Distributed in Europe by
LEHMANNS
Unit E, Viking Business Park
Rolling Mill Road
Jarrow, Tyne & Wear NE32 3DP
England

Distributed in Australia & New Zealand by
GOLDS WORLD OF JUDAICA
3-13 William Street
Balaclava, Melbourne 3183
Victoria Australia

Distributed in Israel by
SIFRIATI / A. GITLER — BOOKS
POB 2351
Bnei Brak 51122

Distributed in South Africa by
KOLLEL BOOKSHOP
Northfield centre, 17 Northfield Avenue
Glenhazel 2192, Johannesburg, South Africa

ARTSCROLL® SERIES
ANI MAAMIN
© *Copyright 2022, by* MESORAH PUBLICATIONS, Ltd.
313 Regina Avenue / Rahway, N.J. 07065 / (718) 921-9000 / www.artscroll.com

ITEM CODE: ANIH
ISBN 10: 1-4226-3164-8
ISBN 13: 978-1-4226-3164-5

Typography by CompuScribe at ArtScroll Studios, Ltd.
Printed in the United States of America.
Bound by Sefercraft, Quality Bookbinders, Ltd., Rahway NJ

*W*ith heavy hearts and gratitude to Hashem for the *zechus* of having had him for 21 years, we dedicate this *sefer* to the memory of our beloved son

Dovi Steinmetz ז"ל
יששכר דוב בעריש ז"ל
בן שלמה עמו"ש
ל"ג בעומר תשפ"א

*H*e was one of the *kedoshim* of Meron, and he was a *kadosh* in life, as well. He was a wellspring of *simchah*, *yiras Shamayim*, and concern for everyone around him, not only in our family, but wherever he was.

Dovi had no desire to be a leader, but all his *chaveirim* were his followers. When someone needed something or something had to be done, it was Dovi who noticed and did it. In the *beis medrash* he was alive in the *sugya*, enthused by a *pshat* in *Tosafos* and a good *sevora*, and the pride of his Rosh Yeshivah. In Mir-Yerushalayim, he was the provider for others, arranging a *chavrusa*, a *dirah* and a bed, finding a Shabbos host for *bachurim* who couldn't do it themselves.

"You don't have a bed? No problem. Here's a bed." It was Dovi's own bed — and he walked 10 minutes in sub-zero weather to a place to spend the night.

He had such a wonderful future ahead of him, but Hashem had other plans. We are left with his inspiring legacy and wonderful memories of a son who lived too few years, but filled them with *kedushah* and accomplishment.

This *sefer* is a fitting tribute to Dovi. Whoever learns from it will come closer to Hashem, as he strived to be all his life.

Shloimi and Feige Steinmetz
and family

שמואל קמנצקי
Rabbi S. Kamenetsky

2018 Upland Way
Philadelphia, PA 19131

Home: 215-473-2798
Study: 215-473-1212

חלה יום שישי פ' עקב

לכבוד בני הנעלה ר' יהבקאל שליט"א
שלו'

הנני לברק כשב על ספרו על עני מזומין
אשר לברק רב ולשפו' הלכות דהלכ"ה
נעשה לאור' שלא ברדה שני ולשראל יתחזקו
הלכמ"ר דהלכ"ה.

כ יגו ספרו וידעכ כל לדורות אמני ולשר
יימן הקהל' יתחזקן רבו להושל פאותם
שלום על יפם לברק קי ישראל דהלכ"ה להושלום,
דורש שלומה ועל טוב'

בע"ה

שמעון אלסטער
ברוקלין, נ. י.

ג' אדר ב' תשפ"ב

כבוד הרב הגאון ר' יחזקאל עליאש שליט"א

ראיתי קונטרוס אשר הוא ספר שלם וגדול
מחמת יוקר ועומק - לבאר וללבן יסודות
ועיקרי הדת כמבואר ברמב"ם - דברים
שנאמרו ונכתבו בטוב טעם ודעת באופן
ברור ומבואר ובלשון צח - וגם יתבארו
עניני יסודות אלו לכל לומד ומעיין - ומעלה
גדולה היא לכל בן ישראל שאינם רגילים בעניינים
כאלה מחמת ילמוד ויקבעו בנפשם ובמחם
אמונתם - וגם לאלו הרגילים בידיעות אלו
העניינים יוסיפו בהירות בהם - ובמיוחד
בדברים כאלו השייכים ביסודו של עולם והדת
חלקים דעשרה דיבורים עיון הדק היטב ומוכח
גם ללימוד מן המקור - שהוא דברים אלו קנויים
ומחוברים בקריאה בעצמו

בהוקרה לכבוד התורה
ולכבוד המחבר
שמעון אלסטער

בס"ד

אליהו ברודנא
RABBI E. BRUDNY
1752 East 18 Street
Brooklyn, NY 11229

אור ליום ג' ה' ניסן תשלב ס"ק

כאתי את החוברת "על נאמ"ן" א' ענג' אמונה
ורבים מ'ל הדברים של אמונה שחיבר הרב הגאון
הר' אורבין והר' אגהר חזק אנא תמודות ה' יתבקשלט
שלום על שם בן יכ' ר' שיע ראש הכל צ' מאמנ'ירו'

הנה שליח' והקונטרט כ'ל הוא אלון ונעש
בדבר' שרם מא'ר'ת ואמאחים ו'ע ההם של
על תמ"ת כבעג "וצ'ק באומנ'ו יחית"
ליבר מאת דב החוברת רום מ'לא תומהר של ס"ו.

כפ' הקבב ההות ס'פ' גבר' הב'נ'ן
ע'נ' הבומת וע'ל' ב'וין
ואין ספק כ' חב הבעלא
וצ'נין ה'ק'ם שרב ב'ר הבלזקל והבפסוג
שא'מ כהאחר ה'א'ר ע'נ'נ' בדבר' חש'כם
והדבשקים ותנ'י לברכו ש'בק לו הקפת
בכתבנו' זאות באתעונ ה'ת'רה וה'את לב'ט' ק'רת
ולהפמ'ית התונם הת'קא הק'דשא
ובארא בא'מ' ס'ם

וליה תו להוקנ'ס'

Rabbi Y. Wosner

5748 Hutchison Ave.

Montreal, P.Q. H2V-4B6

(514)2743414 – Fax (514)274-4940

יוחנן סג"ל ווֹאזנער

ראב"ד דחסידי סקווירא

ודומ"ץ דקהל תולדות יעקב יוסף

דחסידי סקווירא מאנטריאל

בס"ד

יום רביעי לסדר משבצות זהב, ה' אדר א', תשפ"ב לפ"ק

בשמחה רבה ראיתי גליונות של הספר החשוב "אני מאמין"

שחיבר מע"כ ידידי הרה"ג רבי יחזקאל שניאור הלוי עלִיאש שליט"א

בן ידידי הרה"ג רבי דוד מאיר הלוי שליט"א ראש כולל כתר תורה במאנטריאל יע"א

והוא ספר נפלא על כל הי"ג עיקרים של "אני מאמין", שנאמרו בשיעורים בבית המדרש

"מתיבתא ראשית חכמה" בנשיאות ידידי הגה"צ רבי יעקב אליהו אונסדארפער שליט"א.

ונלמדו לע"נ הבחור היקר מו"ה יששכר דוב בעריש ע"ה

בן יבלחט"א ידידי הרה"ח רודף צדקה וחסד ר' שלמה שטיינמץ שליט"א

שעלה ונתעלה לגנזי מרומים יחד עם מ"ה נשמות הקדושות והטהורות בשריפה אשר שרף ה'

באסון הנורא אשר ארע באתרא קדישא מירון בעידנא קדישא של התנא האלוקי רשב"י זי"ע ועכי"א

ל"ג בעומר ח"י אייר תשפ"א ת.נ.צ.ב.ה.

ויזכה ידידי הר"ר שלמה שליט"א ומשפחתו שתחי' לראות נחת מכל יוצ"ח, ברוב שמחה והרחבת הדעת.

ואברך את כבוד מע"כ המחבר שליט"א שיזכה להוסיף לזכות את הרבים מתוך שמחה ונחת, מתוך הרחבת הדעת עד שנזכה במהרה לישועתן של ישראל בב"א.

וע"ז באתה"ח ידידם

יוחנן סגל ווֹאזנער

JACOB E. UNSDORFER

RABBI OF

FIRST MESIFTA OF CANADA
MONTREAL, CANADA

יעקב אלי' אונסדארפער

רב ור"מ

מתיבתא ראשית חכמה
מאנטריאל יצ"ו

בס"ד

יהא רעוא אי"ה אדר כאשר עברו הלך הרבה
ר' תתקבל הנ[...] הלוי שליט"א שליט"א
דן הרב הגאון הא[...] הלה יויב ה' ב[...] שליט"א הלוי שליט"א
היא גדול כבר מרנה הנדבה שלם ותודה
שאמרו להודות לאור טפר[...] לעולם והיו כאור
הביא מרחו[...] כליד שם יצאת לאשרו דברי
ואם ייוו עלי כמה נ[...] דלאם אלא רייו
ולשנו ה[...] נעמו הברית אן נפש זוה
אני לרחמנות הלה הבחור עובר ו[...] זוה
גלזה ל[...] ה[...] תדבא מיכן דיך רייש שה
כן נא[...] ידני רוזף לדבק ואסד ה' שלזוה שישוף אוך
הגו יודבר הידר ה' יצחק כהל' יודל אונף
שתלוי ומגדל' כ[...] שדליך לאיסיך ל[...]ב ג
ישכת התארב להרבל שלה [...] רבוד הלוק
ועזבה גו[...] יצ לברכה שלה כפוב גוזל לדך כבוו

החווים ומכין המזרב ה' כבוד תולד'
יצד[...] אלי' חזים דיא[...]אר

פנחס ירמי' נפתלי רבינוביץ

בן כ"ק מרן אאמו"ר זצללה"ה

מביאלא

בית שמש

יום החמישי בשבת כ"ג אדר ראשון

לסדר אלה הדברים אשר צוה ה' לעשות אותם תשפ"ב

שלומים מרובים מערי יהודה וירושלים, בחודש אד"ר אשר שמחה מרבים, אל מע"כ ידידנו עוז רבות בשנים, וליבו פתוח כאולם לכל דבר שבקדושה, להרבות במפעלת צדקה וחסד, בסבר פנים יפות, ה"ה הרה"ח ר' **שלמה שטיינמץ** שליט"א, עם כל בני ביתו האהבים שיחיו, בטוב ובנעימים.

ישמחו השמים ותגל הארץ, ובתוכם תגל נפשי ולבבי, בשמעי שמועה רחוקה, אבל קרובה ללבי, במפעלכם הכביר, להחדיר י"ג עיקרי אמונה בישראל קדושים, הקטנים עם הגדולים, שהם מאמינים בני מאמינים, מורשה מאבותינו – אברהם יצחק ויעקב הקדושים, וגורמים לתענוג ונח"ר בעולמות העליונים, האיך התחתונים דרי מטה אשר נתונים למכים ולמבך סובלים ומיחדים שמו הגדול תוך עם סגולה באמונה.

וכל זאת לעילוי נשמות של בנך היקר, העומד על זכרונו תמיד, ילד שעשועים, וכולו מחמדים **יששכר דוב בעריש** ע"ה, שנתעלה בגנזי מרומים יחד עם מ"ה נשמות קדושות אשר שרף ה' באתרא קדישא מירון סמוך ונראה למקום מנוחת עמודא דנהורא התנא האלקי רשב"י זי"ע ועכי"א, ל"ג בעומר ה'תשפ"א.

ואתה ידידי ר' **שלמה** השכלת לאור כגיבור חלציך להסתר תחת כנפי השכינה ולהתחזק ב"ה' אלוקינו שהוא המלך טוב ומטיב לכל ומאיתו לא תצא הרעות, י"ג בגימטריא אחד, רומז על הוי"ה אחד, וגם בגמיטריא אהבה שרומז על מאה"כ **אהבתי אתכם אמר הוי"ה** (מלאכי א', ב) – בכל עת ועונה, **וכמאמר הצדיקים** זי"ע על כל המעשים הוא תירוץ על כל הקושיות – דכשאיש ישראל זוכר דהקב"ה הוא קל אדון על כל אדון אזי מקבל הכל באהבה ובאמונה.

וכנודע בשער בת רבים האיך שאאמו"ר הק' מביאלא זצללה"ה – עורר לשנן הי"ג עיקרי אמונה בכל עת מצוא, שלא להיות בכלל תוכחת הנביא, **אבדה אמונה ונכרתה מפיהם** (ירמיהו ז', כח) דיכולים לאבד האמונה באם אין משננים תמיד בחשק ובהתעוררות, **כי קרוב אליך הדבר מאד בפיך ובלבבך לעשותו** (דברים ל', יד).

ומיגו דזכי לנפשיה זכי נמי לאחרינו הפצת ברחבי תבל י"ג עיקרי אמונה מסוף העולם ועד סופו נתחזקו ישראל ב"י"ג עיקרי אמונה שהוא מיסודת אומתנו, ואין אומתנו אומה אלא באמונתם בחשיכה כבאורה – ובכנוסה האקדמות 'עבידנא ליה חטיבא בדנח ושקעתא'.

ועל של עתה קראתי גליונות מהספר **'אני מאמין'** ונתעטר בהסכמת ידידי הגה"צ המפורסם ר' **יוחנן הלוי ואזנער** שליט"א – ראב"ד דקהל סיקווירא, ליקוט משיעורים שנאמרו במתיבתא ראשית חכמה בנשיאות ידידי הגה"צ ר' **יעקב אליהו אונסדארפער** שליט"א ע"י הרה"ג ר' **יחזקאל שניאור הלוי עליאש** שליט"א.

וספר זה לא נצרכה להסכמתי הענ יה, אלא לברך את המחבר שיזכה לברך על המוגמר בלא מכשולות ולהוסיף תמיד בזיכוי הרבים מתוך הרחבת הדעת.

ויעזרנו השי"ת ויברך את בית ישראל ובתוכם ידידי עוז ר' **שלמה** שיחי' עכב"ב, בחודש אשר שמחה וששון ליהודים, ישמח את בני ישראל הנאמנים, ואך טוב וחסד ירדפהו כל הימים, נחת מכל יוצ"ח בבריאות גופא ונהורא מעליא, וגם יגון ואנחה, ויחיש עת ישועה, ותושעין בנחת ובשובה עת ישמע קול מבשר ואומר ואולי לציון צריינה.

הכותב לכבוד התורה ולומדי'

פנחס ירמי' נפתלי הלוי בהרה"ק מביאלא זצ"ל

Rabbi Dovid Elias

1905 Barclay Ave.

Montreal, QC H3S 1J4

(514) 342-8359

דוד מאיר הלוי עליאש

ראה"ב כתר תורה ראדאמסק

מונטריאל

(514) 341-4616

בס"ד

ברוכים לציון

יום ה' ל"הוציא אסר נרבק לאאמ" "ועבר ה' לעצוף

"ויצגב ה'וח והסירות וגו' לחזק כ' ג' הוו הכלא'ת תכא'ת גאול וזו
היצא לנעסב א'ן צוי' " הרי לצדוקת הלאונים א'נג מנק'את
דיצ'עא ברינון, אלא דוקא בהחזרת ה'דצ'ה בנ'שה, ואחייע ול
לבי, כאק דלאג' נפרד מן הצבא צצאגו

וגא כן, אם נצבה השאה והתעצום דטוגע פר' עצוגת דן י'ה'
הרב יתקפל לשלוו ה'ן, חזור שלם שאיקה ונגראמת, גהדה'ר,
להסביר, ובם לאאה'ש על יוצדע הלאונ'ך עד ש'ה' אק'ין נפש' לא
הצוק'א דהב. ואבן ס'גר ל צקר ויצר ל אבון ב'ום כשא'ה,
דל'אומ'ה ועדונ'ם דאפה דרוה, דה'רגת ודאה'ם לפפלא'ל, עד
ש'ה'ו הצא'ק'ם אות'ם ואובג'ם לצל אא וגאו בצד, דפ

ונפ'אקן, שעשע אמל' בע'וגבק חזב, לה'אמד' ספר'ם אחר'ם ולא'ש'ם
לצאב אב חר'ת לאק געא'ה והחזה, ואאק נחב מפ' יוא ה'קר'ת
ר'הב עד וד'ף טנא' - ודכפבא ח'צק הלאונ'ך נצבר כלן'ח
ל'אגא בק'א לאשר ה'צ' (לאק'וס הלא'ע אק'ו") "א'ן הצצ'א אצנ'נת
גע'ם בשוב הלאונ'ך" דדיא אצגא 31 בארה ד'א'ע אגע/

אזרק גלון'

בנה אקבר הלו' אל'אש

Table of Contents

Publisher's Preface

We are proud to present this volume to the Jewish public, for many reasons. The importance of the subject speaks for itself. Rambam formulated the essentials of Jewish belief. Many people can recite all thirteen and many have committed the Thirteen Ami Maamins to memory. Others are familiar with them thanks to the *Yigdal* poem, which is recited by many as part of Shacharis.

But what are these principles in breadth and depth? How do they apply to our everyday lives? How can we explain these profound philosophical concepts in terms that are enlightening to scholar and layman alike?

This volume accomplishes precisely that. It illuminates the Thirteen Principles clearly, engagingly, and accurately. For that we are grateful to **RABBI YECHEZKEL ELIAS**, a newcomer to our roster of exceptional authors, who does justice to this very important topic. There is no doubt that readers will be grateful to Rabbi Elias for enriching their understanding of our eternal faith. It is a particular pleasure to publish Reb Yechezkel's work for another reason. His grandfather, the great thinker and educator Rabbi Yosef Elias, was an early friend and mentor of our work. His Pesach Haggadah, published in 1977, was one of our first volumes. It is still a bestseller and many people still consider it the finest

English-language Haggadah. We also had the honor to publish children's books by Reb Yechezkel's grandmother, Mrs. Miriam Elias. So it is a particular pleasure to welcome another generation of this distinguished family to our roster.

The dedicators of this volume are **MR. and MRS. SHLOIMI STEINMETZ** of Montreal. They are beloved members of their community, and with good reason. They are gracious, generous, and sensitive. They raised a family that notices others, shares a good word, a needed compliment, an encouraging smile. Their home is open to worthy causes and their Shabbos table is a model of *hachnasas orchim*. Mr. Steinmetz exudes emunah and good cheer; to know him is to be inspired with faith that Hashem has a plan for us all.

The Steinmetzes dedicate this volume to their son, **YISSOCHOR DOV BERISH Z"L**, who was taken from this world in the Meron tragedy, on Lag B'Omer, 5781. Very few 21-year olds have such an impact on their *chaveirim*. Dovi was the one they turned to, for *p'shat* in Tosafos, to arrange a trip, find a *chavrusa* or a bed. His roshei yeshivah were proud to call him their *talmid*. May Hashem bring *nechamah* to his parents and siblings. And to Klal Yisrael.

We are sure this volume will bring its readers closer to Hashem by elevating their faith and strengthening their knowledge of the principles of our faith.

Rabbi Gedaliah Zlotowitz / Rabbi Nosson Scherman

Iyar 5782 / May 2022

Acknowledgments

*L*ag B'Omer 5781 was a night that will forever be etched in the memory of Klal Yisrael at large, and of Montrealers in particular. The Montreal community is a warm one, with strong overlap among the broader *tzibbur*, even those not necessarily of the same shuls, schools, or social circles. As word of the tragedy in Meron hit, the entire community, alongside Jewry worldwide, was devastated. When news spread that Dovi Steinmetz *a"h* hadn't been heard from, it suddenly became personal. And when daylight broke and Dovi's fate became clear, the community mourned.

Within the broader community, the *kehillah* of Mesifta Reishis Chochma has a unique place, much like a family unto itself. It is here that the Steinmetzes call home, and it is here that served as the launching ground for R' Shloimi Steinmetz's message of emunah, which he has taken to Jews around the globe.

"Gadol hame'aseh" — great is he who gets things done, and in this regard, credit goes to R' Nuti Meyer, who proposed and arranged for me to deliver a series of *shiurim* in Mesifta Reishis Chochma on the meaning and message of the Ani Maamins. The *shiurim* met a warm reception, and they continue today, as we move through additional topics. It is these *shiurim* that formed the nucleus of this work. May Hakadosh Baruch Hu grant R' Nuti continued success

in all his efforts and endeavors, alongside all the other devoted *shiur* members and the entire Mesifta family.

The next step along this road was my introduction to ArtScroll, thanks to Klal Yisrael's "man of the people," R' Yisroel Besser. Beyond making the initial connection, he has been a steady guide throughout the process. R' Gedaliah Zlotowitz has been remarkable to work with, believing in this project from its inception, and providing constant encouragement, support, and guidance to help this project realize its fullest potential. Rabbi Nosson Scherman graciously provided sage counsel, guiding this work through numerous complexities. Mrs. Heimowitz has invested much time and effort in this manuscript, editing, revising, and polishing each chapter. Above all is my appreciation for her navigating the maelstrom with imperturbable professionalism. An additional review by Mrs. Dick helped raise the caliber of the entire work.

Though at the time of this writing I am but midway through the publishing process, I have been most impressed by the professionalism of the ArtScroll staff, and at the same time, their continually demonstrated desire to ensure the finished product respects and embodies the vision of the author. In particular, R' Mendy Herzberg in skillfully guiding the process, and R' Eli Kroen in producing yet another beautiful cover, have both amply demonstrated the worthiness of their reputations. I am also grateful to Miss Chanie Ziegler, who paginated the book, Mrs. Esther Feierstein, who proofread, and Mrs. Estie Dicker, who entered the corrections. All are professionals of high order.

Throughout my work on this project, many friends and associates have proofread, critiqued, and commented on various chapters and thoughts, and to all of them I am indebted, none of them more so than R' Nachi Hofman. He has painstakingly read and reread every single word of the manuscript, animatedly debating the value of each thought as well as the impact it will have on the reader. He's been a dependable, insightful, and passionate sounding board, for which I am truly grateful.

There is an additional person without whom this work would look very different. He's a man who is willing to step up and take the responsibility to ensure things get done. His tremendous heart is exceeded only by his adamant insistence on remaining out of the public eye. One day, I'm sure, we'll finish Shas together.

Over the past number of years, I have been privileged to be a member of Kollel Keser Torah of Montreal, a vibrant *makom Torah* under the leadership of my father, R' Dovid Elias, and R' Osher Mintz. Being a part of such a *beis midrash*, with the ability to engage in learning with *avreichim* of such elevated caliber, is something for which I am most appreciative.

The value of having a rebbi who knows you well is truly inestimable. It means having someone to turn to throughout the ups and downs of life, a guide to consult with at times of uncertainty, and a watchful eye to ensure that you keep to the proper path. I am privileged to have learned under the Rosh Yeshivah, Rav Shimon Alster *shlita*, and am most fortunate to have kept up that bond ever since. In this work in particular, I have availed myself of the Rosh Yeshivah repeatedly, and the Rosh Yeshivah has been most generous, reading through much of the work, helping to clarify and fine-tune the intricacies of the various concepts, and discussing guidelines and specifics of what should and should not be included. Indeed, although for the most part I did not cite the Rosh Yeshivah specifically, I feel the Rosh Yeshivah's fingerprints are on each and every chapter. May Hakadosh Baruch Hu grant him bountiful *berachah* to continue guiding *talmidim* for decades to come.

In my years living in Eretz Yisrael, I was *zocheh* to develop a most wonderful and unique connection with Rav Yitzchok Berkovits *shlita*, rav of Minyan Avreichim of Sanhedria Murchevet, among many other positions. In addition to being a world-renowned *posek*, Rav Berkovits is a priceless voice of keen, penetrating *machshavah*. Many of the ideas elaborated upon here were either based upon or molded by the countless insights I've heard from him over the years.

Words cannot begin to express man's debt of gratitude to Hakadosh Baruch Hu, but nor can man afford to be silent. Beyond the *siyata d'Shmaya* I have experienced in every aspect of life in general, and in every step of this work in particular, there are two particular gifts for which I am overwhelmingly grateful. Each child is born into a specific family, and Hakadosh Baruch Hu was kind enough to place me in a home characterized not only by a passion for Torah and *yiras Shamayim*, but dedication and responsibility to bringing Torah to the *tzibbur* as well. My grandfather, Rabbi Yosef Elias, a venerated principal for close to sixty years, served first in Yeshiva Beth Yehuda of Detroit, and subsequently in the Rika Breuer Teachers Seminary in New York. His father, Dr. Markus Elias, served as headmaster both in Furth and in Frankfurt, and continued as a *mechanech* in New York. Their light continues to illuminate the way, serving as inspiration not only to our family but to their thousands of students across the globe. This passion has been carried on through the generations, by my father, a long-serving rosh kollel, and my mother, a veteran *mechaneches* of international acclaim, and in turn by their children, who serve as dynamic *klei kodesh* and pillars of their respective communities.

As I slowly progressed through this work, I felt an acute sense of loss for my grandfather *a"h*. I would have loved to have had the opportunity to work through these topics with him and benefit from his vast knowledge and depth of understanding of these concepts in particular. In my humble attempt to carry forward his vision and legacy, I can only hope that this work is one that he would find meritorious.

I must add that as this work goes to publication, I find myself privileged to be forging the next link in the relationship between ArtScroll and the Elias family. Beginning with my grandfather's authorship of *The ArtScroll Haggadah* and continuing with a number of other works, it's a relationship that has spanned nearly half a century, and will *b'ezras Hashem* continue to flourish in the years to come.

Additionally, I feel a tremendous sense of *hakaras hatov* to Hakadosh Baruch Hu for His having gifted me opportunity after opportunity to reach out to Klal Yisrael and share Torah in a wide range of settings, with people across the spectrum of age, background, and education. Whether through intricate *shiurim* in Gemara, basic lessons in *parashah* and halachah, or this very work, I have been *zocheh* to be able to teach and to edify, and hopefully raise people's level of Torah understanding and connection, in ways I would not have imagined. I can only ask that Hakadosh Baruch Hu continue to grant me these opportunities, so that I may one day be truly able to say, "*Kinor ani leshirayich.*"

My parents have invested so much and provided invaluable guidance over all these years. May they be *zocheh* to see the great *nachas* of their children and grandchildren developing into all that they aspired for them to be.

My in-laws have always stood there in firm support and encouragement. They have been there for us and continue to be there in so many ways, doing whatever they possibly can to ensure our greatest *hatzlachah*. May Hakadosh Baruch Hu grant them the joy of their children's success, and may they reap incredible *nachas* from the entire family.

My wife stands behind this and every other endeavor of mine, and my gratitude to her is beyond overwhelming. May we see continued *berachah* and *hatzlachah*, and enjoy *nachas* from our children, raising them to be true *ovdei Hashem*.

I conclude with gratitude to Hakadosh Baruch Hu שׁשָּׂמַת חֶלְקִי מִיּוֹשְׁבֵי בֵּית הַמִּדְרָשׁ, along with my sincere *tefillah* that this continue to be my role — to be devoted to the learning and teaching of Torah, and that my children should follow in this path as well. May we, together with all of Klal Yisrael, be vouchsafed to see the coming of Mashiach speedily.

Yechezkel Elias

Iyar 5782

෨෨

Additional Acknowledgments

*T*hroughout a very dark and difficult year, the light of emunah, faith, has illuminated our lives.

My wife Feige and I are grateful beyond words to the close friends who initiated the *Ani Maamin shiur* and website, and have been an incredible source of *chizuk* for us throughout, Moti and Elisheva Fischer.

The *shiurim* of Rabbi Yechezkel Elias have proven to be clear, informative, and inspiring. He eloquently speaks to both the mind and heart, inspiring his listeners and enhancing their emunah in a very real way.

We appreciate those who join the *shiur* — the *chaburah* who helped us encourage and spread the recitation of Ani Maamin in Dovi's *zechus* — who are doing their part to light up the world with emunah, as Dovi would have wanted.

May Hakadosh Baruch Hu grant fortitude to my wife — the heart of our family, a woman of such kindness and boundless devotion to her children, a woman who presides over a home of *tzedakah* and *chessed* with dignity and grace — and to our children. May we merit to live with emunah and always make Dovi proud, until we are reunited once again at *Techiyas HaMeisim*.

Shloimi Steinmetz

Introduction

*K*lal Yisrael is a nation of *maaminim bnei maaminim*, believers and children of believers. Emunah is the very fabric of who we are. The level of emunah of each Jew certainly varies, but regardless of background, education, or scholarliness, we all share a common core: the kernel of emunah at the center of our being. It's a voice telling us that there's a higher calling, challenging us to live up to our beliefs, and reminding us that an ever-present Higher Being is in control and always watching over us.

We have no shortage of works on emunah. From detailed philosophical discussions to passionate discourses warming hearts gone cold, and from ancient letters penned by Rishonim to far-flung communities to the audiovisual material of our contemporary leaders guiding us through our tempestuous times, we are blessed with a veritable cornucopia of resources in matters of emunah, suited to each level, each personality, and each station in life.

Of all these resources, certainly none is more iconic than the simple and powerful words of Ani Maamin. These Ikkarim, thirteen short, direct statements of creed, have been embraced by all of Jewry, finding their way into nearly every siddur and their place within every committed Jew.

What are these words of Ani Maamin?

The Ani Maamin Text

*T*he standard Ani Maamin text first appeared, to the best of our knowledge, in the mid-sixteenth century. (The earliest instance seems to be in a Prague siddur from 1536. Other early appearances are in a Mantua siddur from 1558, a Krakow siddur from 1578, and a Venice *machzor* from 1599.)[1]

Astoundingly, we have absolutely no information as to the identity of the author. Nevertheless, this text has gained near-universal acceptance and has been embraced by Torah giants and simple Jews alike. Many of our greatest leaders, such as the Chofetz Chaim, went as far as to urge its regular recitation. It is interesting to note that among Sephardic communities, a different version of the Ikkarim exists, varying significantly in wording but enumerating the same concepts.

Ani Maamin delineates thirteen distinct concepts, clearly following the path charted previously by the Rambam.[2] To appreciate the intent of the Ani Maamins, then, it is necessary to turn to the words of the Rambam himself, in his formulation of these thirteen precepts. That is the objective of this work.

The Rambam presented various fundamental tenets of the Torah worldview in his introduction to *Perek Chelek*, the tenth *perek* of *Maseches Sanhedrin*, within his *Pirush HaMishnayos*, a work he completed at the age of thirty, in the year 4248 (1168 CE). There, he delineates thirteen related but independent ideas that together form the foundation of Jewish belief. The Rambam establishes these fundamental principles as the basic hallmark of the observant Jew.

The Rambam concludes by urging the reader to acquire a thorough grasp of these concepts, and to review them repeatedly.

---

1. See *Kenishta* Vol. 4, p. 60.
2. Discrepancies between the Ani Maamin text and the Rambam's version do exist, however, and these are addressed in Appendix C. A poetic rendition of the Ikkarim appears in the hymn of *Yigdal*, which is typically recited before Shacharis. Appendix C examines this version as well.

Describing the prodigious efforts he invested in formulating these precepts, he cautions that if a reader casually presumes to have understood the full intent of these words after reading them "one or [even] ten times," he can rest assured that he has deluded himself.

This listing of foundational beliefs makes another appearance elsewhere in the Rambam. In his *Yad HaChazakah* (*Hilchos Teshuvah* Ch. 3), the Rambam enumerates various categories of nonbelievers, some labeled *apikorsim*, others described as *minnim*, and yet others classified as having forfeited their share in Olam Haba. Although he does not refer explicitly to "Ikkarim" or "Yesodos," the sum total of the various strains of heresy listed is thirteen, and their descriptions are largely in sync with the thirteen Ikkarim. Effectively, these two listings go hand-in-hand, with the *Pirush HaMishnayos* version detailing the thirteen fundamental beliefs, and the *Hilchos Teshuvah* version noting the legal effect of denying any of these thirteen.

In establishing these fundamental underpinnings of our belief system, the Rambam arrived at a total of thirteen concepts. Although some draw various correlations or attach mystical meaning to the number thirteen, a straightforward reading of the Rambam's words seems to indicate that he was not aiming to arrive at any specific number. Rather, having studied and deliberated upon the full body of the Torah's precepts, and whittling down his list of Ikkarim to include only the concepts that met his criteria, the resultant total numbered thirteen. The final number was therefore determined by the inherent role of these Ikkarim, not by a predetermined value.

Ikkarim: The Line of Demarcation

The Rambam establishes these Ikkarim as the defining qualification of whether one is "in" or "out" of Klal Yisrael:

וְכַאֲשֶׁר יַאֲמִין הָאָדָם אֵלֶּה הַיְסוֹדוֹת כֻּלָּם וְנִתְבָּרֵר בָּהּ בֶּאֱמוּנָתוֹ בַּהּ' הוּא נִכְנָס בִּכְלַל יִשְׂרָאֵל וּמִצְוָה לְאָהֲבוֹ וּלְרַחֵם עָלָיו וְלִנְהֹג עִמּוֹ בְּכָל מַה שֶּׁצִּוָּה ה' יִתְבָּרַךְ אִישׁ לַחֲבֵרוֹ מִן הָאַהֲבָה וְהָאַחֲוָה וַאֲפִלּוּ עָשָׂה מַה שֶּׁיָּכוֹל מִן הָעֲבֵרוֹת מֵחֲמַת הַתַּאֲוָה וְהִתְגַּבְּרוּת הַטֶּבַע הַגָּרוּעַ הוּא נֶעֱנָשׁ כְּפִי חֲטָאָיו אֲבָל יֵשׁ לוֹ חֵלֶק לָעוֹלָם הַבָּא וְהוּא מִפּוֹשְׁעֵי יִשְׂרָאֵל.

When one ascribes to all these foundational beliefs, and achieves clarity in his faith in Hashem, he enters the category of "Yisrael," and it is a mitzvah to love him, to show compassion to him, and to behave toward him in accordance with all the interpersonal commandments of Hashem, and with love and brotherhood. Even if someone committed all the sins he possibly could have, due to temptation or to being overcome by his base nature, although he will surely be punished for his sins, he nevertheless maintains his portion in the World to Come, and is categorized as a sinner within Yisrael.

Certainly, by virtue of Jewish birth or halachic conversion, one has full status as a Jew, and cannot lose that status no matter how egregiously he might stray from Jewish belief or observance. There are, however, distinct benefits to being classified as a member of Klal Yisrael's fraternity; these include eligibility for *tzedakah* and acts of *chessed*, as well as the right to having one's lost objects returned. Our obligations to our fellow Jew go far beyond our obligations to humanity at large. After all, we're family, and what wouldn't you do for family? This privileged status, however, is contingent upon a Jew's remaining a member of the "club." Yes, a person who opts out will technically remain a Jew nonetheless, but no longer will he be entitled to the unique benefits associated with being part of the family.

The Rambam also points to the guarantee that each Jew has a share in the World to Come. This, too, he says, is contingent upon belief in all thirteen of these precepts. By rejecting even one, a person inflicts incredible self-damage, causing himself to forfeit this basic portion of Olam Haba.

All about Foundations

*T*hroughout this work, the Ikkarim are referred to as foundational beliefs, rather than the more typical translation of "principles of faith," or the like. This reflects the Rambam's own choice of wording: "Yesodos" (albeit in Arabic). To understand this choice of wording, let's examine how the Rambam viewed these concepts.

The Rambam's establishment of thirteen Ikkarim was met in many circles with strong opposition. This pushback largely fell into two categories. One camp disagreed with the Rambam's methodology in selecting Ikkarim. What litmus test is to be used to determine whether the "Ikkar" tag is to be affixed to a particular concept? If an idea is exceedingly important, yet its removal would not cause the collapse of Torah observance, can this be called a primary belief? Further, many ideas are intertwined and overlap, and are difficult to categorize as distinct concepts. Essentially, this camp opposed not the concept of Ikkarim but rather the specific choice of ideas to be included in this listing. The second camp objected to the entire idea of Ikkarim, arguing that the concept of elevating specific mitzvos or beliefs above others is inherently flawed. We do not arbitrarily affix values to the words of Hashem, for every line and mandate of the Torah reflects Hashem's will and is absolutely incontrovertible. The deliberate demotion of even a single dictate of the Torah, no matter how insignificant it might seem, is enough to deem the denier a heretic.

How did the Rambam view these challenges?

The Rambam provides us with precious little insight into his thought process in evaluating and setting the parameters for the list of Ikkarim. As R' Yosef Albo points out in *Sefer HaIkkarim*, the Rambam's list includes several concepts that do not seem fundamental to the structure of Judaism. Furthermore, the second issue, that of the inherent problem of elevating certain aspects of Judaism to the status of Ikkarim, is particularly difficult to reconcile. The Rambam himself strongly censures those congregations that would deliberately rise for the Torah reading of the portion of the Aseres HaDibros, out of respect for their significance. His opposition related specifically to the potential risk that the public would perceive certain elements of belief as superior to others, which would lessen the rest of Torah in their estimation. Attuned as he was to this concern, how did the Rambam proceed to do something seemingly similar, with the Ikkarim?

The Rambam very clearly avoided mentioning any specific mitzvos in his Ikkarim. He does not classify belief in these Ikkarim as a positive mitzvah, nor does he label failure to believe in them as a violation of any mitzvah (although belief in most of the Ikkarim is indeed a fulfillment of certain mitzvos). The Rambam, apparently, was not coming to promote the value of any particular mitzvah over any other. His objective with the Ikkarim was to highlight specific tenets that are fundamental to the belief system of a Jew, whether or not believing in them constitutes a mitzvah.

In fact, throughout his delineation of these thirteen tenets, the Rambam studiously avoids the word Ikkarim altogether, choosing to label them "foundations": "*hayesod harishon*," "*hayesod hasheini*," and so on. Why?

The term "*ikkar*" connotes something primary, which means that there is something secondary as well. There is an *ikkar*, which is of great importance, and there is a *tafeil*, which is of lesser import. The term *yesod*, foundation, carries an entirely different meaning, however. A foundation is not of greater or lesser importance than any other element of an edifice, but serves as the underpinning upon which the entire building stands. The foundation is not the building. It doesn't boast ornate lobbies, magnificent moldings, or even expansive office space. It's actually not a part of the building that you see at all — but without it, the building crumbles, because the foundation is what sets the parameters of just what can be built, and in what manner. In our lives, what this means is that these thirteen ideas are not the mitzvos. These are not the actions that you'll see a Jew engage in each day. Rather, they're the backdrop, the story behind all the mitzvos, and the ideals that lay the framework for the mitzvos.

Consider any mitzvah at all. Whether it's the obligation to shake a lulav and esrog on Succos or the prohibition against eating species of grasshoppers, if you try introducing these laws to a nonbeliever, you're bound to be bombarded with a slew of questions: Who composed these rules? Further, whoever did so did not relate them to me directly, so how do I know that you're conveying them accurately? In the global scheme, what's the point of these rules, anyway? And what's in it for me personally? Addressing these questions sets the stage for all the commandments that follow.

This, then, is the Rambam's goal — to give us the framework for our mission in this world. The Ikkarim form the backbone of everything we do. I do mitzvos because I have complete emunah in these ideals, which tell me that Hashem runs the world, and that He has assigned me a mission, one that I can be assured has been conveyed to me accurately. Once I have internalized the basic setup of life, understanding why I'm here and what purpose I must strive for, I can then turn to the commandments of the Torah, which are the specifics of how I am to carry out my mission.

This understanding would help mitigate the first issue as well, that of what is an Ikkar and what is not. The Rambam did not seek to assign elevated status to any specific ideals within Judaism. He was looking for concepts that are valuable specifically in regard to laying the groundwork for our everyday mitzvah observance. These thirteen Ikkarim all affect the way we go about each and every mitzvah in our lives. That is what this work seeks to highlight and clarify.

෨෧

In his introduction to *Emunos V'Deios*, Rav Saadiah Gaon offers a number of reasons why people might reject belief in Hakadosh Baruch Hu. One catalyst for this rejection, he writes, is when an audience hears a lecturer expounding on the basics of emunah in an unsatisfactory manner. Since they assume the fault lies with the material rather than with the speaker, they proceed to categorically discard our entire belief system.

For fear of engendering such a reaction, I wish to clarify what the purpose of this work is and what it isn't.

Defining the Objective

For every teacher preparing to enter the classroom, and every lecturer about to deliver a speech to a crowd, the primary question is not what one wishes to say, but what the audience is capable of hearing. What is their level of erudition? What is their vernacular? What will resonate and effect the desired result, and what will simply bounce off their ears and be an exercise in futility? Only after expending the effort to understand the audience can one hope to edify and elevate people to higher levels of understanding.

Presenting a written work to the public is a particular challenge in this regard, as it involves standing up to speak before a crowd the author will never see. It's the classroom of Klal Yisrael at large, a kaleidoscope of many shapes, sizes, and flavors. As such, the goal here was to address a specific need, a heretofore unfilled void where much can be achieved. In aiming for a receptive audience, I have chosen to address those who seek greater clarity in their existing beliefs, and wish to add meaning to the life they already live. This focus means that we will approach each of the Ikkarim with two basic goals. The first is to explain the concept behind each Ikkar in a concrete manner, delineate the parameters of the Ikkar, and highlight the significance it carries in our belief system. The second is to demonstrate how we can incorporate these Ikkarim into our lives, using them to guide our decisions and way of life.

Would some readers benefit from a lengthy philosophical analysis of the Rishonim's varying opinions of what emunah entails, and the intricacies of the Acharonim's treatment of this topic? Certainly. For these, however, there are many fine works available geared to the more academically inclined. For the majority of growth-oriented Jews today, however, tools for enhancing practical understanding and application carry far more relevance and meaning.

There is, however, a far more fundamental reason why I have taken this approach, one that reflects the intent of the Rambam himself. Remarkably, throughout his enumeration of the thirteen Ikkarim, the Rambam provides absolutely no theological or rational proofs of these concepts. His corroboration of these ideas follows one criterion only, that being the sourcing of these Ikkarim to *pesukim* in the Torah. The proof of Hashem's omnipresence is that the Torah says so. The proof that there are consequences for our actions is that the Torah says so. And, most remarkably, the proof that Moshe Rabbeinu's words of prophecy are unassailable is that the Torah itself says so.

This approach seems confounding. How can the Torah prove its own veracity? After all, one who disregards the Torah in the first place certainly wouldn't be impressed. Furthermore, the Rambam himself, in both *Yad HaChazakah* and *Moreh Nevuchim*, presents compelling logical proofs of many of these very concepts. Why, then, would he choose here to ignore those proofs and rely on Torah citations alone?

The answer must be that the Rambam wasn't speaking to non-believers, nor was he seeking to convince those who wished to undermine the pillars of Judaism. He must have been aiming, rather, for the believing but perplexed Jew. A prime example of this audience is the beleaguered communities of Yemen, whom the Rambam addresses in his *Iggeres Teiman*. Beset as they were with terrible hardships, these communities were a prime target for malicious individuals who attempted to ensnare them with all sorts of heretical claims. Some claimed that Hakadosh Baruch Hu had chosen to downgrade the Jewish people from their special status; others falsely asserted that they were the long-awaited Mashiach. The Jews of Yemen believed, but did not know what to believe. The Rambam stepped into this void, clarifying the Torah perspective and bolstering these communities in their loyalty to Hakadosh Baruch Hu and His Law.

The same, we can say, was the Rambam's intention with these thirteen Ikkarim. The Rambam did not come to debate philosophy. He was not attempting to disprove Christianity, Islam, or any other belief system. He was talking to the believing Jew, taking him by the hand and saying, "This is what your Torah says. This is what the Torah you believe in expects of you." For this audience, demonstrating clear Torah sources is sufficient. Yes, there is certainly a need and a place for the proofs and intense philosophical reasoning found in other works, including those of the Rambam himself, but apparently, that was not his goal in his presentation of the Ikkarim.

Similarly, our goal in this work is to stay true to this mandate. We begin with the assumption that the reader already accepts the Torah as axiomatic. Our mission now is to clarify what the Torah expects us to believe, what the fundamental principles of our faith are, and how these beliefs affect our lives.

To this end, this work follows some basic guidelines:

- The emphasis of this work is on understanding the message the Rambam seeks to convey. Each chapter is designed to convey one clear, contained thought. In our discussion of Ikkarim that convey numerous messages, the messages are kept distinct, in separate chapters.

- While the chapters are interrelated, and certainly enhance the understanding of other chapters, each one is freestanding and can be understood without the reader having seen any other chapter.

- In the context of addressing certain ideas, additional

questions often arise. Where these could be addressed without breaking the flow of thought, they were included within the relevant chapter. Where more elaboration was required, the discussions were placed in the Appendix section.

- It is important to note that while there may be views mentioned in the Rishonim that differ from those expressed by the Rambam in his discussion of the Ikkarim, this work does not aim to present these differing opinions, but rather to clarify the Rambam's position alone. Furthermore, to keep the focus streamlined, a number of advanced questions on the Rambam's words were not directly addressed in this work. These issues were not disregarded, though. The astute and erudite reader will be able to discern within the subtleties and nuances of the text that many of these opinions were implicitly addressed.

A Final Note

*H*aving laid the framework for what this work aims to accomplish, one point remains to be addressed.

It's a beautiful day at the Grand Canyon. The radiant sunlight shimmers over the magnificent landscape, as three men who've just arrived engage in a heated discussion on the lookout point where they are perched. The first begins the discussion by noting the ease with which he exchanged the monotonous cityscape of New York for this remarkable scenery. Morning in the city, afternoon at the canyon, no problem at all. Hop on a flight and you're right there. His friend disagrees. To get here, he trekked through the countryside for two months, slowly making his way across the continent. He's seen mountains, he's seen prairies, he's seen glistening skyscrapers and rolling farmland. After such a journey, he claims, he can truly appreciate the stunning beauty of the canyon. Back and forth they argue, as they debate the merits of their respective journeys: a simple, direct, and obstacle-free trip, or a prolonged, challenging trek that offers much more context? Each makes his case compellingly. The third arrival, however, has nothing to offer to this discussion. The only thing on his mind is the glory of the canyon itself. How did he get there? A good question, but that's not his concern. He's soaking in the view, savoring the sight he'll take with him for life.

The question of what is the proper roadmap to emunah is one that evokes passionate responses among Klal Yisrael. Some advocate a simple emunah *peshutah* approach, maintaining that we must accept our fundamental beliefs without question and place firm trust in our ancestors and the heritage they've conveyed. Others insist that true emunah requires a thorough analysis of our beliefs, and that we must question and assess how we've arrived at the truth of these beliefs, and how they stand in contrast to the flawed beliefs of other religions.

Let me be very clear from the outset. This work does not deal with this debate of emunah *peshutah* versus *chakirah*. How the Rambam established these specific points as Ikkarim is not the focus of this work, and the reader who seeks this information can surely benefit from the available bountiful material that addresses this topic. The starting point of this work is that these Ikkarim are absolute, incontrovertible truths. The job at hand, then, is simply to illuminate these principles, clarifying the message of each Ikkar and its practical application. In short, I am not here to discuss how to get to the Grand Canyon; I am here to describe the Grand Canyon.

אני מאמין

Ani Maamin

THE THIRTEEN PRINCIPLES OF FAITH

1   I am steadfast in my absolute belief that the Creator, blessed is His Name, creates and guides all that is brought into existence, and that He alone created, creates, and will create all that is created.

2   I am steadfast in my absolute belief that the Creator, blessed is His Name, is One, and there is no uniqueness like His in any way, and He alone is our Lord, forever having existed, existing, and continuing to exist.

3   I am steadfast in my absolute belief that the Creator, blessed is His Name, has no corporeality, nor can any material qualities be ascribed to Him, and there is nothing at all that is comparable to Him.

4   I am steadfast in my absolute belief that the Creator, blessed is His Name, is the very first and the very last [to exist].

5   I am steadfast in my absolute belief that the Creator, blessed is His Name — to Him alone is it appropriate to pray, and it is inappropriate to pray to any other.

6   I am steadfast in my absolute belief that all the words of the prophets are true.

7   I am steadfast in my absolute belief that the prophecy of Moshe Rabbeinu, may peace be upon him, was true, and that he was the archetype of prophets, both those who preceded him as well as those who followed him.

8   I am steadfast in my absolute belief that the entire Torah now in our hands is the same one that was given to Moshe Rabbeinu, may peace be upon him.

9   I am steadfast in my absolute belief that this Torah [that we have received] will never be exchanged for another, nor will there be another Torah from the Creator, blessed is His Name.

10   I am steadfast in my absolute belief that the Creator, blessed is His Name, knows all the deeds of human beings and all of their thoughts, as the verse states (*Tehillim* 33:15): *He Who fashions their hearts together, Who comprehends all their deeds.*

11   I am steadfast in my absolute belief that the Creator, blessed is His Name, rewards with good those who observe His commandments, and punishes those who violate His commandments.

12   I am steadfast in my absolute belief in the coming of Mashiach, and even though he may delay, nevertheless I await his arrival each day.

13   I am steadfast in my absolute belief that there will be a resurrection of the dead at the time that such will be the will of the Creator, blessed is His Name. [By doing so], His perception [in our world] will become exalted for all eternity.

שְׁלֹשָׁה עָשָׂר עִקָּרִים

א אֲנִי מַאֲמִין בֶּאֱמוּנָה שְׁלֵמָה, שֶׁהַבּוֹרֵא יִתְבָּרַךְ שְׁמוֹ הוּא בּוֹרֵא וּמַנְהִיג לְכָל הַבְּרוּאִים, וְהוּא לְבַדּוֹ עָשָׂה וְעוֹשֶׂה וְיַעֲשֶׂה לְכָל הַמַּעֲשִׂים.

ב אֲנִי מַאֲמִין בֶּאֱמוּנָה שְׁלֵמָה, שֶׁהַבּוֹרֵא יִתְבָּרַךְ שְׁמוֹ הוּא יָחִיד וְאֵין יְחִידוּת כָּמוֹהוּ בְּשׁוּם פָּנִים, וְהוּא לְבַדּוֹ אֱלֹהֵינוּ, הָיָה הֹוֶה וְיִהְיֶה.

ג אֲנִי מַאֲמִין בֶּאֱמוּנָה שְׁלֵמָה, שֶׁהַבּוֹרֵא יִתְבָּרַךְ שְׁמוֹ אֵינוֹ גוּף, וְלֹא יַשִּׂיגוּהוּ מַשִּׂיגֵי הַגּוּף, וְאֵין לוֹ שׁוּם דִּמְיוֹן כְּלָל.

ד אֲנִי מַאֲמִין בֶּאֱמוּנָה שְׁלֵמָה, שֶׁהַבּוֹרֵא יִתְבָּרַךְ שְׁמוֹ הוּא רִאשׁוֹן וְהוּא אַחֲרוֹן.

ה אֲנִי מַאֲמִין בֶּאֱמוּנָה שְׁלֵמָה, שֶׁהַבּוֹרֵא יִתְבָּרַךְ שְׁמוֹ לוֹ לְבַדּוֹ רָאוּי לְהִתְפַּלֵּל, וְאֵין לְזוּלָתוֹ רָאוּי לְהִתְפַּלֵּל.

ו אֲנִי מַאֲמִין בֶּאֱמוּנָה שְׁלֵמָה, שֶׁכָּל דִּבְרֵי נְבִיאִים אֱמֶת.

ז אֲנִי מַאֲמִין בֶּאֱמוּנָה שְׁלֵמָה, שֶׁנְּבוּאַת מֹשֶׁה רַבֵּנוּ עָלָיו הַשָּׁלוֹם הָיְתָה אֲמִתִּית, וְשֶׁהוּא הָיָה אָב לַנְּבִיאִים, לַקּוֹדְמִים לְפָנָיו וְלַבָּאִים אַחֲרָיו.

ח אֲנִי מַאֲמִין בֶּאֱמוּנָה שְׁלֵמָה, שֶׁכָּל הַתּוֹרָה הַמְּצוּיָה עַתָּה בְּיָדֵינוּ הִיא הַנְּתוּנָה לְמֹשֶׁה רַבֵּנוּ עָלָיו הַשָּׁלוֹם.

ט אֲנִי מַאֲמִין בֶּאֱמוּנָה שְׁלֵמָה, שֶׁזֹּאת הַתּוֹרָה לֹא תְהֵא מֻחְלֶפֶת וְלֹא תְהֵא תוֹרָה אַחֶרֶת מֵאֵת הַבּוֹרֵא יִתְבָּרַךְ שְׁמוֹ.

י אֲנִי מַאֲמִין בֶּאֱמוּנָה שְׁלֵמָה, שֶׁהַבּוֹרֵא יִתְבָּרַךְ שְׁמוֹ יוֹדֵעַ כָּל מַעֲשֵׂה בְּנֵי אָדָם וְכָל מַחְשְׁבוֹתָם, שֶׁנֶּאֱמַר: הַיּוֹצֵר יַחַד לִבָּם, הַמֵּבִין אֶל כָּל מַעֲשֵׂיהֶם.

יא אֲנִי מַאֲמִין בֶּאֱמוּנָה שְׁלֵמָה, שֶׁהַבּוֹרֵא יִתְבָּרַךְ שְׁמוֹ גּוֹמֵל טוֹב לְשׁוֹמְרֵי מִצְוֹתָיו וּמַעֲנִישׁ לְעוֹבְרֵי מִצְוֹתָיו.

יב אֲנִי מַאֲמִין בֶּאֱמוּנָה שְׁלֵמָה, בְּבִיאַת הַמָּשִׁיחַ וְאַף עַל פִּי שֶׁיִּתְמַהְמֵהַּ, עִם כָּל זֶה אֲחַכֶּה לּוֹ בְּכָל יוֹם שֶׁיָּבוֹא.

יג אֲנִי מַאֲמִין בֶּאֱמוּנָה שְׁלֵמָה, שֶׁתִּהְיֶה תְּחִיַּת הַמֵּתִים בְּעֵת שֶׁיַּעֲלֶה רָצוֹן מֵאֵת הַבּוֹרֵא יִתְבָּרַךְ שְׁמוֹ וְיִתְעַלֶּה זִכְרוֹ לָעַד וּלְנֵצַח נְצָחִים.

THE THIRTEEN PRINCIPLES OF OUR FAITH
ACCORDING TO SEPHARDIC CUSTOM

Behold! I believe with complete faith in the thirteen principles of the Holy Torah:

1 That the Holy One, Blessed is He, exists and watches over everything;

2 He is One;

3 He has no body nor form of a body;

4 He precedes all precedents;

5 There is no service to any besides Him;

6 He knows the thoughts of mankind;

7 The prophecy of Moshe Rabbeinu, peace be upon him, and of the other prophets is true;

8 Moshe Rabbeinu is the master of all the prophets;

9 The Torah was given from heaven;

10 It will never change, Heaven forbid;

11 The Holy One, Blessed is He, punishes the wicked, and rewards the righteous with good.

12 Messiah, the king, shall come;

13 and the dead will be resurrected.

May it be Your will, Hashem our God and the God of our forefathers, that you compel our inclination to Your service all the days of our lives, forever, Amen. So may it be [Your] will.

שלשה עשר עקרים לאמונתנו
כמנהג הספרדים ועדות המזרח

הֲרֵי אֲנִי מַאֲמִין בֶּאֱמוּנָה שְׁלֵמָה בִּשְׁלֹשָׁה עָשָׂר עִקָּרִים שֶׁל הַתּוֹרָה הַקְּדוֹשָׁה:

א שֶׁהַקָּדוֹשׁ בָּרוּךְ־הוּא מָצוּי וּמַשְׁגִּיחַ.

ב וְהוּא אֶחָד.

ג וְאֵין לוֹ גוּף וְאֵין לוֹ דְמוּת הַגּוּף.

ד וְשֶׁהוּא קַדְמוֹן לְכָל־קְדוּמִים.

ה וְאֵין עֲבוֹדָה לְזוּלָתוֹ.

ו וְיוֹדֵעַ מַחְשְׁבוֹת בְּנֵי אָדָם.

ז וּנְבוּאַת מֹשֶׁה רַבֵּנוּ עָלָיו הַשָּׁלוֹם, וּשְׁאָר הַנְּבִיאִים, אֱמֶת.

ח וְשֶׁמֹּשֶׁה רַבֵּנוּ אֲדוֹן לְכָל־הַנְּבִיאִים.

ט וְשֶׁהַתּוֹרָה נְתוּנָה מִן הַשָּׁמַיִם.

י וְשֶׁלֹּא תִשְׁתַּנֶּה בְּשׁוּם זְמַן, חַס וְשָׁלוֹם.

יא וְשֶׁהַקָּדוֹשׁ בָּרוּךְ־הוּא מַעֲנִישׁ לָרְשָׁעִים וּמְשַׁלֵּם שָׂכָר טוֹב לַצַּדִּיקִים.

יב וְשֶׁיָּבֹא מֶלֶךְ הַמָּשִׁיחַ.

יג וְשֶׁהַמֵּתִים עֲתִידִים לְהֵחָיוֹת:

יְהִי רָצוֹן מִלְּפָנֶיךָ ה' אֱלֹהֵינוּ וֵאלֹהֵי אֲבוֹתֵינוּ, שֶׁתָּכֹף יִצְרֵנוּ לַעֲבוֹדָתֶךָ כָּל־יְמֵי חַיֵּינוּ תָּמִיד, אָמֵן, כֵּן יְהִי רָצוֹן:

What Is Emunah?

*A*ni maamin.
　　Two words.
　　Two powerful words.
Words that have carried us through the generations. Words that reverberate through times of trial and tribulation, words that resonate through times of joy. These words accompanied us in the cattle cars rolling to the concentration camps, and these words will continue to sustain our nation as we joyously go out to greet Mashiach.

What do these words mean? The generic translation is "I believe." In turn, then, the question becomes, what is belief? Although the word "belief" seemingly connotes firm conviction, our usage of the word indicates otherwise. If I see the sun's rays shining through my window, I don't *believe* it's daytime outside; I *know* it's daytime outside. We employ the term belief when we talk of something that we expect or strongly assume to be true, yet lack absolute knowledge of: *I believe it will rain today. I believe he's stuck in traffic. I believe this business venture will be successful.* A strong conviction, perhaps, but far short of absoluteness.

Since the term belief has thus been undermined, let's move away from this term and reassess the word "*maamin.*"

"*Maamin*" finds root in the word "emunah," and *ani maamin* is essentially a declaration that I possess emunah. Emunah is a term associated with religious faith in general, or specific tenets of religion in particular. Yet we find numerous variations of the word "emunah" throughout Tanach without the slightest religious connotation. Let's look at a few of these examples.

אֻמָּן, **Uman** — A worker skilled at his craft is referred to as an *uman*, as in the phrase: מַעֲשֵׂה יְדֵי אָמָּן, *handiwork of the craftsman* (*Shir HaShirim* 7:2). An *uman* can be a talented tailor, a competent carpenter, or a deft computer technician. If he's proficient at his job, he's an *uman*. Does skill have any connection to faith?

אֹמֵן, **Omein** — Esther is an orphan, whose father passed away prior to her birth and whose mother died during childbirth. Mordechai takes Esther into his home, raising her as his own child. In filling the role of a parent, he is described as an *omein*, a variant of the word "emunah." Similarly, the term *omein* in reference to parenting appears in the Torah as well: כַּאֲשֶׁר יִשָּׂא הָאֹמֵן אֶת הַיֹּנֵק, *as a nurse carries a suckling* (*Bamidbar* 11:12). What does childrearing have to do with faith?

אָמֵן, **Amen** — Each time we hear a blessing recited, whether on food, on the performance of a mitzvah, or on anything else, we respond with the word "amen." This variation of the word emunah is clearly intended as an affirmation, proclaiming our agreement with whatever statement was just made. In this sense, amen connects directly with the word *emes*, truth. But this link is quite puzzling. Truth and faith do have a point of intersection, as a person would likely choose to believe in something due to its apparent truth. Yet the two are not the same: Truth is a statement of fact — either it's true or it's false, while faith is a personal statement of where I've chosen to lay my beliefs. If I would simply want to affirm that the blessing is true, wouldn't it be more appropriate to respond, "*Emes!* True," instead of declaring amen?

The key to finding the common denominator here lies in one more intriguing appearance of the word "emunah."

Turning back in history to the Jews' triumphant exit from Mitzrayim, we encounter Amalek, who, fearing the ascendance of this upstart nation, launches an attack. During the ensuing battle, Moshe Rabbeinu, along with Aharon and Chur, ascends to a peak overlooking the battlefield, where Moshe prays intensely for victory. With Aharon and Chur at his sides giving support, Moshe raises his hands heavenward, and remains in that position the entire day, until the victorious culmination of the battle. The Torah describes Moshe's effort with the words: וַיְהִי יָדָיו אֱמוּנָה עַד בֹּא הַשָּׁמֶשׁ, *And his hands were* emunah *until the sun set* (*Shemos* 17:12).

Outstretched? Yes. Upraised? Yes. But emunah? What does that have to do with Moshe's hands?

Clearly, emunah here does not translate as faith. Rather, it refers to an ironclad immovability — something constant, absolute, and faithful. Moshe Rabbeinu's hands did not budge. For an entire day they were locked in one position, steadfast and unyielding. Something that does not change is something with emunah.[1]

Let us return to the other examples.

An expert at his trade is called an *uman*. Why? In truth, any worker can get the job done in a random instance. A novice tailor might construct the perfect suit on occasion. The difference between the skilled professional and the amateur is that the professional doesn't get it right once in a while — he gets it right every time. Give him a task, and you can count on consistently good results.

Similarly, someone raising a child is referred to as an *omein*, because the basis of inculcating our children with proper values is providing them with a clear, unwavering system of principles. If we impart mixed messages, and the definitions of right and wrong that we convey are constantly changing, then we ultimately fail in our *chinuch* responsibility. An *omein* is consistent.

It is this concept of unequivocal fact that we proclaim each time we answer amen. Take the example of someone reciting a blessing on an apple. He picks it up and loudly proclaims his awareness of and appreciation to the One Who created fruits of the tree:

---

1. This explanation is based on *Collected Writings*, Rav Shamshon Raphael Hirsch, Vol. 7, Part 2, Chapter 1.

borei pri ha'eitz. He is referring to Hashem's creation of trees and fruits right now. The one who responds amen does not merely say "*emes*," for to do so would merely be signing on to the exact same statement. By saying amen, he takes his declaration to a whole different level. It's not just true now; it's always true. And it's not a matter of happenstance — it's a truth that is so basic and intrinsic that there is no other way. Fruits of the tree always were and always will be in existence only by virtue of Hashem's creating them. It's an absolute, immutable fact, with no other option. This is the power of amen.[2]

Hakadosh Baruch Hu's Emunah vs. Our Emunah

Hakadosh Baruch Hu is described repeatedly as possessing emunah, such as in the *pasuk*: חֲדָשִׁים לַבְּקָרִים רַבָּה אֱמוּנָתֶךָ, *They are new every morning; great is Your faithfulness* (*Eichah* 3:23). This does not mean He has faith, for in whom would He possibly have faith? Rather, it's a matter of His being eternally reliable, the epitome of unwavering constancy. Since He is not dependent on anything, nothing about Him ever changes, and whatever knowledge we possess with regard to Him is absolutely true yesterday, today, and tomorrow. Likewise, we refer to Him as *ne'eman* — faithful — to allocate proper reward and consequence, such as in the *pasuk*: וְיָדַעְתָּ כִּי ה' אֱלֹהֶיךָ הוּא הָאֱלֹהִים הָאֵל הַנֶּאֱמָן שֹׁמֵר הַבְּרִית וְהַחֶסֶד לְאֹהֲבָיו וּלְשֹׁמְרֵי מִצְוֹתָיו לְאֶלֶף דּוֹר, *You must know that Hashem, your God —*

---

2. Chazal tell us (see *Nazir* 66:2) that in some respect, answering amen is greater than reciting the actual blessing. If the amen response were merely an agreement to the blessing, this would be difficult to understand. Equal, perhaps, but why greater? With the above approach, however, this becomes quite understandable. The one reciting the blessing is laying down the fact as it is here and now. The one responding amen, however, takes that statement and applies it to every time and place.

He is the God, the faithful God, Who safeguards the covenant and the kindness for those who love Him and for those who observe His commandments, for a thousand generations (Devarim 7:9). It's not that He has faith, it's that He is absolutely faithful. If he guarantees something, nothing will disrupt it. Reward will happen. Punishment will happen. He won't have issues delivering due to traffic or a typhoon. He doesn't become tired and He doesn't have moods. He is the ultimate Guarantor, because nothing can shake Him or get in His way.

This knowledge provides us with a powerful tool. We can count on Him as an absolute fixture even when events in our lives might seem to be going haywire. He's right there. He's watching me. He cares about me. He will take care of me. He always has and He always will, whether I'm paying attention or not. Hakadosh Baruch Hu is described as a *tzur*, a rock. He is the one constant, the one entity I can go through life banking on, resting assured that He will never change. All that we are told of Him will forever remain absolutely true.

Our emunah is the other side of the coin. It's not about Him, it's about us and our approach to Him. Our approach must be one of absolute constancy as well. It's easy to believe in Him when everything is smooth and easy, but what about when the lights go out? Can I still hold firm in what I believe when everything seems dark?

There are things in life we absorb as innate truths. We consider these truths so inviolable that we would never stop to question them, and we simply proceed through life taking them as a given.

Let's give this a tangible application. Take a piece of paper and crush it into a ball. Now, with your eyes firmly closed, toss this paper ball directly upward toward the ceiling. Pause. With your eyes still closed, I ask you, where is it now? Undoubtedly, you will confidently respond that the paper ball is now resting on the floor. Are you sure? Are you positive? You threw it upward and yet you believe that ultimately it traveled in the exact opposite direction. Throwing something to the right will never cause it to land on your left, so why do you think that throwing the paper ball up will result in its descent? How can you make this statement with such absolute confidence?

The answer, of course, is that you firmly believe in the power of gravity. It's something you've experienced since your days of throwing cereal off the booster-seat tray. Everything falls down. Do you understand why the law of gravity holds true? Can you provide a precise explanation of how attraction of mass works? If you're part of the vast majority of the world's populace, you safely traverse day after day of your life without thinking twice about these intricate questions. Yet you are eminently confident that gravity is a true force, and you can confidently predict the outcome of your paper ball experiment whether your eyes are opened or closed. It's a fact. Period.

Emunah is our gravity. Our belief in Hashem and His running of the world is a fact. Period. At times I can see His orchestration of events clearly and at times my vision is clouded; at times I can explain things, and at times I stand in silence. Regardless, I live my life confidently, with absolute certainty that this fact is true and inviolable.

David HaMelech extols the singing of Hakadosh Baruch Hu's praises according to the paradigm of לְהַגִּיד בַּבֹּקֶר חַסְדֶּךָ וֶאֱמוּנָתְךָ בַּלֵּילוֹת, *To proclaim by day your kindness, and your* emunah *by night* (*Tehillim* 92:3). Day and night are used here as metaphors, referring to two overarching categorizations of periods in life.[3] Day refers to when times are good. It's sunny, it's bright, life is great, and I can see clearly where matters are headed. Night, on the other hand, refers to the darker times of our lives. Matters are difficult, perhaps gloomy. Our situation lacks clarity, and we have difficulty knowing where to turn. David HaMelech provides us with the recipe for maintaining a true connection to Hakadosh Baruch Hu in both types of periods. By day, when things are clear, and you see and understand the wonderful things Hashem does for

---

3. See *Sefer HaMeshalim* by Rav Yosef Giktilaya, Ch. 97.

you, talk about it: לְהַגִּיד בַּבֹּקֶר חַסְדֶּךָ. Tell the world and tell yourself. When it's nighttime, and you're having difficulty seeing His helping hand, remain steadfast in your emunah: וֶאֱמוּנָתְךָ בַּלֵּילוֹת. Hold strong in your knowledge that nothing has changed, and that He is right there. The facts you saw so often when times were light are just as true now as then. Don't change course. Just as Moshe Rabbeinu's hands held firm, in a state of constancy — emunah, you, too, can hold on unswervingly to what you already know, until daylight once again peeks over the horizon.

Let's take the gravity analogy a step further. How often do you think about gravity? Probably very rarely. Yet it's something you subconsciously factor into every moment of your life. You take a step? Your mind is anticipating gravity. You pass a plate of food? You are calculating the force of gravity. On one hand, you never think about gravity. On the other hand, you're always thinking about gravity. It's not a conscious thought, but it's a basic factor in everything you do. The emunah we maintain is much the same: It's not necessarily about sitting down and delving into philosophy, it's about factoring the truths we believe in into every element of our life.

When I decide which job to take, I do so against a backdrop of His running the world. When I make a medical decision, it's through the prism of His ultimate control and will. All decisions I make are within the range, scope, and possibilities that the rules of emunah dictate, because I understand that there is no option beyond these rules. Much as I can't entertain the idea that I might wake up tomorrow and suddenly float out of bed into the air, I can't entertain the possibility that I will control my health, wealth, or destiny on my own terms.

Ani maamin is a bold statement. It's a proclamation that rings out from our very essence, on two levels. One is that He will never change. He is absolute, dependable, and always there. The second is that I will not change. I hold the truths expressed in the thirteen Ani Maamins to be so deeply rooted that I will live with them every moment of my life, through light and dark, joy and sorrow.

Moving forward, we will come face to face with thirteen unique precepts. These are thirteen basic tenets, fundamentals of how the world operates. We express each one as a credo, with the words *ani maamin*. Each of these thirteen tenets is something I carry with me constantly, incorporating it into the very fiber of my being, so that it guides everything I do and every decision I make.

הָעִקָּר הָרִאשׁוֹן
The First Ikkar

אֲנִי מַאֲמִין בֶּאֱמוּנָה שְׁלֵמָה שֶׁהַבּוֹרֵא יִתְבָּרַךְ
שְׁמוֹ הוּא בּוֹרֵא וּמַנְהִיג לְכָל הַבְּרוּאִים וְהוּא
לְבַדּוֹ עָשָׂה וְעוֹשֶׂה וְיַעֲשֶׂה לְכָל הַמַּעֲשִׂים.

I am steadfast in my absolute belief that the
Creator, blessed is His Name, creates and
guides all that is brought into existence, and
that He alone created, creates, and will
create all that is created.

In the Rambam's Words

הַיְסוֹד הָרִאשׁוֹן מְצִיאוּת הַבּוֹרֵא יִשְׁתַּבַּח וְהוּא שֶׁיֵּשׁ שָׁם
מָצוּי בִּשְׁלֵמוּת בְּיוֹתֵר שֶׁבְּאָפְנֵי הַמְּצִיאוּת וְהוּא עִלַּת מְצִיאוּת
הַנִּמְצָאִים כֻּלָּם וּבוֹ קִיּוּם מְצִיאוּתָם וּמִמֶּנּוּ הַתְמָדַת קִיּוּמָם
וְאִלּוּ יָכֹלְנוּ לְשַׁעֵר סִלּוּק מְצִיאוּתוֹ הָיְתָה בְּטֵלָה מְצִיאוּת כָּל
נִמְצָא וְלֹא יִשָּׁאֵר מֵחֲמַת עַצְמוֹ בִּמְצִיאוּתוֹ וְאִלּוּ יָכֹלְנוּ לְשַׁעֵר
סִלּוּק הַנִּמְצָאִים כֻּלָּם זוּלָתוֹ לֹא הָיְתָה בְּטֵלָה מְצִיאוּתוֹ
יִתְעַלֶּה וְלֹא תִגָּרַע כִּי הוּא יִתְעַלֶּה קַיָּם מִצַּד עַצְמוֹ וְאֵינוֹ
נִזְקָק בִּמְצִיאוּתוֹ לְזוּלָתוֹ וְכָל מַה שֶּׁזוּלָתוֹ מִן הַשְּׂכָלִים
כְּלוֹמַר הַמַּלְאָכִים וְגִרְמֵי הַגַּלְגַּלִּים וּמַה שֶּׁלְּמַטָּה מֵהֶם הַכֹּל
נִצְרָךְ בִּמְצִיאוּתוֹ אֵלָיו וְזֶה הַיְסוֹד הָרִאשׁוֹן הוּא שֶׁהוֹרָה עָלָיו
בַּדִּבּוּר אָנֹכִי ה' וְכוּ'.

The first foundational belief is that of the nature of the existence of the Creator, may He be praised, and that is that there exists an Entity of ultimate perfection beyond any other existence, and He is the source of everything that exists. The ability of all creations to come into existence, and to continue to exist, is entirely reliant upon Him. Were we able to conjure a situation where He would no longer exist, all other matter would immediately cease to exist. Conversely, if the entire universe would cease to exist, it would not cause Him to stop existing, nor would it mitigate Him in any way, for His existence is completely independent and self-sufficient and He requires nothing at all from anybody or anything else. Even all spiritual beings that exist, such as angels and other forces, of varying levels, are all entirely dependent on His existence. This first foundational belief is established by the proclamation of *I am Hashem, etc.* (*Shemos* 20:2).

הוּא לְבַדּוֹ עָשָׂה וְעוֹשֶׂה וְיַעֲשֶׂה
Hashem Alone Created, Creates, and Will Create

In this, the first Ani Maamin, we are introduced to the core feature of Hakadosh Baruch Hu, that of His integral existence. He alone is the only Entity that can and does exist independent of any other being. With this declaration, we draw a side-by-side comparison to the rest of the universe. Unlike Him, our continued existence is eminently dependent on a myriad of factors, such as oxygen, food, and much more. Yet our deficiency is far more profound: We are creations, and can exist only because we were created by something that preceded us. He alone required no creation, and He alone requires no support.

*A*rriving at belief in Hakadosh Baruch Hu by analyzing our own creation is an eminently logical process. You, I, and everything around us came to be only by virtue of something that preceded us. I was born to parents. My parents, likewise, were born to parents. The same can be said of everything with which we are familiar. My table started as wood, which came from a tree, which in turn began as a seed. The chain keeps going.

Matter does not spontaneously burst into existence. It comes from a source. This, of course, leaves us with a question mark — if everything comes about from something before it, where did the original entity come from? If man is born to parents, where did the first parent come from? Ultimately, we have no way of defining or describing what the originator looks like. What we can say definitively, however, is that there is something, some force out there, that does not conform to the rules of our universe. There is something that doesn't need a creator, and doesn't require any of the factors on which we are dependent.

By way of analogy, suppose you sat down one day, and with your knowledge of coding, created some sort of computer game. In this game, you create a town full of people. Understandably, whether these people are tall or short, how many eyes or ears they have, the color of their hair, or if they have any hair at all, and all their other features and abilities, as well as the broader rules and parameters of the town, are totally at your discretion. You write the code, and you get to set up your town any way you wish.

Now let's say someone could come along and somehow interact with the characters in your computer-game town. Picture him asking one of these characters to describe the programmer who created them. Obviously, this would be rather impossible. The only thing these characters have experienced is whatever exists in the world you created. That's the only frame of reference they have. If the only color you used in your town is blue, there's no way for them to picture red. If you didn't create anyone with a nose, it would be impossible for any character to fathom a sense of smell. There's no way for them to have any concept of anything outside of their bubble. What they can comprehend, however, provided they have some level of intelligence, is that there is somebody, or something, who created the program. They won't have an inkling as to the methods of writing code, nor any description of the one who wrote it, but they will be quite certain that something exists outside their bubble, and that something created the bubble and all that is in it.

We live in this bubble. We were created — and therefore, something must exist completely outside our bubble, and that something is the One Who created our bubble. This is our Creator, Hakadosh Baruch Hu. He is not bound by any of the rules or contingencies in our universe — on the contrary, He is the One Who wrote the entire code.

We will return to this idea further along the road, as we deal with facets expressed in some of the other Ani Maamins. For the time being, let's focus on the wording of this first Ani Maamin.

In this Ani Maamin, Hakadosh Baruch Hu is described as one who created, creates, and will create. Past, present, future. What does this mean? Yes, he created the world a few millennia back, but to say that he is actively creating seems a bit strange. Where is all this new creation happening? Doesn't the world seem to exist pretty much the way it always has?

There are two methods of creating an entity. The first model is by far the most familiar to us. If I make a table, a chair, a watch, or anything else that we know of, the moment I've finished making it, I can walk away. My handiwork is complete. It exists. It's a free-standing item that no longer requires any input. Yet there is another model of creation, one that does require constant input. Perhaps the best example we have in this regard is that of light. Electricity runs through wires, arriving from a power source and fueling a glowing lightbulb. This light that is now here cannot continue on its own. As long as a continuous current is provided, there will be light. Stop the flow of the current, and the light goes out. In fact, we never actually "turn off" a light. By flipping a switch, we break the flow of electricity; consequently, the light no longer exists.

Similarly, our existence is incapable of perpetuating itself. Cut the current, and the world will simply cease to be. Hakadosh Baruch Hu wants us, and His world, to exist, and He is the constant, radiant energy Source that keeps us going, refreshing us anew each moment. Put differently, if He were to decide He no longer wants our universe, He would have no need to destroy it by nuclear apocalypse or any other means. Simply stopping to provide the universe its energy would cause it to instantly cease to exist. You, I, and every atom of the world as we know it exists only because at every moment Hakadosh Baruch Hu creates the world for yet another instant. Proof of this, as we say every day in *Birchos Krias Shema*, is found in the present-tense formulation of the *pasuk*: לְעֹשֵׂה אוֹרִים גְּדֹלִים כִּי לְעוֹלָם חַסְדּוֹ, *To Him Who makes great lights, for His kindness endures forever*.[1]

Creation didn't merely happen back then. It's happening at every moment.

How Does This Affect My Daily Life?

*W*hile we may be in a constant state of re-creation, it's certainly not something we can easily perceive. After all, to all appearances, the world looks to be functioning in quite a state of constancy. Truthfully, though, this appearance is but a masterful illusion. Think for a moment of a video. It runs for a couple of minutes, depicting some scene or other. While the video flows quite smoothly, there is actually no continuity throughout the images it portrays. A video merely comprises an extraordinary number of still photos, shown in rapid succession. Moving through relatively similar frames at such quick speed fools the eye into viewing the scene as continuous action.

We move through the milliseconds of a constantly recreated world with rapid speed. The scene created each second is very similar to the one that preceded it, but in reality, each moment is a brand-new picture, a brand-new world.

The mirage of constancy is compelling, but if we take the time to understand and internalize the true nature of the world, we will view the elements of our lives in a different light.

Suppose someone is in a bit of a rough situation. Perhaps he faces a tough job market, difficulty with shidduchim, or bills

---

1. For a discussion of the Rambam's view of constant creation, see Appendix A.

piling up. Sure, it's nice to be hopeful, but after a while, despondency can begin to set in. I'm in a rut. The situation is dragging on, with no ray of light on the horizon. Sure, I'll daven and perform all the motions of Yiddishkeit, but can anything really change?

Stop. There is no real status quo. The world is being recreated. It wouldn't take much for Hashem to create it this moment just a little bit differently than a moment ago. So talk to Him, ask Him to help you out, because nothing is set in stone. Everything is beginning afresh.

The same goes for the other side of the equation. Suppose life is good. There's money in the bank. Family, children, *nachas*… But is everything so set? Are we buying into the mirage of constancy, or do we understand that everything stays the way it is only because He chooses to create the world in a manner that feeds that mirage? If we understand and internalize the mechanics of recreation, we certainly shouldn't be taking anything for granted. It is imperative to keep talking to Him, acknowledging Him, thanking Him, and asking Him to continue showering us with blessing.

We can take away two lessons. One is the core awareness that Hakadosh Baruch Hu has never walked away from the world post-creation. He is constantly holding His hand upon the world, feeding the electric current that sustains it. We are utterly dependent on His doing so, and would not exist for a moment without it. Secondly, the world is not bound to an absolute status quo and is open to change at any moment. Knowing this, if you are experiencing something positive, do not take it for granted. Talk to Him, and ask Him to keep giving you all the goodness you've received until now. Conversely, if you are experiencing something difficult, nothing mandates that it will stay that way. He is recreating the world again in a moment. Just ask Him to create the next moment a bit better than this one.

וּמַנְהִיג לְכָל הַבְּרוּאִים
Guiding Our Lives

With these words, we are introduced to the concept of Hash-gachah: the idea that Hakadosh Baruch Hu does not merely suffice with His role as Creator and Maintainer of our universe, but actually intervenes in the day-to-day occurrences within our world, guiding events and circumstances.

The theme of the first Ani Maamin is not the manner in which Hakadosh Baruch Hu conducts Himself, but rather how His very essence differs so dramatically from the nature of everything we know and experience, as discussed in the previous segment. Nevertheless, since the author of the Ani Maamins chose to insert the concept of Hashgachah within this Ani Maamin, this would be an opportune time to provide some framework for understanding this concept, by delineating what it is and isn't, as well as what purpose it serves.[2]

---

2. Remarkably, not only does the Rambam himself make no mention at all of Hashgachah within this Ikkar, he seems to have opted to leave this concept out of the Ikkarim entirely. For further analysis of the discrepancies between the text of the Ani Maamins as found in our siddurim and the Ikkarim articulated by the Rambam, see Appendix C, "Comparing the Words of the Rambam, Ani Maamin, and Yigdal."

The basic premise we start with is our knowledge that Hakadosh Baruch takes a hands-on approach to our world, intervening directly and altering the course of all occurrences to fit His goals. Though He does so from behind a curtain, veiling His actions in a cloak of nature, He is very much present and active. While the methods of His intervention are many and complex, on a basic level we are told that He employs two forms of conduct, referred to as Hashgachah Klalis and Hashgachah Pratis. At risk of oversimplification, it can be said that Hashgachah Klalis refers to a broad or more generalized involvement, whereas Hashgachah Pratis connotes a more nuanced and specific form of intervention.

Broadly, the divide between the two approaches can be explained as follows. At times, Hakadosh Baruch Hu's intervention serves a broad purpose — say, for example, His plan requires a herd of mountain goats to graze in a certain area. There may not be a particular need for any one specific goat to end up there, as the objective can be satisfactorily achieved by any random group of goats. On the other hand, at times He deliberately guides matters with pinpoint precision, such as by ensuring that a specific person ends up in a specific place at a specific time so that at that precise moment he will — seemingly accidentally — encounter a friend he hasn't seen in years, leading to a shidduch or business deal.

It must be emphasized, however, that in no way should this imply that Hakadosh Baruch Hu on occasion deals only with details, while in other scenarios He limits His interaction to the broader picture and leaves the minutiae to evolve untended. Such an approach is absolutely false. Indeed, it is downright impossible. As mentioned previously, we know that we exist each moment because at this specific moment He is granting us life. The same holds true for everything in the universe. If He would not want that rock in that place, it wouldn't be there. If He would not want this specific animal to exist, it wouldn't. The question here is not whether He is involved in every detail. Of necessity, he is eminently involved in even the most minute details of every particle in the universe at every moment or fraction thereof. The question is only what style of involvement He will employ. He can guide matters based on the highly specific needs of an individual, or He can guide them based on the broader requirements of a group at large. All the pieces are being moved, but they may be moved to satisfy either the broader needs of the universe or the specific needs of that particular piece.

Generally, the greater a role a piece of the puzzle plays in fulfilling Hakadosh Baruch Hu's master plan, the more significantly Hakadosh Baruch Hu tailors the experience to assist that piece in playing its role. Humanity certainly receives a greater degree of precise intervention than do animals or inanimate objects. Above humanity at large, Klal Yisrael benefits from an infinitely greater dosage of Hashgachah Pratis custom guidance. After all, Klal Yisrael are the ones who fulfill the purpose of the world's creation.

Even within Klal Yisrael, the degree of personalized Hashgachah each person receives can differ tremendously. The Ramban (*Iyov* 36:7) explains that the level of Hashem's Hashgachah over any specific person is directly tied to the degree that the person himself chooses to focus on and draw close to Hakadosh Baruch Hu. If a person strengthens his own emunah, even if only within a specific moment or situation, he will earn far more personalized intervention and assistance.

We may wonder, however, why Hakadosh Baruch sees fit to intervene directly in this world and maneuver the course of people's lives. What is the purpose of His doing so? We might assume that the objective would be to reward those who follow the correct path in life, ensuring they are well taken care of, while meting out punishment to those who fail to heed His will. The difficulty with this, however, is that ultimately this world is not where reward and retribution are dispensed. This world is for playing the game, doing as best as we can before the clock expires. Only when we move on to the next world will the score be finalized and the results brought to bear. Indeed, we see many wonderful Jews who seem to be quite upstanding and scrupulous in their mitzvah observance yet suffer rather difficult lives. We know that they will receive inestimable reward in Olam Haba, so the metric of reward and punishment certainly doesn't seem to provide rationale for Hashgachah in this world.

There are several different approaches to resolving this question. These approaches are not mutually exclusive, and may all be true. I would like to focus on one specific line of thought.[3]

We know we were put in this world for a purpose. We are each given challenges, along with the ability to freely decide which actions to take and from which actions to desist. The decisions in our lives have value precisely because we find these decisions to be challenging. If the correct course of action would be exceedingly clear as well as easy to undertake, I would receive no credit for choosing the proper path. Likewise, if I were confronted by a situation where I would have no ability to avoid the path of wrongdoing, I would not be faulted. For that reason, an angel cannot be credited for serving Hakadosh Baruch Hu, since to an angel, right and wrong are clear and obvious, and has no draw to disobedience. Conversely, a Jew lying unconscious in a hospital ward would bear no liability for failing to don tefillin, daven, or perform other mitzvos, since he is beyond the point of *bechirah*, free choice.

Taking this a step further, for most observant Jews, the decision of whether to eat a bacon sandwich is not a matter of practically exercising free will. It's simply beyond the range of any real internal conflict. It is precisely for the battles we face, when we are torn and pulled in opposite directions, that we were put into this world. During the moment of standing on the precipice, when we have two ways to go and we decide which of the paths to take, we truly define who we are, and we either elevate or lower ourselves with each decision. The entire universe is structured in such a way as to provide us with opportunities to exercise our *bechirah* and earn Olam Haba.

---

3. Based on Ramchal, *Derech Hashem*, Ch. 3.

Human beings, however, are not static. We have ups and we have downs. We learn to conquer mountains, yet we also turn molehills into mountains. Each day of life, our point of balance keeps shifting, and what was nearly insurmountable a year ago might at this point have become quite doable. How, then, can it be ensured that the system of free choice is at perfect equilibrium? How can we constantly be ensured the right level of challenge?

If Hakadosh Baruch Hu would simply plunk us down here in this world, leave us here for a number of years without any intervention, and then call us upstairs for a reckoning, there would be a serious flaw in the entire design of the world. A person could conceivably live for many years, yet end up with relatively few true free-choice opportunities over the course of his life. He might have encountered numerous situations that were simply out of his range of free will, either due to their extreme ease or due to their extreme difficulty. Furthermore, even in situations where a person does make a choice, the challenge may be present, but not truly all that difficult. The entire purpose of our traversing this world is to capitalize on our opportunities to exercise *bechirah*, and yet it would be quite feasible that a person could end up with only a limited number of situations in which he could truly choose between right and wrong.

To this end, Hakadosh Baruch Hu becomes involved. He micromanages my life and custom tailors my experiences to ensure that my life never becomes too easy, or too difficult. The challenges I face in my day are custom-made, right at the point of pushing my skill level. Tough, but eminently doable. As I move through life, with my many ups and downs, He'll keep customizing the difficulties I encounter, always keeping my struggles at the perfect keel for me to be both challenged as well as able to grow through the difficulty. He'll confront me with challenges, but at the same time He'll be right there ensuring I have all the requisite emotional and material tools to be able to succeed.

How Does This Affect My Daily Life?

When we think of Hashgachah Pratis and what it means to feel the hand of Hashem, our thoughts typically gravitate to stories of miraculous salvations and supernatural occurrences that we have experienced or heard about. Yet these extraordinary events do not happen every day.

The Ramban (*Shemos* 13:16) explains that Hakadosh Baruch Hu is generally loath to perform open miracles that show His hand in plain view. He did, however, perform a vivid display of grandiose miracles at the time of our exodus from Mitzrayim, as well as on sporadic occasions thereafter. The function of these open displays was for us to take note and learn to recognize Him as well when He operates in a more concealed mode.[4]

In the previous section, we compared the constant re-creation of the world to a video that is composed of a series of still images, with each image slightly different from the previous one. Revisiting this analogy, an open miracle would constitute an abrupt, jarring change to the film. What we call "nature" is really a series of small, subtle miracles that are barely perceptible, resulting in a smoothly running screenplay that does not conclusively demonstrate Divine involvement. Hashem prefers to run the world according to the dictates of nature, rather than performing wonders that jolt us into awareness of His involvement, because He wants to leave room for us to *choose* to notice Him. This is also why He expects us to invest the requisite effort — *hishtadlus* — into achieving our life goals, whether by working to support our families, seeking medical treatment when we are ill, or visiting shadchanim in our quest for a marriage partner. When these

---

4. For further elaboration on why Hakadosh Baruch Hu generally refrains from performing visible miracles, as well as why certain select individuals in previous generations were privileged to experience miracles on a regular basis, see Appendix D, "Miracles vs. Free Will."

processes unfold subtly and "naturally," the frames of the video that is creation come together seamlessly, allowing Hashem's involvement to remain under the radar. This maintains the illusion of nature that sets the stage for *bechirah*, free choice.

On occasion, however, we are privy to events that involve Hashem's unmistakable intervention. A few years ago, my father *shlita*, the rosh kollel of the Montreal Community Kollel, was involved in a car accident where his vehicle flipped over, crashed into a light pole, and erupted in flames. In a stroke of Divine serendipity, two Muslims who were passing at that very moment stopped their car and pulled my father from his vehicle just a few seconds before it exploded. The two had not even planned on being in the area altogether. Having stumbled on some excellent sales, they had wrapped up an extended shopping trip a full day earlier than expected, and they used some of their extra time to take a more circuitous route back home, a route that brought them to that exact spot at that precise moment. The hand of Hashem was certainly evident at that time and continued to be most evident in every subsequent twist and turn until my father's full recovery.

This story continues to inspire us, serving as an eye-opener that helps us go through life with the awareness that He is always watching us from the shadows. It does not, however, show me His involvement in my daily life. Where, then, can I find His Hashgachah every single day?

Within the above idea, we find a solution: The challenges we face are the manifestation of Hashem's constant Hashgachah. Suppose you are having a really hard day: tough meetings at work, trouble with the bank, yelled at by the boss. You escape from the office and begin your ride home, only to be stuck behind a slow-moving tractor, tripling the time of your commute. Finally, you walk through your front door, ready to collapse, and are greeted by a cacophony. Supper isn't ready, the kids are fighting, and some sticky substance seems to have spilled all over the floor. Freeze. This is a Hashgachah Pratis moment. You were just sent a challenge custom-tailored to your unique talents and abilities.

You may be down and out, but you have the power to choose. He's right there. He's setting you up for the challenge, and He's telling you, "You can do this!"

הָעִקָּר הַשֵּׁנִי
The Second Ikkar

אֲנִי מַאֲמִין בֶּאֱמוּנָה שְׁלֵמָה שֶׁהַבּוֹרֵא יִתְבָּרַךְ
שְׁמוֹ הוּא יָחִיד וְאֵין יְחִידוּת כָּמוֹהוּ בְּשׁוּם
פָּנִים, וְהוּא לְבַדּוֹ אֱלֹהֵינוּ, הָיָה הֹוֶה וְיִהְיֶה.

I am steadfast in my absolute belief that the
Creator, blessed is His Name, is One, and
there is no uniqueness like His in any way,
and He alone is our Lord, forever having
existed, existing, and continuing to exist.

וְהַיְסוֹד הַשֵּׁנִי אַחְדוּתוֹ יִתְעַלֶּה וְהַיְנוּ שֶׁזֶּה שֶׁהוּא עָלַת הַכֹּל
- אֶחָד. לֹא כְּאֶחָד שֶׁל מִין וְלֹא כְּאֶחָד שֶׁל סוּג וְלֹא כִּפְרָט
הָאֶחָד הַמֻּרְכָּב שֶׁמִּתְחַלֵּק לַאֲחָדִים רַבִּים וְלֹא אֶחָד כַּגּוּף
הַפָּשׁוּט הָאֶחָד בְּמִנְיָן שֶׁמְּקַבֵּל הַפְּרָדָה וַחֲלָקָה עַד אֵין סוֹף,
אֶלָּא הוּא יִתְעַלֶּה אֶחָד בְּאַחְדוּת שֶׁאֵין כְּמוֹתָהּ אַחְדוּת בְּשׁוּם
פָּנִים. וְזֶה הַיְסוֹד הַשֵּׁנִי הוּא שֶׁהוֹרָה עָלָיו בְּאָמְרוֹ שְׁמַע
יִשְׂרָאֵל ה' אֱלֹהֵינוּ ה' אֶחָד.

The second foundational belief is that of the Exalted One's singularity. This means that this entity that is the cause of everything is One. This does not mean one in the sense of one species or one of a type, nor does it refer to an entity that is an amalgamation of many parts, or a singular unit that can theoretically be split and divided infinitely. Rather, the Exalted One is One in the sense of absolutely unparalleled singularity. This is this second foundational belief, which is attested to in the verse (*Devarim 6:4*): *Hear, O Israel: Hashem is our God, Hashem is the One and Only.*

הוּא יָחִיד וְאֵין יְחִידוּת כָּמוֹהוּ
There Is Only One Power

The first five of the Ani Maamins comprise a set, present-ing different facets of a unified concept of how we view and interact with Hakadosh Baruch Hu. Although these facets overlap, each one emphasizes a specific tenet and lesson that warrants its own focus. This particular Ani Maamin dis-cusses Yichud Hashem, which means that beyond the idea that Hakadosh Baruch Hu exists and created the world, He alone is the Creator and Controller. He has no partner or co-creator, and nothing else exists on par with Him; every-thing exists only because He chose to create it.

One of the most complex and intricate of the Ikkarim is the one we have before us, that of Yichud Hashem. Since we are focusing on the practical application of these Ikkarim, we will not delve into the subtleties of this Ikkar, but we must nevertheless understand some basic concepts regarding Hash-em's Oneness in order to glean the lessons it yields.

What do we mean by *Yichud*, Oneness, of Hashem?

We already know that Hakadosh Baruch Hu created the entire universe; the first of the Ikkarim established that. Yet that does not necessarily indicate that He is acting alone. After all, a company may be launched by one person independently, but it may just as well be established by multiple partners, all of whom are involved in the formation of this corporate entity. A person could, God forbid, believe in the *Borei Olam* but think that maybe there is more than one. Maybe there are two, three, or more powers out there? This is where the most basic level of Yichud Hashem comes in: There is One. One and only One. It is He and He alone.

If we turn back the pages of history, we will encounter many civilizations — Rome, Greece, Persia, Egypt, and more — that did in fact worship multiple deities. Hardly an ancient civilization existed without a convoluted system of gods, each of which supposedly controlled this or that, and many of whom were in continual conflict with the others.

On the surface, it might seem that the basic difference was one of numbers. We believe in monotheism, they believed in polytheism. We believe in One, they believed in six, seven, ten-and-a-half, or a hundred.

It is critically important to realize that the difference is far more significant than simple mathematics. It's not just that we don't believe in more than one deity; we believe it's utterly impossible for there to be anything but One. The most elementary understanding of Hakadosh Baruch Hu dictates that there simply can't be any multiplicity.

Put it this way: It is possible for someone to be the absolute top player of a game or sport. He might be the best ever at pitching, chess, or equestrian jumping. But it is not possible for two people to both be the top player ever. If we say that two people are statistically tied as the best ever, that means neither is truly unique.

Hakadosh Baruch Hu is *kol yachol*, all-powerful. He is in absolute and total control of everything that exists. That said, an unchallengeable entity can exist only if there is one such entity. The moment a second such entity enters the scene, neither of the two is unchallengeable. They can't both have absolute control. It's completely paradoxical. Likewise, Hakadosh Baruch Hu is *ein sof*, unlimited. You can't have two coexisting powers that are unlimited. Having two necessarily means that each will invade the other's territory, causing each one to be limited.

In other words, to claim belief in anything more than one higher authority is to miss the entire concept of God altogether. By creating multiple gods, those civilizations diminished the whole perception of a god, reducing it to nothing more than a glorified version of a human being.

Not Like an Egg, or a Skyscraper

*T*his Ikkar describes Hakadosh Baruch Hu's Oneness as incomparable to any other oneness. In what way is this uniqueness so incomparable? Take an egg out of a carton. You're holding one. True. But this Oneness is a rather poor level of uniqueness. After all, any other egg you would pick up is also only one. Furthermore, you could pick up a second egg, and now there are two, not one. In other words, the egg is in a position of singularity simply as a matter of circumstance, but there is nothing intrinsic about this oneness. Moving up a notch, we can take the example of the tallest skyscraper in the world. Here, there is something intrinsically unique, as the building itself possesses a distinguishing feature: No other such structure exists anywhere in the world. Nevertheless, here, too, the oneness is not absolute. Yes, right now this tower is the tallest, but another, higher tower could foreseeably be constructed. Indeed, ever-taller skyscrapers are constantly being built, shattering previous records. While the building does boast uniqueness, that is incidental, as nothing dictates that its uniqueness will endure.

Hakadosh Baruch Hu doesn't happen to be one. It's so intrinsic to Who He is that it can't be any other way. He is the unlimited, all-powerful One, rendering the existence of any other power an impossibility.

As believers in Hakadosh Baruch Hu, we maintain the firm

conviction that He alone is the Creator, and He never relinquished any control to another force. The idea that He created the world independently means that every iota of matter, every particle and every quark, was fashioned by Him personally. But we can take this concept much further. Our world is not composed merely of physical matter; it is filled with all sorts of metaphysical and non-physical entities as well. Concepts, thoughts, emotions, and all other intangibles are also elements of His handiwork. Happiness and sadness, the pain of defeat and the thrill of triumph — these, too, were created by Him. After all, since there is only one Creator, without Him these elements simply could not exist.

We tend to mentally categorize events and circumstances into certain boxes. Some occurrences we tend to view as acts of Hashgachah, a function of the hand of Hashem, while other events we casually accept as somewhat random happenings. An appreciation of Yichud Hashem eviscerates this distinction, however.

To illustrate, let's examine how we make sense of the challenges, or even tragedies, that confront us. These events can be quite difficult to come to terms with intellectually. In our mind, a strong believer in Hakadosh Baruch Hu would fortify himself with trust in Hashem in the face of such a difficulty, and turn to Him asking that He fix what is broken and make everything right: He should cure this ill person. He should help that person land a job. He should find the other person a shidduch.

Yet asking that Hakadosh Baruch Hu save me from sickness in the sense that the sickness exists out there, as some sort of independent entity, is a completely flawed perspective. Yichud Hashem means that every single thing comes from Him. Not just the cure I hope for, but the illness as well. Not just my next job, but the challenges I experienced in the last one as well. Sickness and hardship are creations, too, and could not exist without His wanting them to exist. Every single thing we experience originated through the will of Hakadosh Baruch Hu.

His Signature in Every Color

*A*t times we experience *middas hadin*, when Hashem deals with us in a manner we perceive as difficult. Other times, we experience *middas harachamim*, when Hashem showers us with boundless kindness. Contrary to the popular conception of what constitutes Hashem's Hashgachah, however, it's not only the good times that show Hashem's involvement in our lives. He deals with us in different ways, some that we perceive as more enjoyable than others, but behind each and every experience is His hand alone. That recognition is Yichud Hashem.

Rav Gedalia Schorr, in an oft-quoted essay,[1] illustrates this point with a beautiful analogy.

If you look at a beam of pure white light, you will see no color at all. Yet if you shine this beam through a prism, you will suddenly notice a whole spectrum of color.

Looking back at the beam of light just before it enters the prism, you see nothing but white. How, then, did you end up with red, orange, yellow, green, blue, indigo, and violet? Where did these colors come from? The answer is that the beam of light contains the amalgamation of all the colors of the rainbow. When fully combined, however, they cannot be individually discerned. Only when you refract the light, isolating a ray of a specific color, will you be able to perceive the characteristics of that particular ray.

Similarly, *middas hadin* and *middas harachamim* are not two distinct forces, but rather two rays emanating from a single beam of light. There is but One force. We merely experience different facets of His singular manner of conducting our world.

Accordingly, the person who experienced a miraculous recovery courtesy of Hakadosh Baruch Hu was given the illness by Him as well. Hashem put him into the crisis, Hashem took him out of the crisis. He put us into Mitzrayim and He took us out of Mitzrayim. All aspects of our lives, whether difficult or pleasant,

---

1. *Ohr Gedalyahu, Mo'adim,* "*Yom HaKippurim b'Bechinas Shabbos,*" section 2.

are but different angles of the same beam of light. They all emanate from the One Source: *Hashem Echad.*

When Bad Things Happen

*I*n the aftermath of the Holocaust, many people's emunah was badly shaken, as they grappled with the harrowing question of how Hakadosh Baruch Hu could have allowed such painful and horrific tragedies to occur. When this issue was posed to our *gedolim*, their responses followed a common thread: The question is not how did Hakadosh Baruch Hu let this occur, but rather why did He want this to happen? He didn't "let" anything occur. Nothing can happen without Him, and if it in fact happened, of necessity He directed it to take place.[2]

This idea can be quite troubling. After all, if my approach to dealing with the problems in my life is, "This happened to me by chance, and I look to Hakadosh Baruch Hu to save me," then I can easily write off the difficulty as a random life occurrence; why it happened is irrelevant to me. If, however, I look the challenge in the eye and say, "Hakadosh Baruch Hu Himself is sending me this *tzarah*," then I'm confronted with a real dilemma. He is not cruel. He loves me. He wants to take care of me. Why, then, is He sending me this hardship? How can I wrap my brain around this?

At this point, the question of why He is sending me this hardship then turns away from Him and toward... me. Suddenly, I'm forced to confront a rather discomfiting question: What does He

---

2. The commentators debate whether a human being, who has free choice, has the power to impact the life of another person in the absence of Hakadosh Baruch Hu's direct dictate to that effect. For additional perspective on this matter, see Alshich, *Bereishis* 37:21; Rabbeinu Chananel (*Chagigah* 4b), *Sefer HaChinuch* (Mitzvah 241): Netziv, *Harchev Davar Bereishis* 37:13, Chazon Ish, *Miluim L'Maseches Bava Basra, siman* 21, *daf* 14a; and *Teshuvos Rashbash siman* 195, cited as halachah by *Pischei Teshuvah, Yoreh Deah* 116. What is unequivocally clear, however, is that no person can impact another against Hashem's will.

want from me? What message is He sending me? Am I properly deciphering the message?

A life challenge may be Hashem's way of prodding me to do *teshuvah*. It might be intended to serve as a catalyst to help me grow into a bigger, better person. Regardless of why the trouble befell me, the first step in coming to terms with it is to acknowledge that nothing happens by itself. It's just one more facet of that same beam of light.

How Does This Affect My Daily Life?

Everything in our lives, whether we perceive it as good or bad, is a manifestation of the hand of Hashem. Rather than merely pinning our hopes on Hakadosh Baruch Hu's salvation — the end of the tale — we need to see His handwriting on every single page of the story. Each twist and turn is Hashem, yet again. Because there is no other power in the universe, every detail must necessarily be set in motion by Him alone.

Don't just grow from happily-ever-after endings. Don't limit your connecting to Hashem to seeking the cure. The difficulty itself is His doing as well. He is reaching out to you. It is your job to figure out how to interpret that message, and how to respond to it. Grow from the challenge. He is talking to you.

שְׁמַע יִשְׂרָאֵל ה׳ אֱלֹהֵינוּ ה׳ אֶחָד
Shema — Our Eternal Rallying Cry

No one sentence has taken on as much meaning to the Jewish people as that of Shema Yisrael. At the youngest age, as a toddler haltingly expresses his first tefillos, the words of Shema play a starring role. Each night, as a child is tucked into bed, he murmurs the words of Shema. As he grows older, the twice-daily recitation of Shema becomes a central pillar of his day. During his last moments on this world, the words of Shema close a life of many years, turning the page to the next world.

The Jew calls out "Shema Yisrael" at the climactic fading moments of Yom Kippur, and before the Torah is read on Shabbos. Whether he was about to be burned at the stake during the Inquisition or being led to the gas chambers, the cry of Shema Yisrael always accompanied him.

The Rambam says that the words of *Shema* attest to the concept of Yichud Hashem. When we declare "*Shema Yisrael,*" then, we are essentially affirming our belief in Yichud Hashem. It is this conviction we carry with us at all times.

What is the meaning of *Shema Yisrael*? And why does it occupy such a prominent place in Judaism?

Much of the discussion surrounding the concept of Yichud Hashem focuses on the intricacies of Hakadosh Baruch Hu's Oneness. This discussion commonly revolves around scholarly issues such as the true definition of "one," analysis of where others went wrong in this regard, the various opinions as to whether *shituf* (a belief system with "partners" to a deity, such as in the "Trinity" of Catholicism) constitutes *avodah zarah*, and *l'havdil* the question of whether we can truly grasp aspects of His nature. These themes relate primarily to the understanding of Hashem; we human beings don't factor much into this discussion.

But Yichud Hashem features another major angle, a perspective whose lens is focused firmly on us and our way of life. How so? Picture for a moment two scenes, side by side. In each one, someone is beginning his morning by catching up on the news. Both individuals hear the same stories: Civil war is about to erupt in Venezuela, a virus is triggering a lockdown in some provinces in China, elections are being held for governor in three different states, and a hurricane is approaching the Gulf of Mexico.

The first individual is a plumber, who is busy fixing pipes and installing fixtures around town most of the day. He hears these stories with a yawn. World news doesn't affect him that much. He does have some strong opinions about viruses and lockdowns, and perhaps a few thoughts about hurricanes and global warming, but these are just conversation topics to hash out with his friends. None of this has any real bearing on his life, and he sees no connection between one story and the next.

The second fellow is the CEO of a large, multinational corporation. He needs supply chains, he needs oil delivered, he needs state regulations that foster a workable environment. Every story he hears on the news ends, for him, with one question: How does this affect my business? Lockdown in China — how will this impact my ability to restock? War in Venezuela — will that drive up oil prices? Someone won an election — what does that mean for my subsidiaries in that state?

To him, the main question is not which candidate is more

qualified, more talented, or more eloquent. It's about who's good for the business. He filters every news item, every discussion point, through one constant prism: What does this information mean for my business?

It's all about the business.

If we recognize that every single thing we see and experience is from Hashem alone, and no other force exists that can cause anything to happen, then we must constantly view every occurrence — personal, communal, or global — through the prism of His directing these events. Our follow-up question, then, will always be the same: What does He want now? What can I do to fulfill His plan? My mind constantly assesses each vicissitude of life through the viewpoint of Hakadosh Baruch Hu's running of the world. Whether I'm pondering the election, the weather, or my day at work, my opinions and decisions are molded based on what's good for Hakadosh Baruch Hu's corporation.

The Race Matters More Than the Race Car

The recognition of Hashem as the sole force in the universe impacts more than just our views and opinions. It's something that should serve as the motivational energy behind our every action.

As devoted Jews, we constantly give of our time, money, and resources for the sake of fulfilling Hashem's will, in both our daily and seasonal obligations. We spend hours every day learning Torah and davening. We donate money toward communal causes, supporting institutions of Torah and *chessed*, and we pay premium prices for glatt kosher food, yeshivah tuition, a lulav and esrog, and so many other items. Often, we forfeit something, big or small, to actualize our values and live a truly fulfilling life.

The ultimate sacrifice, of course, is that of life itself. Jews throughout the ages have willingly gone to their death rather than renounce their allegiance to Hakadosh Baruch Hu. In those final moments, *Shema* was invariably on their lips. For instance, the Gemara (*Berachos* 60b) teaches that as R' Akiva was being tortured to death in a grotesquely painful manner, he recited *Shema*, moving on to the next world as he recited the word *echad*.

Chazal (*Midrash Tehillim* 9:17) actually describe this act of sacrificing one's life with the intriguing words, *"mosrim nafsham l'misah al yichud Hashem"* — they give their lives for Yichud Hashem. This choice of terminology is rather curious. People sacrificed their lives for their belief in Hashem. They sacrificed their lives for adherence to His Torah. They sacrificed their lives *al kiddush Hashem*, in sanctification of His Name. But they sacrificed their lives for the *unity* of His Name? What does that mean?

Yichud Hashem is not what they sacrificed their lives for, but rather how they were able to sacrifice their entire being for their beliefs. They understood that Hashem is One, meaning that there is nothing in the world but Him. Since He is all I have, I'll give up anything, even life itself, for His sake.

To illustrate this idea, imagine that you're watching the last lap of a car race, as several cars hurtle at high speed toward the checkered flag. One driver is in the lead, but the race is tight. To maintain his lead down the final stretch, the driver can floor the pedal, pushing his car beyond its limits to cross the finish line in a burst of record speed. Doing so, however, will destroy the car's motor, necessitating expensive repairs. The tires and numerous other parts will likely be damaged as well. Should he go all out, at the cost of demolishing his vehicle? To the driver, the answer is obvious: He's in it to win. Will his car suffer damage? The whole point of having a car is to win the race! The car is just a detail, a means of carrying him to victory. He's not destroying the car; he's using it for its ultimate purpose.

The core of every individual is not our money, our possessions, or our social standing. It's not even our bodies. It's our *neshamah* and our *neshamah* alone. After all, our bodies are a part of us for but a finite number of years, while our *neshamah* defines us forever.[3]

My body is no more than a glorified race car, a tool given to me to carry me to the finish line of Olam Hazeh. Without a body, I couldn't accomplish anything in this world. But once the race is over and I cross the finish line into Olam Haba, I hop out of the car and continue being whoever I am. If I'm properly hyper-focused on the race, then my body, my financial resources, and all of my abilities take on value only insofar as they propel me toward the finish line. Essentially, giving up one's life *al kiddush Hashem* is not giving up anything. It's a brilliant rush across the finish line. I'm not destroying my body — I'm using it to win the race!

Yichud Hashem means that nothing matters but Him and His will. If I have this clarity of focus, I can do anything for Him. I can give up my money. I can give up my own ambitions. I can even give up my life. My goal is to do whatever I can to best serve Him.

This is our call of *Shema Yisrael*.

Shema Yisrael — Hear what we're about to say. Listen well. Internalize it.

Hashem Elokeinu — Hashem is the absolute Controller[4] of every single thing that transpires in our world. He runs the world in a unique manner for us, the Jewish people, because we alone have a special bond with Him.

Hashem Echad — Looking beyond the face value of everything we experience in life, we realize there's only one force behind it

---

3. Remarkably, the Radvaz rules (*Hilchos Sanhedrin* 18:6) that a person has no legal monetary right to his bodily organs, for this very reason — your body is not you or yours. It's on loan to you from Hashem for use as a tool to accomplish whatever you need to accomplish.

4. The Name Hashem (יְ־הֹ־וָ־ה) refers to Him as an everlasting and infinite entity. The Name *Elokim* refers to the concept of control. The term *"elohim"* is also used in reference to human rulers, as well to judges, since both exert control. Effectively, Hashem Elokeinu is a statement that Hashem is not merely an entity on high, but is Elokeinu, actively involved in running and controlling everything in our lives.

all. He is the One. He is the only One.[5]

As the world hustles and bustles, inundating us with a cacophony of news and events, we need to look past the smokescreen of randomness and realize that everything we experience is due to His pulling the strings. Whatever happens or exists in our world is a reflection of Him alone. There is nothing else.

What comes after *Shema*? *"Ve'ahavta es Hashem"* — love Him. Connect to Him. Bond with Him through learning Torah, doing mitzvos, and emulating His kindness and goodness. Follow His guidance in every area of life.

If He is all that matters, I will channel all my abilities and resources, from morning to night and from cradle to grave, to do anything I can to fulfill what He asks of me.[6] Ultimately, He's all that exists in my life; everything else fades into the backstage.

How Does This Affect My Daily Life?

*M*esirus nefesh is not just a way to die. It's a way to live. The Rambam (*Hilchos Mezuzah* 6:13) writes that we affix a mezuzah to the doorpost of our home so that every time we enter or leave we will encounter Yichud Hashem. This, says the Rambam, serves as a constant reminder of Hakadosh Baruch Hu's love for us. The mezuzah provides a wake-up call, shaking a person from the stupor of life's trivialities and spurring him to develop a real sense of purpose. This awareness of Yichud Hashem — I have One God, and my one goal is to do His will — keeps a person focused and determined and helps him chart a true and proper course through life.

We each occupy two worlds. One is the realm of home and family, and the other is the big world out there. When I step out of

---

5. For further elaboration on the concepts of *Shema* and *Echad*, see Appendix A.

6. This idea, as well as a broader explanation of *Shema*, is presented by the Rashba, *Teshuvos* Vol. 5, *siman* 55.

my house, I touch the mezuzah, and focus on Yichud Hashem. I remind myself that whatever I encounter and whomever I meet, ultimately the one thing that matters is not whether I aced my job interview or whether I made a successful sales pitch to prospective clients, but whether I made Hakadosh Baruch Hu proud. Ultimately, He is the only One Who counts. And when I step back into my house, I touch the mezuzah again and remind myself of Yichud Hashem. My personal life, my family, my values when no one is watching me — it's all centered around how Hakadosh Baruch Hu wants me to guide my home. His is the only standard to which I have to aspire.

Mesirus nefesh comes in many shapes and sizes: giving up a big contract due to the risk of a *ribbis* violation, forgoing the enticing fare at a family event when the kashrus certification is questionable, even simply getting out of bed promptly for Shacharis and resisting the urge to hit the snooze button. Each time I put aside something I crave because deep down I know it's not right, I've given up something for the sake of Hashem.

It takes exceptional fortitude and motivation to do this. What fuels the ability to consistently triumph and stay true to our values is Yichud Hashem.

Avoid becoming distracted by all the noise of life and stay focused on the core goal. There is only one factor to consider, and that is His will.

הָעִקָּר הַשְּׁלִישִׁי
The Third Ikkar

אֲנִי מַאֲמִין בֶּאֱמוּנָה שְׁלֵמָה שֶׁהַבּוֹרֵא יִתְבָּרַךְ
שְׁמוֹ אֵינוֹ גוּף וְלֹא יַשִּׂיגוּהוּ מַשִּׂיגֵי הַגּוּף וְאֵין
לוֹ שׁוּם דִּמְיוֹן כְּלָל.

I am steadfast in my absolute belief that
the Creator, blessed is His Name, has no
corporeality, nor can any material qualities
be ascribed to Him, and there is nothing
at all that is comparable to Him.

In the Rambam's Words

וְהַיְסוֹד הַשְּׁלִישִׁי שְׁלִילַת הַגַּשְׁמוּת מִמֶּנּוּ וְזֶה כִּי הָאֶחָד שֶׁזְּכַרְנוּ
אֵינוֹ גוּף וְלֹא כֹּחַ בַּגּוּף וְלֹא יַשִּׂיגוּהוּ מְאֹרְעוֹת הַגּוּפִים כְּמוֹ
הַתְּנוּעָה וְהַמְּנוּחָה לֹא מִצַּד עַצְמוּת וְלֹא בְּמִקְרֶה וְלָכֵן שָׁלְלוּ
מִמֶּנּוּ הַחֲכָמִים ז״ל הַחִבּוּר וְהַפֵּרוּד וְאָמְרוּ אֵין לְמַעְלָה לֹא
יְשִׁיבָה וְלֹא עֲמִידָה וְלֹא עֹרֶף וְלֹא עִפּוּי... וְאָמַר הַנָּבִיא ״וְאֶל מִי
תְּדַמְּיוּן וְאֶשְׁוֶה יֹאמַר קָדוֹשׁ״... וְכָל מַה שֶּׁבָּא בַּכְּתוּבִים בְּתָאֳרָיו
מִתָּאֳרֵי הַגּוּפִים כְּגוֹן הַהֲלִיכָה מִמָּקוֹם לְמָקוֹם וְהָעֲמִידָה וְהַיְשִׁיבָה
וְהַדִּבּוּר וְכַיּוֹצֵא בָזֶה כֻּלָּם הֵם דֶּרֶךְ הַשְׁאָלָה וּכְמוֹ שֶׁאָמְרוּ דִּבְּרָה
תוֹרָה כִּלְשׁוֹן בְּנֵי אָדָם... וְהַיְסוֹד הַשְּׁלִישִׁי הַזֶּה הוּא שֶׁהוֹרָה עָלָיו
בְּאָמְרוֹ כִּי לֹא רְאִיתֶם כָּל תְּמוּנָה כְּלוֹמַר לֹא הִשַּׂגְתֶּם אוֹתוֹ בַּעַל
תְּמוּנָה לְפִי שֶׁהוּא כְּמוֹ שֶׁאָמַרְנוּ לֹא גוּף וְלֹא כֹחַ לַגּוּף.

The third foundational belief is the negation of His having any material properties. The One we have mentioned has no physical body, nor any forces associated with physicality; and no physical functions, such as movement or rest, can be attributed to Him, whether intrinsically or incidentally. As such, the Sages spurned any depiction of Him as potentially joining [with other forces or beings] or dissociating, and they said that Above there is neither sitting, nor standing, nor merging or dissociating... As the prophet says, *"And to whom shall you compare Me and find any parallel?" says the Holy One* (Yeshayah 40:25).

The Scriptural descriptions that attribute corporeal properties to Him, such as movement from place to place, standing, sitting, speaking and the like, are all borrowed terms, in accordance with the principle that "the Torah speaks in the human vernacular."

...This third foundational belief is expressed in the verse (*Devarim* 4:15): *For you have not seen any image [of Me]*, meaning that you cannot possibly perceive any likeness of Him, because He, as we have said, possesses neither physicality nor forces associated with physicality.

אֵינוֹ גוּף
Hashem Defies Description

Hakadosh Baruch Hu has neither a body, nor any shape or size. In fact, we cannot possibly describe Him, because He is entirely different from anything in our universe. He is absolutely infinite; we are absolutely finite. There is nothing we can compare Him to because we have nothing with any true resemblance to Him. It's not just difficult to picture Him, it's impossible.

"Tachlis hayediah shelo neida" — the ultimate understanding of Hashem is attained by reaching an awareness that He is truly incomprehensible.

On what basis can we say with certainty that Hakadosh Baruch Hu has no physical attributes or properties?

We have already established that Hakadosh Baruch Hu is *ein sof*, truly infinite. In contrast, all physical matter is by nature limited. A chair is a chair because it conforms to a certain basic shape. It has an endpoint, beyond which it does not extend. A beam of light has certain parameters that it does not exceed. For instance, a single ray of light doesn't immediately light up the entire world. Everything in our universe has limitations. Hakadosh Baruch Hu has no limitations whatsoever. As such, describing

Him as possessing the limited features of humans is not just a matter of comparing apples to oranges, it's a matter of comparing two systems that differ so fundamentally that they share no point of comparison whatsoever.

Attempting to comprehend the nature of something infinite is not for the faint of heart. But perhaps the concept of His lacking any physical form can be expressed in more relatable terms.

Let me ask you a question. Is Hakadosh Baruch Hu strong? Assuredly, you will reply in the affirmative, with utmost confidence. Likely, you will regard the question with credulity. Strong? Why, of course, He's stronger than all of us combined! And yet maybe it's not that simple. Maybe He really isn't stronger than you or I. The Rambam declares unequivocally clearly that Hakadosh Baruch has absolutely no physical dimensions or properties. Since physical strength falls into those categories, we would have to conclude that He does not, in fact, possess any physical strength. How can that be?

In the first chapter, we used an analogy comparing Hakadosh Baruch Hu's creation of the world to a computer programmer's creating an imaginary world in a computer game. Let's return for a moment to that analogy. The programmer sits down and begins creating his virtual city, filling it with all sorts of interesting characters. Character One in the game is a standard person, not particularly powerful. Character Two is a big tough guy, and Character Three has superpower strength and can destroy his surroundings with his bare hands. We onlookers can compare the three, noting which one is stronger than the others. It would be ridiculous, however, to compare the strength of any of these characters to the strength of the person who wrote the computer program. The programmer can eliminate all these characters with ease, but that's not because he's stronger head-to-head. It's because he's the one who created the whole metric of strength in the first place. As far as he's concerned, the strength of the respective characters is utterly meaningless, and represents nothing more than a line of code, or a manifestation of his whim.

Hakadosh Baruch Hu cannot be described as stronger than you or I. He is the One Who created strength. It would be completely wrong, therefore, to attribute strength to Him in any comparative terms.

Put otherwise, the ability of Klal Yisrael to defeat enemies who possessed clear military superiority, against overwhelming odds, stemmed not from Hakadosh Baruch Hu being stronger than any army. Rather, an army's entire ability to function rests upon His discretion. His abilities are not just superior by comparison, but in absolute terms, as He is the controlling force without which nothing would exist. As far as He's concerned, whether water flows downstream or upstream makes no inherent difference.

What emerges, then, is that aside from the information given to us via the Torah, we have no way of describing the essence of Hakadosh Baruch Hu. All that we do know about Him can be summed up by stating that there is some entity that created our entire system, and therefore is not part of our system. It is not bound by any rules of our system, nor does it possess any of the characteristics of creatures found in the system. It is simply above and beyond the whole system.

This brings us to the thorny question posed above, by the Rambam. We are told in no uncertain terms that Hakadosh Baruch Hu has no physical properties. He has no body, nor any bodily features. He performs no human behaviors, such as sitting or standing, walking, or talking. For that matter, He experiences no emotions and He does not become angry, distressed, or overjoyed. And yet the Torah is replete with such references to Hakadosh Baruch Hu. We find repeated mention of His hand, arm, and body. We encounter many descriptions of His being happy or upset. How can we understand this? If believing that Hakadosh Baruch Hu possesses any level of corporeality is a violation of a basic tenet of our faith, then why would the Torah describe Hakadosh Baruch Hu in such terms?

The Rambam explains that these are merely borrowed terms, not true descriptions. This, he says, is in line with Chazal's principle that *"dibra Torah k'lashon bnei adam"* — the Torah speaks in terminology familiar to mankind. In other words, these descriptions of Hakadosh Baruch Hu are fundamentally inaccurate.

What does this mean? What value is there in speaking in our lingo if these terms could quite easily be misconstrued? Furthermore, if these descriptions are merely borrowed human terms, what are they meant to convey?

If I want to describe something that is unfamiliar to you, of necessity I must resort to comparing that item to something in your realm of experience. By portraying the new item in relatively comparable items, I can convey a basic understanding of what it is. If I'm describing a piece of furniture, I can say it's as long as this, or as tall as that. Even terms such as strong, sturdy, or heavy have meaning only because the person is familiar with these concepts in other settings.

If, however, I describe to you something for which you have no frame of reference, my descriptions will be utterly useless. The classic example of this is trying to describe color to a person who has been blind from birth. What words would I use? What meaning do the words blue, black, or white have to him? These words belong to a realm to which this person has no connection, and therefore no point of comparison. Consequently, he has no way to process these terms.

Outside Our Bubble

Hakadosh Baruch Hu, and to a large degree all spiritual beings, exist on a different plane, one that is completely removed from our world. We live in a bubble, in a created reality that carries certain rules and properties. Those who exist outside this bubble don't have these properties and don't play by the rules of our physical universe. Essentially, then, for us to achieve any understanding at all of Hakadosh Baruch Hu should be utterly and completely impossible. How can we comprehend a world for which we have no parallel?

And yet, Hakadosh Baruch Hu wants us to understand. He wants us to acquire at least a basic knowledge of what He is all about, and He wants us to emulate His ways. He wants us to appreciate the importance of His mitzvos, and He wants us to be acutely aware of the special bond He has with us. He wants us to understand the concept of Olam Haba, of Gan Eden and Gehinnom. So how can He help us out? How can we attain even a rudimentary grasp of these concepts?

To this end, Hakadosh Baruch Hu speaks in our terms, and ensures that our world is replete with parallels that serve as tools for understanding the spiritual universe. The structure and operating procedures of the world, and the physical and emotional realities of the human being, provide us with some minimal frame of reference to the spiritual dimension.

At times, Hashem acts with a show of strength, meting out punishment. How could He describe this conduct to us? He provides us with an arm, and infuses it with strength. An outstretched arm, in our world, is one that is poised to strike. Now that we have this point of comparison, He turns to us and says, "You may not truly understand Me, but know this. The course of action I'm about to take is much the same as the one you take when you stand with an outstretched arm."

Sometimes, Hashem will alter the natural course of world order due to corruption on humanity's part. The Torah describes this as a change of heart. Does He have a beating heart? Most definitely not. Yet we human beings also experience shifts of perspective that cause us to redirect our course of action. We refer to this as a change of heart, and therefore so does He.

Hakadosh Baruch Hu has an intense bond with each and every one of us. How can He describe this to us? How can He help our minds grasp just how connected to us He really is? To this end, He created the concept of love and endearment. Now that this concept exists between humans, and we have some glimpse of the extremes to which people will go for love, He can tell us that He is *oheiv amo Yisrael* — He loves His nation, Klal Yisrael. Having experienced relationships with our loved ones — parents, siblings, a spouse, a friend — we now have a basis of comparison for a relationship that transcends all of those bonds.

What we refer to as the Kisei HaKavod is not actually a chair or throne (*Moreh Nevuchim* 1:9), nor are angels the winged cherubic beings we commonly see depicted (ibid 1:43). The spiritual realm is an entirely different world, one that defies any physical characterization. Is Gan Eden a place of physical enjoyment? No. Is Gehinnom an actual fire? No. But by familiarizing us with concepts such as intense pleasure and searing pain, Hashem gives us a comparative tool that provides a glimmer of understanding of what awaits us in the World to Come.

Returning to our question, we can now understand that although Hakadosh Baruch Hu most definitely does not have a body, when the Torah describes His hand, foot, or nose, it is giving us a frame of reference. We have hands. What He is doing is what we would use our hands to do. We walk and talk, shift gears and change focus. He does none of those things; He is not physical. But all those activities can be viewed as metaphors that provide a very minimal glimpse into what He does.

The same is true of the emotions the Torah attributes to Hashem. He does not have emotions, but these descriptions of His emotions open a window into processes we otherwise could not grasp. As an example, R' Avraham ben HaRambam writes (*HaMaspik L'Oveid Hashem*, end of Ch. 6) that every time the Torah refers to Hashem as being in a state of anger or vengeance, the statement is immediately followed by His taking action. He explains, in line with the above, that Hakadosh Baruch Hu does not become angry, nor does He feel any urge to take revenge. Even in our world, however, if someone denigrates another person, and certainly a person who is of higher rank, his action will necessarily draw a reaction. It is inappropriate to casually let such an affront pass, as doing so would indicate a lack of recognition of the severity of the offense. For example, if someone were to witness his father being slapped across the face and respond with a flippant comment to the effect of, "Oh well, live and let live," he would be displaying a lack of basic respect for his father. If a country were to absorb a massive missile attack that kills hundreds of people and its government would respond with a "We're pro-peace" shrug, that would rightly be construed as a serious lack of concern for the citizenry.

Hakadosh Baruch Hu is not insulted by our behavior, even when we flagrantly defy His commands. His reaction to our behavior is not dictated by emotion. He never becomes angry. When the Torah describes Him as angry, it is alerting us that our notion of warranted anger, and our recognition of the necessity of appropriate retaliatory action, can help us understand Hashem's response to the action that was just performed. Hashem's anger is not a reality, it's merely a vehicle for simplifying concepts to our terms.

How Does This Affect My Daily Life?

*W*e are certainly aware of the issue with having any physical items somehow representing a manifestation of Hakadosh Baruch Hu. It is prohibited to create or own any statues, depictions, or renderings intended to represent Hakadosh Baruch Hu or a facet of Him.

Strangely, many places where Jews settled over the years somehow came to be bedecked with artwork, such as tile mosaics, depicting various scenes containing some image representing Him.[1]

---

1. In recent decades, for instance, a number of ancient "synagogues" have surfaced around Eretz Yisrael, some of which feature intricate floor mosaics that depict scenes from the Torah or other Jewish sources. Aside from other halachic issues with these images, many contain a central "God" figure. Most likely, these sites were frequented by groups who worshiped some form of *avodah zarah*, not by Torah-observant Jews at all. Regardless of who these worshipers were, however, these depictions are absolutely forbidden.

Not only are these images forbidden, they are nonsensical. There is nothing about Hashem that can be portrayed in a physical likeness — and attempting to create a physical likeness of Him evinces a fundamental misunderstanding of what He is.

In genuine Jewish tradition, any sort of icon or physical representation of God was unconditionally shunned. In fact, the *Meshech Chochmah* explains that for this reason, Moshe Rabbeinu destroyed the Luchos upon his descent from Har Sinai. Seeing that Klal Yisrael had created a physical item, the Golden Calf, and ennobled it as a manifestation, on some level, of Hakadosh Baruch Hu, he feared that the Luchos would be appropriated for that same role, becoming the next object of worship. Indeed, he feared that he himself had somehow been misperceived as some sort of Divine figure, as evidenced by the extreme panic the Jewish people experienced upon his presumed demise, which resulted in their fashioning the Eigel. Similarly, says the *Meshech Chochmah*, even the Beis HaMikdash carries no inherent *kedushah* or value. Its only value lies in its role as a point of connection between Hakadosh Baruch Hu and His people. As soon as it ceased to fill that role, all its holiness dissipated, making it possible for our enemies to destroy it, as all that was left was merely an edifice of wood and stone.

Beyond our rejection of any physical representation of Him, however, we need to banish any likeness of Him from our own headspace. We stand in *tefillah* each day, charged with developing a true awareness that we are in live conversation with the ultimate King, the Creator of the world. So you close your eyes — and what do you picture? Our minds tend to jump to the nearest point of association, so we naturally gravitate toward imagining ourselves standing before a human king on a bejeweled throne. This, however, is incorrect. Hashem is not a person. He has no physical dimension that we can visualize, and we may not picture Him as such. Yes, we can use our conceptualization of standing before a king, judge, or other authority figure as a springboard for understanding the awe required when speaking to Him. It must be exceedingly clear, though, that this is a tool to initiate the thought process, but not at all what we are meant to visualize during *tefillah*. The wording of the *Shulchan Aruch* (*Orach Chaim* 98:1) is impeccably precise in this regard: "One should think that if he were speaking before a human king, he would arrange his words and concentrate on them well so that he should not stumble — all the more so before the King of kings, Hashem." Picturing a mortal king is but the first step in the thought chain, not the final objective.

Are we stuck, then, without any means of visualizing Whom we are addressing? Perhaps a suggestion worth considering would be to picture that we are facing a curtain behind which He stands. What goes on behind the curtain? We have no idea. Some entity is there, and that entity is Who we are addressing. This is a means to envision some sort of tangibility without running afoul by actually picturing Him in a proscribed manner.

Moving a step further, we need to expand this concept to our understanding of Chumash and the words of Chazal. When we encounter Hakadosh Baruch Hu's role in various incidents — He spoke, He asked, He was happy, He was upset — our natural tendency is to view the incident through our own frame of reference. We must remember, however, that none of our human realities apply to Him. These are all but illustrations meant to convey more elevated concepts. We need to constantly remind ourselves that He is totally out of our realm and on a different plane. Hakadosh Baruch Hu — and, for that matter, all spiritual entities, such as angels or even our own *neshamos* — are part of a vastly different system, a profound world that exists above and beyond our physical one.

Some years ago, I was davening Shacharis in a certain shul one Shabbos morning. As the chazzan brought the *sefer Torah* toward the *bimah*, he noticed a young child holding his father's hand, waiting to kiss the passing *sefer Torah*. Noting the child's height, the chazzan bent down and lowered the *sefer Torah* to the child's level. A *mechanech* who observed this noted wryly, "In my line, we don't bring the Torah down to the child — we raise the child up to the level of the Torah."

Let us not reduce Hakadosh Baruch Hu to the level of a glorified human. Instead, let us develop and expand our minds to grasp the concept of a Higher existence.

הָעִקָּר הָרְבִיעִי
The Fourth Ikkar

אֲנִי מַאֲמִין בֶּאֱמוּנָה שְׁלֵמָה שֶׁהַבּוֹרֵא יִתְבָּרַךְ שְׁמוֹ הוּא רִאשׁוֹן וְהוּא אַחֲרוֹן.

I am steadfast in my absolute belief that the Creator, blessed is His Name, is the very first and the very last [to exist].

וְהַיְסוֹד הָרְבִיעִי הַקַּדְמוּת וְהוּא שֶׁזֶּה הָאֶחָד הָאָמוּר הוּא
הַקַּדְמוֹן בְּהֶחְלֵט וְכָל הַנִּמְצָא זוּלָתוֹ הוּא בִּלְתִּי קַדְמוֹן בְּיַחַס
אֵלָיו וְהָרְאָיוֹת עַל זֶה בַּסְּפָרִים הֵן רַבּוֹת וְהַיְסוֹד הָרְבִיעִי הַזֶּה
הוּא שֶׁהוֹרָה עָלָיו בְּאָמְרוּ מְעֹנָה אֱלֹהֵי קֶדֶם.

The fourth foundational belief is first existence, meaning that the aforementioned One is of necessity the absolute first to exist, and everything else could not possibly have predated Him. Many proofs of this are found in our sources, and this fourth foundational belief is attested to in the verse (*Devarim 33:27*): *[The heavenly spheres are] the abode of God immemorial.*

הוּא רִאשׁוֹן
The Cause of the Cause of the Cause

In this Ikkar, we deal with the concept of origination. Hakadosh Baruch Hu predates the entire universe. He existed at a point when nothing else existed.

In our universe, children are born to parents, who in turn were born to their parents. Paper comes from a tree, which came from a seed. Words are expressed by my mouth after originating as a thought in my brain. Everything we know and encounter follows a chain of development, emanating from a prior source. Everything, that is, except for Hakadosh Baruch Hu. He is the ultimate original source.

In this Ani Maamin, we are told that Hakadosh Baruch Hu is not only the first, but He will also endure eternally, even should all else cease to exist. *Hu rishon vehu acharon.* These words are somewhat obscure. That He existed before He created us we can understand, but what is the flip side of that? Is there a point when the universe will entirely cease to exist?

While there is much debate among the early sources about the ultimate endgame of our universe, perhaps the most straightforward way to understand this Ani Maamin is not to wade into that debate at all. Rather, the intent here is seemingly to stress that just as Hashem existed before creating us, His existence continues to be completely untethered to our world, and He would continue to exist just as well should we ever disappear. "He is first and He is last" simply highlights His independence from our universe. He is not at all reliant upon us and is not bound by our existence in the slightest. Our world can come and go and it would affect Him not a whit.

Turning to the words of the Rambam, however, we notice a marked discrepancy, which yields a very different emphasis. The Rambam establishes that Hakadosh Baruch Hu is the Kadmon, the point of absolute origination, but he makes no mention of His being the Acharon, the final One, Who will exist even after the cessation of the universe. The stress is squarely on the point of origination: He was there first. We were not.

The intent of the Rambam, as he expressed in numerous other writings, was to utterly negate the idea that the world always existed, an erroneous approach referred to as "Olam Kadmon." At a specific moment, Hashem chose to create a brand-new universe that previously did not exist in any shape or form whatsoever.

Hashem's being first is not merely a matter of chronology, with His existence predating ours. It's a matter of causation. Everything in our universe traces back to something that brought it to be. Man is born to parents, who were born to the previous generation, going back to the original creation of humanity by His hand. The fascinating panorama of nature that we witness — waterfalls, canyons, the Northern Lights — are all brought about by specific causes. Their causes as well are brought about by other causes. If we keep tracing the cause of the cause of the cause, we will ultimately arrive at a point where He himself created the original matter. Everything we know — be it ecosystems, rules of physics, sociological patterns, or any other object or concept — originated with Him. He is the first in every chain of existence.

Finding Our Niche

*W*hat lesson can we derive from this? Perhaps we can suggest that this Ikkar provides the context for our entire life's work.

If He existed without us, and decided to create us, that must mean He had a specific reason to do so. He created us for a purpose. The question then stares us straight in the face: Why did He create the world? Why did He create me? What role am I supposed to fulfill in the grand scheme of the universe?

The proper course of life encompasses many correct and viable routes. Some people excel in one aspect of Yiddishkeit, others find their niche in another. Regardless, every individual must cement within himself the concept that he is here for a purpose. He has work to do and goals to achieve.

Arriving at this understanding transforms my entire value system. Instead of asking what I would like to accomplish in life, my question becomes, what does Hashem want from me? All my efforts, goals, and accomplishments will be ranked and assessed by one metric only, that of how well I've fulfilled the goals I was handed.

Suppose you are at a job fair, seeking new opportunities. A fellow approaches you, peruses your resume, exchanges some talk about your qualifications, and offers you a job at a large Amazon warehouse he oversees. The next day, bright and early, you walk through the front doors, ready to work. There's just one issue: The boss never told you which of his many job openings you would be filling. He's nowhere in sight, and the place is massive. What now? You walk around and explore the warehouse, enjoying the fascinating sights and sounds, and then head over to a nearby vending station and buy some breakfast. Eventually, you figure you might as well make constructive use of your time. Looking around, you see hundreds, maybe thousands, of workers engaged in all sorts of activities, but the vast majority are absorbed in moving inventory and packing items into boxes. If that's what everyone else is doing, you think, you probably can't go wrong joining them. You spend the next few hours huffing and puffing, heaving loads and running back and forth.

Suddenly, you see a familiar face. The man from the job fair has arrived. Rushing over, you proudly inform him how much you have accomplished, and how much effort you exerted. He looks at you with a mixture of puzzlement and shock. "Packing boxes? I'm paying you to be part of the managerial team. I wanted you to help in the corporate offices! You're supposed to help manage the company, not run around the warehouse filling orders."

We learn Torah, we daven, we perform countless acts of *chessed* and other good deeds. But beyond the basic obligations that apply to every Jew, each of us has a specific task to perform, a unique mission that is ours alone. Hashem is our employer, and we are His employees. The question we have to constantly ask ourselves is not what good deed we can do next, but rather, what does He want me to be doing with my life? What does He expect from me today? This question cuts to the core of what we are doing in life, and creates the framework for our relationship with Him.

Sometimes, answering this question involves evaluating my conduct and implementing changes to bring it up to par. Other times, it involves adjusting my perspective. Rather than helping others simply because I enjoy doing *chessed*, I focus on helping others because that's the mission I was assigned.

Rabbeinu Yonah (*Shaarei Teshuvah* 3:17) highlights the extraordinary potential each Jew possesses, in many different areas. At the same time, he writes, we have been charged with monumental responsibility, and much is expected of us. "What hope is there for a person," Rabbeinu Yonah asks, "if he does not direct his energies primarily toward the matters for which he was created?"

Imagine that a person invests his heart and soul, and every ounce of his energy, into succeeding at a particular sport, only to discover that he was playing according to the wrong set of rules, and all his efforts were worthless. Now consider how much time and energy we invest into succeeding in life. We all have goals, ambitions, and pictures of what success looks like. How tragic would it be if after the game is up we would discover that we've been totally off track. The only way to avoid this is to stop for some introspection and assessment before charting our daily or lifelong path. What's the game all about? What are the rules? What truly counts as an accomplishment, and what actions don't rank on the scoreboard? How do I know I am answering these questions correctly?

If He was here first, and He chose to initiate my creation and bring me into existence, then He must have had a goal for me. Some things are in alignment with that purpose and some things aren't. To consistently achieve the goal for which I was created, I need to continually ask myself: What does He want from me? Am I on track toward achieving my purpose?[1]

Asking these questions will not necessarily result in clarity. Even if we are determined to figure out what He wants, and are fully willing to align our priorities and values with His will, it can nevertheless be difficult to verify that we are on the right path. Try as we may to decipher His messages, we live in a time of *hester panim*, a dimly lit era in which discerning right from wrong can be bewildering. The Vilna Gaon (*Mishlei* 16:4) describes how, in times gone by, *nevi'im* were readily available, and a person seeking direction in life would approach his local prophet and receive personalized guidance. Today, we don't have a *navi*. We don't have the clarity to arrive at absolute answers. We are held accountable, though, for putting in all the effort we can to find those answers.

Ask yourself: What is the basis for my values? Are my actions governed by halachah, or by the dictates of society? Sometimes, we can verify whether our course of action reflects Hashem's will through our own Torah knowledge, or by consulting with those who possess greater Torah knowledge — *daas Torah*. Other times, we try our best to pinpoint His will, but come up emptyhanded.

---

1. For a discussion of the connection between this message and this Ikkar, see Appendix A.

Then, we must look to Hakadosh Baruch Hu, Who knows how we have tried, and implore Him for greater clarity.

Regardless of whether we ultimately find answers, the first and most important part of the process is asking the question.

How Does This Affect My Daily Life?

*H*akadosh Baruch Hu created the world with a purpose, and placed every human being into this world to help reach that goal. Some people will be executives, while some will suffice with packing boxes. As Jews, we must look ourselves in the eye and contemplate why we are here. We each have sterling qualifications and have been Divinely chosen for an executive position, with a serious level of responsibility. We need to wake up each morning and ask, "What does the Boss want from me today?"

While we are not prophets, the decision of how to structure our day, and our life, will look vastly different if our priorities reflect those of Hashem.

Asking myself what He wants will help me determine, for instance, how to divide my time between Torah learning and engaging in *hishtadlus* at work. It will help me identify which social interactions to welcome and which to shun. It will help me decide which tradeoffs I need to make for the sake of my wellbeing and that of my family — and which compromises I refuse to make. These and other life questions should be decided not on the basis of our own feelings, or the opinions of those around us, but through the prism of what He wants from us. Our value system must reflect His preferences, not our own, and our definition of success must be how well we are meeting the job description He assigned us.

Will we always know precisely what He wants from us in any given situation? Of course not! Thankfully, however, we today enjoy unparalleled access to information and Torah erudition. Wise people with the knowledge and perspective necessary to guide us are only a phone call away. We can find answers, and we can receive the guidance we need — but it all starts with asking ourselves the question.

הָעִקָּר הַחֲמִישִׁי
The Fifth Ikkar

אֲנִי מַאֲמִין בֶּאֱמוּנָה שְׁלֵמָה שֶׁהַבּוֹרֵא יִתְבָּרַךְ
שְׁמוֹ לוֹ לְבַדּוֹ רָאוּי לְהִתְפַּלֵּל וְאֵין לְזוּלָתוֹ
רָאוּי לְהִתְפַּלֵּל.

I am steadfast in my absolute belief that
the Creator, blessed is His Name —
to Him alone is it appropriate to pray,
and it is inappropriate to pray to any other.

וְהַיְסוֹד הַחֲמִישִׁי שֶׁהוּא יִתְעַלֶּה הוּא שֶׁרָאוּי לְעָבְדוֹ וּלְרוֹמְמוֹ
וּלְהוֹדִיעַ רוֹמְמָתוֹ וַעֲבוֹדָתוֹ וְלֹא לַעֲשׂוֹת כֵּן לְמִי שֶׁהוּא
לְמַטָּה מִמֶּנּוּ בַּמְּצִיאוּת כְּגוֹן הַמַּלְאָכִים וְהַכּוֹכָבִים וְהַגַּלְגַּלִּים
וְהַיְסוֹדוֹת וּמַה שֶׁהֻרְכַּב מֵהֶן לְפִי שֶׁכֻּלָּם הֵם מְטְבָּעִים
בִּפְעֻלּוֹתֵיהֶם אֵין לָהֶם יְכֹלֶת וְלֹא בְּחִירָה אֶלָּא רְצוֹנוֹ יִתְעַלֶּה
וְאֵין לַעֲשׂוֹת אוֹתָם אֶמְצָעִים לְהַגִּיעַ אֵלָיו אֶלָּא אֵלָיו לְעָמְתוֹ
יִתְעַלֶּה יְכַוְּנוּ הַמַּחֲשָׁבוֹת וּמַנִּיחִים כָּל מַה שֶׁזוּלָתוֹ וְזֶה הַיְסוֹד
הַחֲמִישִׁי הוּא אַזְהָרָה עַל עֲבוֹדָה זָרָה וְרֹב הַתּוֹרָה הִיא
בְּאַזְהָרָה עָלֶיהָ.

**The fifth foundational belief is that He, the Exalted
One, is the One Whom it is appropriate to serve and
to treat with elevated stature,** as well as to proclaim to
others His loftiness and how to serve Him, and not to
do so to any other entity or force beneath Him, such as
angels, stars, constellations, the core elements of nature,
or anything that consists of these elements, for natural
law governs the activities of all of these. They have no
independent capabilities, nor free will, but function only
according to His will. These forces are not to be treated as
intermediaries to enable one to reach Him; rather, people
should direct their thoughts straight to Him, abandoning
anything aside from Him. This fifth foundational belief is
a warning against idolatry, which much of the Torah comes
to proscribe.

לְעַצְמוֹ יִתְעַלֶּה יְכַוְּנוּ הַמַּחֲשָׁבוֹת
To Hashem, and Hashem Alone,
We Channel Our Hearts and Minds

Exclusivity. Hakadosh Baruch Hu is not merely the One we turn to, but the only One we turn to. The role He occupies in our life is uniquely His and shared by no other. In our tefillos, we turn to Him and Him alone. In our avodah, we serve Him and Him alone. There is no other address. There are no intermediaries. He is the only appropriate address.

In the Ani Maamin version of this Ikkar, we declare that we address our prayers to Him alone. *Tefillah,* including both the standardized texts we recite three times a day as well as the personal discussions we have with Hakadosh Baruch Hu, generally encompasses two integral facets. The first is that of praise and gratitude. We speak of the remarkable world He has created, and the fascinating way He conducts the universe. As we stand in awe before Him, expressing praise and appreciation, we internalize, in our hearts and minds, all that He has done and continues to do for us. The second facet is that of making requests. Acknowledging that He is the One Who controls everything, from health and wealth to intelligence, childbearing, and the weather, we turn to Him asking that He fill all our needs, alleviate any difficulties we are encountering, and bless our efforts with success. Both of these facets must be squarely focused on Him: He is the only One Who truly warrants praise, and He is the only One Who can grant what we need and desire.

The Rambam expresses this Ikkar more broadly, as a reference to the general category of *avodah*, not specifically to *tefillah*. Presumedly, he is referring to both *avodah* in action — fulfilling His commandments and refraining from transgression — as well as prayer, which is referred to as *avodah shebalev*, service of the heart, since supplication is an act of subservience and humbling oneself before a Higher authority. Both of these forms of service must be directed to Him alone, since He alone controls the world and determines what is right and wrong, and He alone is with Whom we seek to find favor.

From the choice of wording in both versions of this Ikkar, it is clear that the emphasis is not on the necessity to daven to Hakadosh Baruch Hu. That's a given. The directive here is to direct our prayers to Him alone: Ensure that the conversations you have when you turn to a Higher Being are focused on the correct address, and limit them to that address alone.

Clearly, this Ikkar is not addressed to an atheist or to a person who worships something other than Hakadosh Baruch Hu. It is addressing someone who believes in Hakadosh Baruch Hu and already turns to Him in prayer, cautioning him to avoid bringing any other entity into that relationship. Talking to Hakadosh Baruch Hu is not enough. Our relationship with Him must remain exclusive.

Why, though, would there be a need to tell someone not to serve something else in tandem with Hakadosh Baruch Hu? If a person acknowledges Hashem's sovereignty and worships Him, why must he be cautioned to avoid turning as well to other entities?

Remarkably, as we study the works of the *nevi'im* and peer through the history of Klal Yisrael, we find this startling scenario to be quite common. In many, if not most, of the instances when Jews turned to *avodah zarah*, they did not decide to abandon Hakadosh Baruch Hu in favor of a whole new track of belief. Rather, they still proclaimed fealty to Hakadosh Baruch Hu, but simply added additional entities to which to pay homage.

Each Tishah B'Av, we read the painful *kinnah* that describes the bubbling blood of the murdered *navi* Zechariah. Why was he killed? Apparently, the Jews decided to set up an *avodah zarah* right in the middle of the courtyard of the Beis HaMikdash. Zechariah, watching this travesty unfold, objected, but his was a lone voice against the public will. With his murder, that voice was silenced, and the idol continued to stand, as Zechariah's blood bubbled on the floor of the Azarah in protest.

This incident transpired more than a century before the destruction of the Beis HaMikdash, which means that the Mikdash was defiled with idolatry for over one hundred years — a century living with a glaring, astounding paradox.

Of all places, why worship *avodah zarah* in the Beis HaMikdash? If you don't believe in our system, if you don't want to serve Hakadosh Baruch Hu, go choose a different venue.

Evidently, the goal was to create some sort of hybrid system, in which the people could worship both Hashem and *avodah zarah*.

This notion of attempting to create a hybrid system famously presents itself in Eliyahu HaNavi's dramatic showdown with the prophets of the Ba'al on Har HaCarmel. Eliyahu confronts these prophets, laying down a challenge to prove which is the true deity. He then turns to the masses of Jews gathered to witness the event and accuses them of vacillating between both sides, trying to have what they thought was the best of both worlds. "How long will you continue to straddle both sides of the fence?" he demands. Eliyahu was demanding intellectual honesty: Which side are you on? If you are on our side, great; if you are on the other side, I can talk to you and argue with you. But at least pick a side. Be clear with regards to which side you stand on. Here as well Klal Yisrael was sitting on this very same fence. They believed in Hakadosh Baruch Hu, but somehow sought to intertwine this with belief in the Ba'al as well.

Paying Homage to the Assistants

*H*ow could the Jews think they could simultaneously serve both Hashem and other deities?

The Rambam writes (*Hilchos Avodas Kochavim* 1:1) that the first people to stray after *avodah zarah* did not intend to create a new belief system at all. Rather, they felt that in deference to Hakadosh Baruch Hu, the recognized Supreme Force, it would be appropriate to accord honor to His "assistants" as well. Obviously, showing respect to cabinet members bespeaks an admiration for the president himself.

This first step was inherently flawed. These perceived "assistants" are simply tools that Hashem uses, and warrant no recognition in their own right. Nature boasts awesome beauty and brilliance, and when marveling at these manifestations of the Divine, we are meant to praise the Creator, not pay tribute to the creations themselves. When a chess master pulls off a stunning checkmate, the winning move may technically be executed via a castle, knight, or queen, but the praise is reserved for the person who orchestrated the victory, not for the piece itself.

This venture into the dangerous territory of honoring Hashem's "assistants" continued to evolve, morphing from a problematic approach into full-fledged *avodah zarah*. The intermediaries came to be viewed as holding some of the cards in their own hands, as if they maintained some element of control. And with that, the door was opened to beseeching, serving, and attempting to "win favor" with these forces.

Still, the masses viewed these forces not as independent elements, but as powerful delegates of Hakadosh Baruch Hu, whose worship was therefore somehow compatible with *avodas Hashem*.

Understandably, this approach was fatally flawed long before it reached the full-fledged *avodah zarah* stage, as Hashem has never relinquished any control to any other entity. He maintains full command of even the most minute occurrences, at all times and in every place. Furthermore, He specifically tells us that we need no go-between, and that He is not at all distant from us. We have direct, unfettered, guaranteed access to Him anytime we want. He is right here listening to anything we want to discuss with Him.

The question then arises: Even if these hybrid worshipers truly believed in some convoluted form of duality, why did they keep turning to the various forms of *avodah zarah*, instead of praying directly to Hakadosh Baruch Hu?

To answer this question, we must understand that idol worship was perceived as a way to achieve results, on some level. The world operates in accordance with certain natural and supernatural forces — powers that Hashem Himself vested in the universe, in much the same way as the forces of gravity or magnetism operate. Whether it was indeed possible to harness metaphysical forces, or whether this was simply an accepted misperception, the prevalent — and at times dominant — belief was that desired outcomes could be achieved by appealing to these forces, instead of turning to Hakadosh Baruch Hu directly.

The reason people opted to go the *avodah zarah* route now begins to seem less confounding. A person contracts a devastating illness. In his mind, there are two choices of how to proceed: He can turn to Hakadosh Baruch Hu, or he can appeal to his local *avodah zarah*. If He turns to Hakadosh Baruch Hu, he might get a rather discomfiting response. After all, Hakadosh Baruch Hu would never cause one of His children pain needlessly. The illness might be a wake-up call to do *teshuvah*, and make difficult corrections to one's life. It might be a challenge for the person, forcing him to rise to the occasion by finding and developing strengths that lay dormant within him. In short, resolving the issue will often require serious work. The other choice would be to seek immediate relief by turning to *avodah zarah* — problem-solving with no introspection necessary. This was the catalyst for adopting a conflated belief system.[1] People's belief in Hakadosh Baruch Hu was marred by their inability to face the message behind their

---

1. This idea is discussed at length in Rav Yitzchak Berkovits's *The Six Constant Mitzvos*, Mitzvah 2.

difficulties, and instead of stopping to consider the root causes, they sought quick-fix solutions to these problems. *Avodah zarah*, then, was the outgrowth of the drive for gratification unaccompanied by the willingness to stand up to challenges and grow from them.

In some instances, such as in the tragedy that was the Eigel HaZahav, there was an additional motivation. Recognizing that Hakadosh Baruch Hu is so exalted and lofty, people viewed Him as remote, and deemed it necessary to establish some sort of intermediary to bridge the gap. By way of analogy, imagine that you need to meet with the CEO of a company to swing a deal, but since gaining access to him is tough, you approach a company representative who is lower on the chain of command, yet has access to the CEO. You send this representative a gift here and there, cultivate a relationship with him, and hope that this back-door approach will garner you the meeting you covet. This strategy might work in the business world, but vis-à-vis Hashem it is categorically wrong. He is not far. He informs us clearly and emphatically that He is always close to us, and is waiting to hear from us. While an outsider or even an employee might need to devise strategies to gain an audience with the boss, his children can barge right in. A child who turns to others to gain access to his father simply doesn't understand what a relationship with one's loving parent is all about.[2]

How Does This Affect My Daily Life?

*A*ll this discussion of worshiping idols might seem wholly arcane and irrelevant to modern times, but these concepts are actually very relevant to us. Often, people encounter difficult or painful situations: illness, death, unemployment, and so on. In addition to davening for a *yeshuah*, a sincere Jew also seeks *berachos* from *gedolim*, performs mitzvos as

---

2. See *Teshuvos Chasam Sofer*, OC 166.

a merit for salvation, and travels to *kivrei tzaddikim* and other holy sites to give his *tefillos* added potency.

Yet while these interventions are certainly noble, we must understand clearly that nothing and no one other than Hakadosh Baruch Hu Himself holds any capability to alter a situation. He maintains full and absolute control, and has never relinquished any of it. Nothing, and no one, can force His hand. The traditional strategies that we employ in times of misfortune can, if utilized properly, bolster our case, adding reasons for Hakadosh Baruch Hu to ameliorate whatever issue we are facing. Yet they are nothing more than advocates standing on the sidelines. Ultimately, it's all about you and Him. There are divergent approaches in halachah as to how and whether requests may be made of non-physical entities, such as *malachim* and departed *neshamos*, but all agree that the supplicant must always know clearly that his petitions are addressed to Hashem alone.

Moreover, people in distress will often embrace all sorts of omens, *segulos*, or random acts that can ostensibly help bring about a cure or remedy. Truthfully, there is a time and place for *segulos*, and there is merit in many of the other wonderful practices that are out there. When and if properly sourced, these are Torah-approved and at times recommended. Oftentimes, however, they can cloud our perspective. We become convinced that the *segulah* alone is the perfect salve for what ails us: I have a problem, I perform a *segulah*, and presto, problem solved. Such an approach is indicative of a basic error in reasoning. We are hyper-focused on the problem and the practical methods of ameliorating the issue: How do I get rid of the sickness? How do I find a job? How do I solve the shidduch crisis?

Stop. Are you seeing the bigger picture?

There's a root cause behind every problem. The problem is Hakadosh Baruch Hu's means of calling out to you. He loves you tremendously, beyond any human concept of love, and if He is sending challenges your way, it can only be for your own good. Is it a call to *teshuvah*? A call to growth? Sometimes it's tough to tell, but the first step is realizing that the difficulty has a tailor-made purpose. One thing is certain: Hakadosh Baruch Hu cares for us to a degree we cannot begin to comprehend, and He most definitely did not cause us pain in order to inspire us to wear a red string or march around a *kever*. Yes, *segulos* and *berachos* have their place. When deemed proper, they fall under the heading of *hishtadlus*, efforts we may or must invest in our quest to deal with challenges. If we align our efforts with the Torah's guidance, that will certainly serve to improve our situation. But these forms of *hishtadlus* are peripheral, not a replacement for focusing on what Hashem is trying to tell us.

Motrin may provide pain relief, but it won't perform the root canal that will put an end to the pain and save the tooth. You are allowed to seek relief, but think big. Think deeper. Think about why you might have been put in this situation, and how you can use it to grow.

Don't focus on the problem. Focus on the One who sent it. Talk to Him. Listen to Him. Grow.

לוֹ לְבַדּוֹ רָאוּי לְהִתְפַּלֵּל
To Hashem Alone We Pray

Hide-and-Seek

In the previous segment, we discussed the general approach to dealing with the various issues we face: Our primary focus should not be on achieving pain relief, but rather on what Hashem, Who created the issue, wants from us.

There is another element within this Ikkar, one that pertains to tefillah specifically. Prayer must be addressed solely to Him. If we truly understand the concept of tefillah, we recognize that beseeching any other person, force, or entity for assistance as if control lay in their hands is entirely senseless.

*D*irecting prayers toward anything other than Hakadosh Baruch Hu leads a person into serious *avodah zarah* territory, as the Rambam establishes. Aside from the *avodah zarah* aspect, however, looking elsewhere for assistance involves another fundamental issue: It undercuts the entire essence of *tefillah*.

How so?

Let's have a look at the function of *tefillah*.

Tefillah plays a central role in every day of our life. We address our Creator in Shacharis, Minchah, and Maariv, and many times in between. Why? What are we trying to accomplish? For one thing, we are thanking Him for all that He has done for us personally and for the world at large. This aspect is understandable. By praising the myriad facets of His world, from the mind-boggling complexity of the solar system to the intricacy of each cell, we express our gratitude and appreciation for these wonders, which helps us focus on His many gifts and truly enjoy the environs He has created for us.

Yet the most basic component of *tefillah* is our requests for the varied items we need. "Could You please help me out with my *parnassah*, with my health, with *shidduchim*, with *shalom bayis*, with raising my children?" We turn to Him regularly with our litany of requests, asking Him to provide for us.

Here we run into a roadblock, a conundrum that cuts to the core of all our *tefillos*. Hashem is in charge, and He understands the situation far better than I do. So He already knows what I need before I open my mouth. And if He wants to give it to me, He can certainly do so. Conversely, if He doesn't want to give it to me, there's no getting around Him. So why should I bother asking?

The Ramchal and others explain that indeed, Hakadosh Baruch Hu knows what we need, and He has no problem giving it to us straightaway. He loves us deeply, and wants to make our lives as pleasant as possible. To understand the purpose of prayer, then, we must take a step back. Before we can think about asking for assistance, let's think about why we have a problem in the first place. Why is that person lacking health, money, or anything else? The answer is that He withheld it in the first place. Hashem created the challenge.

But why?

Our job down here in this world, and the overall purpose in everything we have to do, can be summed up as a quest to find

Hakadosh Baruch Hu. He put us down here, in a murky world where His hand is not readily apparent, with the task of finding Him. It's one ongoing quest of hide-and-seek.

How do we go about finding Him? Suppose a person's life is going well on every front, and he has all the money and resources he requires. In such a situation, people tend to take matters for granted. They are comfortable, they are content, and they ask no questions. Where does all this goodness come from? Who cares, just pass the Coke. How, then, are they going to find Hakadosh Baruch Hu? Along He comes and takes things away. Now people start to open their eyes. Now they're looking. Who's in charge? Who can help me? And with that, they can find Him.

Once I realize that prosperity is a gift from Him, wellbeing is a gift from Him, intellect is a gift from Him, I will turn to Him and ask for these things. I got the message. I'm connecting. There's no longer a need for Him to withhold anything.

Essentially, the goal of *tefillah* is not to convince Hashem to grant me a bonus. It is for me to receive what He planned to give me all along. Hashem took it away to spur me to come and find Him, which I can accomplish through prayer. There's a saying attributed to Rav Yitzchak Hutner *zt"l*: *Tefillah* wasn't invented to get us out of problems — problems were invented to get us into *tefillah*.

The Avos were childless for decades. This, we are told, is because Hakadosh Baruch Hu yearned for their prayers. What does that mean? Would Hakadosh Baruch Hu inflict pain just to hear a *tefillah*? And why does He need their prayers at all? The answer is that He needs absolutely nothing. He wanted the Avos to grow far beyond what they were. Only by lacking something critical, which prompted them to engage in heartfelt prayer and connect with Hashem on a profound level, could they attain such heights. In other words, for a Yitzchak Avinu to emerge, his parents had to connect to Hakadosh Baruch Hu on an intense level that could be attained only by yearning for a child for so many years.

This concept of *tefillah* serving as a means of connecting us with Hashem is evident throughout the wording of *Shemoneh Esrei*.

Looking through the various *berachos* of personal requests, we find a recurring structural pattern: In many of these *berachos*, after making the initial request, we conclude with a statement beginning, "*Ki atah* — because You are." We ask for health — "because You are the faithful Healer." For livelihood, "because You are the One Who blesses the years."

I understand that You are the One in charge, I get it. Now that I attained this understanding, there's no longer a reason for You to withhold these benefits from me. Now, I ask You to grant them to me.

If the whole essence of *tefillah* is to forge a connection between Hakadosh Baruch Hu and myself, it would be utterly absurd to respond to His withholding something from me by turning to someone or something else for help. The whole reason He took it away was to motivate me to draw near to Him! Turning to someone else and viewing that other person or entity as exerting some control over my life completely defeats the purpose and just digs the hole I'm in even deeper.

How Does This Affect My Daily Life?

*L*ife appears, to the casual observer, to be running on a course of its own. People make money. People lose money. People are healthy. People become sick. People have it easy. People deal with endless stress. Can we peer through the veil to understand that there's a hand pulling the strings in everything we see?

Each experience in life, whether enjoyable or difficult, is His doing. Our mission is to see through the smokescreen and to keep drawing everything we see back to its source. Through prayer, we rewire our vision of how the world is truly run.

Tefillah is fundamental to our day, and not just as a shopping list. Set yourself straight each morning. Remind yourself midday, and then again when your day draws to a close. Hashem wants you to notice Him in health and in sickness, in the business deal you close and in the one that falls through. Through *tefillah*, you find Him everywhere.

הָעִקָּר הַשִּׁשִּׁי
The Sixth Ikkar

אֲנִי מַאֲמִין בֶּאֱמוּנָה שְׁלֵמָה שֶׁכָּל דִּבְרֵי נְבִיאִים אֱמֶת.

I am steadfast in my absolute belief that all the words of the prophets are true.

וְהַיְסוֹד הַשִּׁשִּׁי הַנְּבוּאָה וְהוּא לֵידַע שֶׁבַּמִּין הָאֱנוֹשִׁי הַזֶּה
אֶפְשָׁר שֶׁיִּמָּצְאוּ בְּנֵי אָדָם שֶׁיֵּשׁ לָהֶם תְּכוּנוֹת מְעֻלּוֹת מְאֹד
וּשְׁלֵמוּת רַבָּה וְכוֹנְנוּ נַפְשָׁם עַד כְּדֵי קַבָּלַת צוּרַת הַשֵּׂכֶל
וְאוֹתוֹ הַשֵּׂכֶל הָאֱנוֹשִׁי מִתְדַּבֵּק בַּשֵּׂכֶל הַפּוֹעֵל וְנֶאֱצָל מִמֶּנּוּ
עֲלֵיהֶם אֲצִילוּת נִכְבָּדָה וְאֵלֶּה הֵם הַנְּבִיאִים וְזוֹ הִיא הַנְּבוּאָה
וְזֶה הוּא עִנְיָנָהּ. וּבֵאוּר יְסוֹד זֶה עַל בֻּרְיוֹ יֶאֱרַךְ מְאֹד וְאֵין
בְּכַוָּנָתֵנוּ לְהָבִיא מוֹפֵת עַל כָּל יְסוֹד מֵהֶם וּבֵאוּר אָפְנֵי
הַשָּׂגָתָם לְפִי שֶׁזֶּה הוּא כְּלַל הַחָכְמוֹת כֻּלָּם אֶלָּא אַזְכִּירֵם דֶּרֶךְ
הוֹדָעָה בִּלְבַד וּכְתוּבֵי הַתּוֹרָה מְעִידִים עַל נְבוּאַת נְבִיאִים
רַבִּים.

The sixth foundational belief is that of prophecy: to know that within humanity it is possible to find people of exceptional, rarefied character who have molded their souls to the degree that they fully absorb [and act strictly in accordance with] the dictates of intellect — and this human intellect then bonds with the [higher] intellect of He Who runs the world, which causes an extremely elevated level of intellect to rest upon them. These people are the prophets, and this is what is referred to as prophecy.

A comprehensive explanation of this foundational belief would be extremely lengthy, and our intention is not to bring proof of each principle within this concept, nor to explain the methods of attaining them, for that would require the amalgamation of all the various forms of wisdom. Rather, I mention this concept as general information alone; and the verses of the Torah attest to the prophecies of many such prophets.

נְבוּאָה
Prophecy: A Window Between Worlds

*The term nevuah, prophecy, conjures up images of myste-
rious foretelling of the future, and performance of nature-
defying feats. Why would such activities play a role in our
lives? How can they claim center stage as one of the fundamentals of our belief system?*

*In truth, nevuah is not about magical abilities. It is about
opening a whole new window — not into other worlds, but
into our own.*

*W*hat exactly is *nevuah*?

We tend to associate *nevuah* with the ability of a
human to somehow foretell the future. The prophet
sees that which ordinary people cannot, and can therefore provide useful information regarding future events. We also associate
nevuah with the ability to perform supernatural wonders, whether
to bring about miraculous cures and solutions or to mete out punishment.

Looking through the treasure trove of the *sifrei Nevi'im*, though,
we come away with a very different picture. Yes, such achieve-
ments did occur, but by and large they were few and far between. In fact, most of the words and actions of the *nevi'im* are

remarkably unexceptional, and fall into two categories. One is reproach, with the *navi* serving as the critical eye and voice of reason as he warned his fellow Jews of the dangers of the path they were choosing. The other is comfort, with the *navi* standing by the masses in times of tragedy, guiding them toward a brighter future, and assuring them all was not lost. Hardly a shock-and-awe presentation.

If these two roles constitute the primary work of the *navi*, then we must ask ourselves what a *navi* really is.

One of the first times the concept of *nevuah* appears in the Torah is when Hakadosh Baruch Hu instructs Moshe Rabbeinu to approach Pharaoh, setting the wheels of redemption in motion. Moshe Rabbeinu protests this assignment, pointing to his speech impediment. Hakadosh Baruch Hu responds that Moshe must nevertheless go to Pharaoh, but he will be accompanied by Aharon HaKohen: וְאַהֲרֹן אָחִיךָ יִהְיֶה נְבִיאֶךָ, *Aharon your brother will be your navi* (*Shemos* 7:1). *Navi*? Aharon was to serve as a mouthpiece, voicing the message that Moshe was bearing. How can this be construed as prophecy?

Rashi, citing Chazal, explains that the word *navi* is to be understood as *meturgeman*, an interpreter. Furthermore, says Rashi, every instance of the word *navi* in the Torah denotes conveying a message.

The mystery intensifies. Our prophets have been reduced to interpreters?

From the various pieces of information we've been given, as well as the Rambam's depiction in numerous places of the workings of *nevuah*, the following understanding emerges.

Hakadosh Baruch Hu created this magnificent universe, and charged us with a mission when He placed us into it. Our task is to act as He wants us to, and steer clear of actions He wants us to avoid. What makes this a challenge, though, is that He remains hidden. Were He to reveal himself openly, allowing us to perceive the full scheme of how the world functions and easily discern right from wrong, there would be no point in having us live within this system. Remove the challenge, and we would effectively be reduced to robotic creatures. Every sane person will avoid poison. If we understood the harm wrought by an *aveirah*, we would never dream of sinning.

Hashem placed us into a murky world, where His existence is hidden. Finding Him is a real challenge, and making the right choices is difficult. To compound the challenge, we were created as a composite of two forces that pull us toward two opposite poles. Essentially, we are half-angel and half-animal. The angel within us, our *neshamah*, is motivated by altruistic logic, and forever tugs us upward. Our animalistic bodies, however, tug us earthward, as the passions and drives raging within us spur us to enjoy the here-and-now without a thought to the consequences. With the conditions in place for a true challenge, our life's work can begin.

Portal of Communication

*T*he setup poses a risk, though. Put a person in such a situation and he can lose all focus. He can easily take a wrong turn, and then heap error upon error until he is lost beyond return.

One way to deal with this potential risk would be for Hashem to place a person into this world with a basic set of instructions and then leave him to his own devices. For better or for worse, he'll fare in his task however he fares. At the end of his life, he'll be judged on his performance, acknowledging and taking into account that he was left on his own.

Rather than do so, though, He decided to actively assist us, by keeping open a small but active portal of communication to convey directions. Not enough to derail the challenge. Not enough to unmask Hakadosh Baruch Hu. Just enough to give a helping hand, a push in the right direction, to enable humanity to avoid going off the rails.

Hakadosh Baruch remains hidden, but He actively reaches

across the divide and communicates with our world. Historical-
ly, the recipients of these communications were the *nevi'im*. The
message of this Ikkar is not merely that the words of the *nevi'im*
are true; it is that the basic concept of *nevuah* exists, granting us a
portal of communication with Hakadosh Baruch Hu.

The Rambam writes that qualifying for *nevuah* was no simple
feat. It required arduous character development: A would-be *navi*
would have to invest years into self-perfection, while striving for
lofty levels of closeness to Hashem and utilizing every aspect of
his life to its maximum potential. He would have to be free of
petty motivations, untethered by drives for the mundane, and la-
ser-focused on *avodas Hashem*. Once a person reached this point,
he could aspire for *nevuah*. Even then, not all *nevuah* was created
equal. A prophet could always achieve greater levels of closeness
to Hashem, and, commensurately, greater levels of *nevuah*.

The basis of *nevuah*, then, is the work a person does to completely refashion himself. Having molded himself to live, act,
and think exactly as Hakadosh Baruch Hu wants him to, the *navi*
would gain a worldview that often differed dramatically from
that of the people. The view of the masses may have been essentially altruistic, but it was colored by other motivations, such as
prestige, wealth, or physical pleasure. Each time they weighed a
decision, there were other factors on the scale aside from *avodas
Hashem*. Even if only minimal, these factors could nonetheless tip
the scales in critical decisions.

To illustrate with a contemporary example, say a person is deciding in which of two shuls he should daven Minchah. One has
an environment conducive to proper tefillah, while the environment in the other leaves much to be desired. Technically, this decision should be made purely on the basis of in which shul will the
tefillah experience be enhanced, but the fact that one location is a
block and a half further than the other, or has fewer parking spots
available, will likely influence the person's decision, whether consciously or subconsciously.

Not so the *navi*. Having risen above his personal desires, his perspective is untarnished, and he sees the world in its true light. His job, then, was to turn to the rest of Klal Yisrael and explain to them, in their terms, why their vision was distorted.

Repackaging the Message

*L*et's step back to the description of the *navi* as a *meturge-man*, an interpreter. What is an interpreter? Suppose someone was giving you some necessary information, in his native Norwegian tongue. Assuming you belong to the vast majority of the world population that has not the faintest understanding of Norwegian, his words will sound like complete gibberish. Truthfully, however, there is nothing nonsensical about what he is saying. His statement might even be brilliant and profound. The issue is the listener's inability to process what is being told to him. Enter the interpreter. His job is not to provide new information, but to take the message — which he understands clearly — and present it in a way that the listener can understand.

This is precisely the task of the *navi*: to turn to the masses, the people who want to understand but whose comprehension is limited, and convey Hashem's perspective, the true understanding of what is transpiring, in terms they can understand.

Visualize a life-size maze, an intricate combination of paths in which it is difficult to find one's way or reach the exit. People are circulating, turning here and there, trying mightily to calculate a route to the exit using only their limited vision. Now, picture a person standing on a platform overlooking this maze. Seeing some hopelessly lost individuals, he calls down to them and directs them to the turns that lead to the exit. His power is not magical; his is not an otherworldly vision. Rather, from his elevated viewpoint he enjoys a panoramic perspective. With a true grasp of the layout, he can make accurate decisions. This is the *navi*. He's up there on the platform, looking down and guiding us through the labyrinth of life from a point of clarity.

As mentioned, the *sifrei Nevi'im,* for the most part, contain words of reproach and comfort. At times, Klal Yisrael strayed dangerously, positioning themselves on the fast lane to self-destruction while confidently reassuring themselves that all was right. They saw no error in their ways and no reason for concern. It was the *navi's* role to shake Klal Yisrael awake, opening their eyes to their mistakes before they would be hopelessly lost.

Sadly, the message often went unheeded, and the dire predictions of the *nevi'im* invariably materialized. Then, as Klal Yisrael trudged down a road of tears, leaving their homes, their land, and their Mikdash for a future filled with pain, slavery, and suffering, it was again the *navi* who provided the masses with a different perspective. This time, it was a message of hope and survival: Yes, to your eyes everything looks bleak. It looks like we've reached the end of the road, a point of no return. In truth, though, Hakadosh Baruch Hu will never abandon us, and these times, difficult as they may seem, are simply additional stops on the road back to a glorious future.

The *navi* is not a magician. He is a guide, here to keep us on track. Yes, he is endowed with special abilities. Yes, at times his actions venture into the supernatural, as he performs remarkable feats, reveals hidden information, or predicts the future. But these abilities do not define his role — they are merely enhancements that Hakadosh Baruch Hu grants him, to be used only in specific situations. His role is to interpret how the world, and all the events we encounter, should be understood.

How Does This Affect My Daily Life?

The existence of *nevuah,* in which Hakadosh Baruch Hu actively bridges the divide to communicate with our world, is a core principle of our faith, and is counted among the Thirteen Ikkarim. Yet we have gone thousands of years without this form of communication. Where, then, is *nevuah* manifest in my life?

For one thing, the veracity of *nevuah* remains a critical concept for us whether or not new prophecies are actively being transmitted. After all, the linchpin of the entire Torah is this ability to receive instructions from Hakadosh Baruch Hu. The Torah we have in our hands came to us via Hakadosh Baruch Hu's communication, whether to Moshe Rabbeinu or to other *nevi'im*. Belief in *nevuah*, therefore, is a basis of our trust in the Torah, which we received so many millennia ago, when that portal was still active.

Yet even today, there remains an active form of communication with the Divine.

The last of the *nevi'im* to be recorded in Tanach is Malachi. His final prophecy contains the exhortation: זִכְרוּ תּוֹרַת מֹשֶׁה עַבְדִּי, *Remember the Torah of Moshe, My servant*. Rather cryptic words with which to close out the chapter of *nevuah*.

The Malbim offers the following explanation. The power of prophecy had guided Jewry for generations. At times of need, the *nevi'im* of each generation would stand by, serving as a beacon of clarity, guidance, and leadership. Now, the window was closing. The gates of *nevuah* were being sealed until the era of Mashiach. What hope remained? Without prophets showing the way, how could people discern the correct path in life?

"Zichru Toras Moshe avdi" — turn to the Torah. Hakadosh Baruch Hu still wants to connect with us. He is still communicating with us. But now, the transmission follows a different track. It's no longer as easy as stopping by the *navi* on the corner. Perceiving Hashem's communications requires concerted effort and determination, but for the one who dives into the sea of Torah, immersing his mind and energy in the *dvar Hashem*, the voice of Hashem will still resonate, imbuing him with clarity and providing guidance for every situation.

In each generation, we are blessed with true Torah giants: rabbanim and roshei yeshivah who dedicate themselves to lifelong immersion in Torah. These individuals strive to rise above physicality and the mundane, aligning their lives completely with the Torah's values and perspective. We still have whom to turn to for guidance. Indeed, today we enjoy unparalleled access to great men. These leaders still exist, and are tailored to our generation's needs. From their elevated plateau, they possess a clear view of the world and a profound understanding of the unique challenges of our time, making them ideally positioned to guide us who are of limited vision.

At times, we might struggle to follow the directives of our leaders, or fail to understand the wisdom behind the guidance they have provided to us individually or collectively. Still, we are commanded to obey the instructions of Torah sages, as the verse states: לֹא תָסוּר מִן הַדָּבָר אֲשֶׁר יַגִּידוּ לְךָ יָמִין וּשְׂמֹאל, *Do not stray from the word they will tell you neither right nor left* (*Devarim* 17:11). Chazal interpret this to mean that we must listen to them even if they tell us that left is right and right is left.

What does this mean? We are a nation that places supreme value on intellect, on the ability to distinguish right from wrong. If someone tells us to do something ridiculous, shouldn't we have the good sense to disregard his advice? Are we really supposed to suppress all logic in favor of blindly following Torah leaders?

The answer, suggests Rav Yitzchak Berkovits, lies in Chazal's choice of terminology. Right and left — not east and west. East and west are absolute values. If the person guiding you tells you that east is actually west, seek counsel elsewhere. Right and left, though, are subjective. If I'm facing you, your right is not my right. When *chachamim* tell you that right is left, they're not defying logic. They are simply telling you that your perspective is all wrong. Your priorities or worldview need to be recalibrated. Turn around to face a different angle. Get your views in sync with the Torah's vision, and suddenly, right will be right.

There is, however, one dramatic difference between hearing Hashem's voice through the Torah and hearing it via *nevuah*. *Nevuah* was the domain of the select few. Either a person was of the elite few who qualified, or he was not. Until someone succeeded at attaining that plateau, he could not receive any *nevuah* at all; were he to claim that he had experienced a prophetic vision, he could potentially face capital punishment. Torah, on the other hand, is immediately attainable by any Jew, regardless of his level of scholarship or piety. It is a majestic staircase rising toward Hakadosh Baruch Hu, with an infinite number of levels to climb. Some people take but a few steps, while others invest every iota of their energy to ascend as high as they possibly can. Yet every person can take steps. Everyone can grow in Torah, and with that growth will come *siyata d'Shmaya*, a supernatural dose of Heavenly guidance.

Hearing Hashem's voice, and identifying the Divine perspective, is not solely the domain of the *gedolei hador*, the towering giants of each generation. Through Torah, the portal of Hashem's communication remains open, ready to be accessed by each and every one of us. Take a step up, no matter where on the Torah staircase you find yourself, and with every bit of effort you invest, you will draw that much closer to Hakadosh Baruch Hu. In the process, your perspective on life will be calibrated, and you will enjoy a special infusion of Divine guidance that will illuminate your path forward.

הָעִקָּר הַשְּׁבִיעִי
The Seventh Ikkar

אֲנִי מַאֲמִין בֶּאֱמוּנָה שְׁלֵמָה שֶׁנְּבוּאַת מֹשֶׁה רַבֵּנוּ עָלָיו הַשָּׁלוֹם הָיְתָה אֲמִתִּית וְשֶׁהוּא הָיָה אָב לַנְּבִיאִים לַקּוֹדְמִים לְפָנָיו וְלַבָּאִים אַחֲרָיו.

I am steadfast in my absolute belief that the prophecy of Moshe Rabbeinu, may peace be upon him, was true, and that he was the archetype of prophets, both those who preceded him as well as those who followed him.

In the Rambam's Words

וְהַיְסוֹד הַשְּׁבִיעִי נְבוּאַת מֹשֶׁה רַבֵּנוּ וְהוּא שֶׁנַּאֲמִין שֶׁהוּא
אֲבִיהֶן שֶׁל כָּל הַנְּבִיאִים שֶׁקָּדְמוּ לְפָנָיו וְאֵלֶּה שֶׁאַחֲרָיו
כֻּלָּם הֵם לְמַטָּה מִמֶּנּוּ בְּמַעֲלָה וְהוּא הַנִּבְחָר לַה' מִכָּל הַמִּין
הָאֱנוֹשִׁי אֲשֶׁר הִשִּׂיג מִמֶּנּוּ יִתְעַלֶּה יוֹתֵר מִמַּה שֶׁהִשִּׂיג וְיַשִּׂיג
כָּל אָדָם שֶׁנִּמְצָא וְשֶׁיִּמָּצֵא וְכִי הוּא עָלָיו הַשָּׁלוֹם נִתְעַלָּה
בְּתַכְלִית מִן הָאֱנוֹשִׁיּוּת עַד שֶׁהִשִּׂיג אֶת הַמַּעֲלָה הַמַּלְאֲכִית
וְנִהְיָה בְּמַעֲלַת הַמַּלְאָכִים לֹא נִשְׁאַר לוֹ מָסָךְ שֶׁלֹּא קְרָעוֹ וְלֹא
מְנָעוֹ מוֹנֵעַ גּוּפָנִי וְלֹא הָיָה בּוֹ כְּלוּם מִן הַחֶסָּרוֹן מְעַט אוֹ
הַרְבֵּה וּבָטְלוּ מִמֶּנּוּ הַכֹּחוֹת הַדִּמְיוֹנִיִּים וְהַחוּשִׁיִּים בְּהַשָּׂגוֹתָיו
וְנֶאֱלַם כֹּחוֹ הַמִּתְעוֹרֵר וְנִשְׁאַר שֵׂכֶל בִּלְבַד וּלְעִנְיָן זֶה
הִתְבַּטְּאוּ עָלָיו שֶׁהוּא מְדַבֵּר עִם ה' שֶׁלֹּא בְּאֶמְצָעוּת.

The seventh foundational belief is the prophecy of Moshe Rabbeinu. We believe that he is the archetype of all other prophets, both those who preceded him as well as those who followed him. All those were of lesser stature, and he was the one chosen by Hashem from all of humanity to perceive more of Hashem than any human who ever lived or will ever live. He, may he rest in peace, rose to the pinnacle of humanity, to the point that he attained an angelic level and indeed existed on the plane of angels, leaving no dividing screen that he did not pierce. No physical impediment restrained him, and he possessed no character failings, major or minor. By virtue of his elevated level, he was devoid of natural desire and physical impulses, and his emotional urges were completely muted, leaving him with pure intellect alone. This is why Chazal described him as speaking to Hashem without any intermediary.

אִסְפַּקְלַרְיָא הַמְּאִירָה
Crystal Clear Vision

*The previous Ikkar established the basic premise of nevuah:
Hakadosh Baruch Hu actively communicates with humanity. In this Ikkar, the concept is clarified further. There are
varying levels of seeing and understanding Hashem's prophetic messages, and not all nevi'im experience the same
clarity of vision. The paragon of nevuah was Moshe Rabbeinu. No other prophet attained the absolute clarity of communication that he experienced.*

*I*n describing the difference between the *nevuah* of Moshe
Rabbeinu and that of every other prophet, the Rambam
enumerates four key points of contrast:

1. **Direct connection**: All *nevi'im* were required to achieve an
   exceptional degree of closeness to Hakadosh Baruch Hu
   in order to be qualified for prophecy. Nevertheless, they
   were still unable to receive communication directly from
   Hashem. Divine messages had to be transmitted through
   several levels or phases, such as angels or other intermediaries, to become accessible to the *navi*. Moshe Rabbeinu,
   on the other hand, stood "face-to-face" with Hashem, who
   communicated with him directly, without any go-between.

2. **Fully alert:** Generally, a *navi* could attain *nevuah* only when his physical capacities were subdued, such as during sleep. If a *navi* received a prophetic vision by day, he would first fall into a sleep-like trance. Yet Moshe Rabbeinu remained fully alert, awake, and cognizant throughout the *nevuah*.

3. **Bodily control:** While experiencing *nevuah*, a person would lose control of his faculties, with his body appearing to undergo convulsions and enter a state of near-morbidity. Moshe Rabbeinu remained in full control of his faculties throughout the entire *nevuah*, looking much the same as a person involved in a normal conversation.

4. **At will:** After years of preparatory work, which involved laboring to achieve spiritual growth and character perfection, a person could attain a level at which he qualified for *nevuah*. But even then, there was no way to guarantee that he would merit to receive a Divine communication. A *navi* could prepare himself to draw close to Hashem, and achieve the necessary focus, concentration, and determination, and yet he could wait days, months, or even endlessly to receive a *nevuah*. In contrast, Moshe Rabbeinu maintained an open connection with Hakadosh Baruch Hu, and was able to initiate prophetic dialogue whenever expedient.

Chazal (*Yevamos* 49b) sum up the distinction between the prophecy of Moshe Rabbeinu and that of all other prophets by stating that Moshe viewed his *nevuah* in the manner of a person seeing through an *aspaklaria hame'irah* — a clear, well-lit lens, while all the others had only a limited view, described as peering through an *aspaklaria she'einah me'irah*, an unclear lens.[1]

---

1. Although some sources seemingly equate Bilam's level of prophecy with that of Moshe Rabbeinu, this is not to say he achieved true parity. The reference is merely to one or more specific elements, but the overall quality of Bilam's prophetic transmission was certainly far inferior. See Ramban, *Bamidbar* 24:4 and Rabbeinu Bechaye; see also *Akeidas Yitzchak* Ch. 82; Abarbanel, *Devarim* 24:10; and Maharal, *Tiferes Yisrael* Ch. 21.

    For further discussion of the possibility of prophets attaining a level equal to that of Moshe Rabbeinu, see Appendix A.

Imagine that you are looking through a telescope at Niagara Falls, the Grand Canyon, or any other spectacular landscape. Understandably, a clear lens will provide a perfect view, while a blurred lens will yield a distorted view. If the lens is tinted, then the greater the degree of color, the more the viewer's perception will be impaired. The Grand Canyon is not altered in the slightest; it is equally magnificent no matter which lens you use. The lens determines only how well *you* can view that glorious reality.

Moshe Rabbeinu perceived the brilliance of Hashem's communications with full transparency, seeing the full, detailed picture exactly as it was. Other prophets witnessed this incredible brilliance as well, but only via a blurred lens, which yielded a clouded vision. For them, there were gaps, areas of the message that could not be seen or deciphered.

What was this blurred lens? And why was it clouded?

The Power of Self-Interest

*I*n the previous Ikkar, we explained that our view of life and our determination of right and wrong are heavily swayed by our desires and emotions, which can color our opinions, distort our perception of reality, and influence what we consider morally correct. All sorts of decisions, such as where to live, with whom to associate, and how to spend our leisure time are often based not so much on objective logic and reason as on impulse and emotion.

When I was a young teenager in yeshivah, a more senior *bachur* served as my *mussar-seder chavrusa*. I recall him making an incisive observation. Many times, during a basketball game, the ball bounces on the line marking the edge of the court. In or out? Invariably, five of the players will vociferously argue that the ball landed inside the court, while five others will ardently insist that the ball bounced out of bounds. Each side is adamant, convinced that they saw exactly what happened — and the divide is always right down the line between the two teams.

The players he observed were good boys. None of them would ever deliberately tell a lie, or sacrifice their credibility for some points in an inconsequential game. They all honestly believed they were telling the truth.

Yet there is only one reality: Either the ball landed inside the line, or it bounced out. Five of the people who are claiming to have seen where the ball landed must be wrong. A straightforward event they witnessed just moments earlier was rewired in their brain, which told them they experienced an entirely different, and nonexistent, reality.

Apparently, our emotions and desires can blind us to the truth that's right in front of our eyes.

This explains why doctors, or even patients in cancer wards, continue to smoke. It also explains how a person can eat any food that is clearly detrimental to his health. Our internal desires throw up a wall in front of logic and reality, blocking the truth from our vision. We become blinded, simply unable to see things that don't conform to our personal settings.

A *navi* is someone who has labored to perfect his character to the point that he rises above his natural inclinations and desires. By freeing his mind from the shackles of self-interest, he trains himself to value only what is truly meaningful in life and to crave that and that alone. By syncing his views, and the way he lives, with Hakadosh Baruch Hu's values, he attains an untainted perspective on life. This enables him to guide others, and chart a course for the masses, as he perceives the true path of goodness and justice, while others cannot. Once he has done his part to purify his vision, he can then be imbued with supernatural dosages of Divine inspiration and knowledge, which turbocharge his ability to perceive and to lead.

Yet as great as a *navi* is, he is still a human being. He may have climbed mountains, but he still has challenges to overcome. While his human drives are under control and minimized, they nevertheless exist, and although he follows the path his *neshamah* charts, his physical body still exerts some pull. It is this residual draw toward physicality that stands between him and Hakadosh Baruch Hu.

Moshe Rabbeinu attained such a degree of elevation that uniquely in his case, physical desires and drives did not exist at all. In this sense, as the Rambam writes, he was essentially an angel.

What is the *aspaklaria*, the mysterious glass through which a *navi* views Hashem?

It's not some distant, mystical item.

It is the person himself.

The more a human being follows his heart's desires, and the more drawn he is after his animalistic tendencies, the less able he is to see Hashem's point of view. When a person is pulled toward the pleasures of life, it's as though he's throwing mud at a glass window. Eventually, the mud hardens, and his vision is obscured.

Moshe Rabbeinu's body functioned only as a tool to serve Hashem. It operated exclusively according to the dictates of pure *seichel*, logic, and did not pull him off course in the slightest. He perfected himself to the extent that he was not motivated by any physical desires or ego — "the humblest of men," the Torah calls him (*Bamidbar* 12:3). Nothing was left to distort his vision; he was purely an *eved Hashem* (*Devarim* 34:5), existing only to fulfill his Master's dictates. There remained only one barrier, however: After all was said and done, he was ensconced within a physical body. Elevated as it was, it still created a layer that separated him from a perfect view. A glass remained — but it was crystal clear.[2]

This does not mean that other *nevi'im* experienced a distorted or mistaken vision. On the contrary, we are assured that when Hakadosh Baruch Hu imparts a *nevuah*, he grants the *navi* supreme clarity.[3] The *navi's* message is a guaranteed truth. The effect of the lens is that it reduces the depth or scope of what can be

---

2. Rambam, *Shemonah Perakim*, Ch. 7.
3. Rambam, *Moreh Nevuchim* 3:24. For a further discussion of this idea, see Appendix A.

seen. Levels of information might be inaccessible, and additional insights might be lacking.

Imagine that two identical photos lie side by side, but one is black and white, while the other is in rich color. They depict the same scene, both accurately, but the black-and-white photo is missing so much depth and detail. Similarly, although every *nevuah* from a bona fide *navi* was absolute truth, the other *nevi'im* had access to less detail than Moshe Rabbeinu, due to the blockages within them. Moshe Rabbeinu, who had no internal barriers, saw his prophetic visions in full, vivid detail.

The four differences that set Moshe Rabbeinu's *nevuah* apart from that of other prophets all hinge on the same basic concept. Since Moshe Rabbeinu had no internal barriers, he could engage in a perfect conversation, while the others still had to contend with a level of obstruction brought on by their ties with physicality. This obstruction was manifest in several ways. First, unlike Moshe Rabbeinu, who heard Hakadosh Baruch Hu directly, the other *nevi'im* were too far removed to receive these communications directly, so the *nevuah* would have to be transmitted through angels or other intermediaries in order for the *navi* to comprehend it. Second, for a *navi* to receive his prophecy, the impediment that was his body would have to be subdued so that it would not obstruct the communication. To this end, *nevuah* was transmitted when the *navi* was asleep or in a sleep-like state. With the body dormant, the mind would stand unshackled and ready to communicate. The body of Moshe Rabbeinu, however, posed no impediment, and he therefore received his *nevuah* when fully alert and awake. Third, since the body of a *navi* was not fully primed to receive a purely spiritual communication, this experience would cause the body to convulse or enter other extreme states. In contrast, Moshe Rabbeinu's body was solely a tool for spiritual *avodah*, so receiving a *nevuah* was quite natural. Posing no conflict, it did not cause any negative effect on the body. Lastly, Moshe Rabbeinu's unique closeness and devotion to Hashem brought him to a state of proximity in which he could seek and attain communication at any time. All others, however, could prepare themselves and draw as close as they could, but with a distance still remaining, they could only hope that Hashem would bridge the gap from His end, as they could not cross the divide on their own.

Why Is This So Important?

Our entire Torah, encompassing both the written and oral elements, emanates from the communication Moshe Rabbeinu received from Hashem at Har Sinai, which he then transmitted to us. Had any information been missing, had any aspects been omitted, had any ambiguity crept into the transmission, the integrity of the Torah would have been jeopardized. If our Torah were based on the word of a different *navi*, as noble and elevated as he may have been, we would still be missing the total picture. Not so with Moshe Rabbeinu. His perfectly clear vision was the ultimate guarantee that the Torah we have is the precise and unadulterated expression of Hakadosh Baruch Hu's will.

Moshe Rabbeinu's *nevuah* was the epitome of clarity. As the Torah tells us (*Devarim* 34:10), there never was and never will be another *navi* of such caliber. The message to us is unequivocal. Some values are measured on a relative scale. One person runs fast, another runs faster. The door is always open for yet another person to run even faster. Since the runner's speed is measured against the speed of others, there is no final, absolute point of "fast" that cannot be exceeded. If something is absolute, however, we know with certainty that it can never be exceeded. Once an archer hits the bullseye dead center, no one can challenge his achievement. There's simply nothing to improve.

Other *nevi'im* were on a path to closeness with Hakadosh Baruch Hu. Some were very close, others even closer. Moshe

Rabbeinu wasn't close; he was there. No specks clouded the glass. His vision conveyed the absolute truth. One simply can't do better than that. No one ever will.[4]

How Does This Affect My Daily Life?

*W*hen we open a Chumash, or sit down to a Gemara, we step into a whole different world. While studying Torah, we are introduced to new concepts, new thought processes, and new assertions about the world and everything in it. Some we understand readily, while others take more time to grasp. As intelligent human beings, we are naturally skeptical of anything we can't immediately process and digest.

Go slow. You're not hearing some random person's opinion or studying the minuscule intellectual offering of another human — you are looking at Hakadosh Baruch Hu's personal diary. This is His wisdom, and He is opening a window for you to peer directly into the deeper truths of the world and discover how the mechanisms of the world and humanity function. Proceed with humility. The words of the Torah before you are an exact reflection of His will, encompassing every nuance — as recorded with absolute precision by the ultimate prophet.

---

4. This explains only why Moshe Rabbeinu's level cannot be exceeded; it does not address the question of whether that level could be matched. The answer is that after working to reach a lofty spiritual level, the *navi* then receives special Divine assistance, which propels him to a higher plateau of *nevuah* and closeness from Hakadosh Baruch Hu (see, for example, *Seforno, Devarim* 34:10). Moshe Rabbeinu received a unique measure of this Divine assistance, whose purpose was to facilitate the perfect transmission of the Torah to us for all time (see *Sefer HaIkkarim* 3:12). This was a one-time, specific requirement, and once the requirement was met, there was no longer a need for Hakadosh Baruch Hu to communicate with any *navi* this way, even if he were to attain a level identical to that of Moshe Rabbeinu. (See *Derashos HaRan, Derush* 4; Rambam, *Moreh Nevuchim* 2:39; and *Ohr Hashem*, by Rav Chisdai Crescas, *Maamar* 2, *Klal* 4, Ch. 3.)

הָעִקָּר הַשְּׁמִינִי
The Eighth Ikkar

אֲנִי מַאֲמִין בֶּאֱמוּנָה שְׁלֵמָה שֶׁכָּל הַתּוֹרָה הַמְצוּיָה עַתָּה בְּיָדֵנוּ הִיא הַנְּתוּנָה לְמֹשֶׁה רַבֵּנוּ עָלָיו הַשָּׁלוֹם.

I am steadfast in my absolute belief that the entire Torah now in our hands is the same one that was given to Moshe Rabbeinu, may peace be upon him.

In the Rambam's Words

וְהַיְסוֹד הַשְּׁמִינִי הוּא תּוֹרָה מִן הַשָּׁמַיִם וְהוּא שֶׁנַּאֲמִין שֶׁכָּל
הַתּוֹרָה הַזֹּאת הַמְּצוּיָה בְּיָדֵנוּ הַיּוֹם זוֹ הִיא הַתּוֹרָה שֶׁנִּתְּנָה
לְמֹשֶׁה וְשֶׁהִיא כֻּלָּהּ מִפִּי הַגְּבוּרָה כְּלוֹמַר שֶׁהִגִּיעָה אֵלָיו כֻּלָּהּ
מֵאֵת ה' בְּהַגָּעָה שֶׁנִּקְרֵאת עַל דֶּרֶךְ הַשְׁאָלָה דִּבּוּר וְאֵין יוֹדֵעַ
הֵיאַךְ הִיא הַהַגָּעָה אֶלָּא הוּא עָלָיו הַשָּׁלוֹם אֲשֶׁר אֵלָיו הִגִּיעָה וְכִי
הוּא נֶחְשַׁב כְּסוֹפֵר שֶׁמַּקְרִיאִים לְפָנָיו וְהוּא מַעְתִּיק וְכוֹתֵב אֶת
כֻּלָּהּ דִּבְרֵי הַיָּמִים שֶׁבָּהּ וְסִפּוּרֶיהָ וּמִצְוֹתֶיהָ וְכָךְ נִקְרָא מְחוֹקֵק
וְאֵין הֶבְדֵּל בֵּין וּבְנֵי חָם וּמִצְרַיִם וּפוּט וּכְנַעַן וְשֵׁם אִשְׁתּוֹ
מְהֵיטַבְאֵל בַּת מַטְרֵד אוֹ אָנֹכִי ה' וּשְׁמַע יִשְׂרָאֵל ה' אֱלֹהֵינוּ ה'
אֶחָד הַכֹּל מִפִּי הַגְּבוּרָה וְהַכֹּל תּוֹרַת ה' תְּמִימָה טְהוֹרָה קְדוֹשָׁה
אֱמֶת וְלֹא הָיָה מְנַשֶּׁה בְּעֵינֵיהֶם כּוֹפֵר וּמְחַלֵּל קֹדֶשׁ חָמוּר יוֹתֵר
מִכָּל כּוֹפֵר אֶלָּא לְפִי שֶׁחָשַׁב שֶׁיֵּשׁ בַּתּוֹרָה פָּנִים וּקְלִפָּה וְשֶׁדִּבְרֵי
הַיָּמִים אֵלּוּ וְהַסִּפּוּרִים אֵין תּוֹעֶלֶת בָּהֶם וְשֶׁהֵם מֵאֵת מֹשֶׁה וְזֶהוּ
עִנְיַן אֵין תּוֹרָה מִן הַשָּׁמַיִם אָמְרוּ הוּא זֶה שֶׁסּוֹבֵר שֶׁכָּל הַתּוֹרָה
כֻּלָּהּ מִפִּי הַגְּבוּרָה חוּץ מִפָּסוּק אֶחָד שֶׁלֹּא אֲמָרוֹ הקב"ה אֶלָּא
מֹשֶׁה מִפִּי עַצְמוֹ וְזֶה הוּא דְּבַר ה' בָּזָה יִתְעַלֶּה ה' מִמַּה שֶּׁאוֹמְרִים
הַכּוֹפְרִים אֶלָּא כָּל אוֹת מִמֶּנָּה יֵשׁ בָּהּ חָכְמָה וְנִפְלָאוֹת לְמִי
שֶׁהֱבִינוֹ ה' וְלֹא תֻשַּׂג תַּכְלִית חָכְמָתָהּ אֲרֻכָּה מֵאֶרֶץ מִדָּה וּרְחָבָה
מִנִּי יָם וְאֵין לְאָדָם אֶלָּא לְהַלֵּךְ בְּעִקְּבוֹת דָּוִד מְשִׁיחַ אֱלֹהֵי יַעֲקֹב
שֶׁהִתְפַּלֵּל גַּל עֵינַי וְאַבִּיטָה נִפְלָאוֹת מִתּוֹרָתֶךָ וּכְמוֹ כֵן פֵּרוּשָׁהּ
הַמְּקֻבָּל הוּא גַם כֵּן מִפִּי הַגְּבוּרָה וְזֶה שֶׁאָנוּ עוֹשִׂים הַיּוֹם אֶת
אֹפֶן הַסֻּכָּה וְהַלּוּלָב וְהַשּׁוֹפָר וְהַצִּיצִית וְהַתְּפִלִּין וְזוּלָתָן הוּא
אוֹתוֹ הָאֹפֶן עַצְמוֹ שֶׁאָמַר ה' לְמֹשֶׁה וְהוּא אָמַר לָנוּ וְהוּא מוֹסֵר
הַשְּׁלִיחוּת נֶאֱמָן בְּמַה שֶּׁמָּסַר וְהַמַּאֲמָר הַמּוֹרֶה עַל יְסוֹד הַשְּׁמִינִי
הַזֶּה הוּא אָמְרוֹ בְּזֹאת תֵּדְעוּן כִּי ה' שְׁלָחַנִי וְכוּ' כִּי לֹא מִלִּבִּי.

The eighth foundation is that Torah is Divine. That is, we are to believe that this entire Torah that is currently in our possession is the one that was given to Moshe, and is entirely from the mouth of the Almighty, meaning that it

all came from Hashem, through the interaction we refer
to, in borrowed terms, as "speaking" [to Moshe]. No one
knows the exact nature of this interaction, except [Moshe
Rabbeinu] of blessed memory, who was the one addressed.
He served as a scribe, before whom dictation is given, and
he transcribed all of the Torah, including historical events,
stories, and commandments. It is in this context that he is
referred to as a lawgiver.

[Since every word of the Torah emanates directly
from Above,] there is no disparity between [seemingly
insignificant verses such as]: *The sons of Cham: Cush,
Mitzrayim, Put, and Canaan* (*Bereishis* 10:6) and: *And
his wife's name was Mehetavel, daughter of Matred,
daughter of Me-zahav* (ibid. 36:39) or [the understandably
transcendent] verses of *I am Hashem* (*Shemos* 20:2)
and *Hear, O Israel: Hashem is our God, Hashem is the
One and Only* (*Devarim* 6:4). It is all directly from the
Almighty, and it is all the Divine Torah: complete, pure,
holy, and true. [In fact,] King Menashe would not have
been considered more of a heretic and desecrator of
holiness than any other heretic had he not thought that the
Torah contains an interior "fruit" and an exterior "inedible
shell," meaning that the Torah's historical records and
stories serve no purpose, and were inserted by Moshe. This
is one who maintains that Torah is not Divine: He believes
that the entire Torah was communicated by Hashem
except for one verse that was not said by Him, but was
said, rather, by Moshe, of his own accord. Regarding such
a person we say, "He has disgraced the word of Hashem";
may Hashem be exalted above what these heretics say.
Rather, every single letter in the Torah contains wisdom
and wondrousness, for those to whom Hashem granted

comprehension. One can never reach the endpoint of the Torah's wisdom, for *its measure is longer than the earth and wider than the sea* (*Iyov* 11:9). A person can only follow in the footsteps of David HaMelech, the anointed one of the God of Yaakov, who prayed: *Unveil my eyes that I may perceive wonders from Your Torah* (*Tehillim* 119:18).

Likewise, the Oral Torah, too, is the direct word of the Almighty. With this knowledge, we observe [the mitzvos of] succah, lulav, shofar, tzitzis, tefillin, and all others, [confident] that this is the precise form that Hashem instructed Moshe, and that he conveyed these instructions to us, as a faithful messenger whose transmission was accurate.

This eighth foundation is expressed in the verse (*Bamidbar* 16:28): *Through this shall you know that Hashem sent me to perform all these acts, that it was not from my heart.*

תּוֹרָה מִן הַשָּׁמַיִם
Every Word Is Divine

Torah has been transmitted from father to son and from rebbi to student throughout the ages, spanning millennia. We have carried our sifrei Torah, and the Torah lessons that were faithfully passed down from teacher to student and from father to son, to each of the many stops on our journey. Through it all, we maintain a direct chain back to the original source. The Torah is no mere lesson book or legal system contrived by a human being. Yes, we have been blessed with remarkable leaders, brilliant individuals with outstanding minds. The Torah, though, is something far greater. It is Hashem's wisdom — every single word of it. Entering the world of Torah is tapping into the source of wisdom, which is infinitely beyond human comprehension.

In this Ikkar, we affirm that Torah is *min haShamayim*: It is the word of Hashem, not something contrived by humans. The Rambam states clearly that this status is not limited to the Written Torah, but applies to the Oral Torah as well. All of it is the direct word of Hashem.

To understand this Ikkar, we must view it as part of a sequence, linked with the two Ikkarim preceding it as well as the Ikkar that follows.

This four-part sequence, spanning the sixth Ikkar through the ninth Ikkar, provides a complete perspective on the Torah that guides every detail of our lives.

How do we know what Hakadosh Baruch Hu wants from us? How do we determine our goals in life? How can we assess whether our actions are propelling us toward those goals?

We are given a Torah, whose truth is built on these four principles. Step one is the concept that Hakadosh Baruch Hu communicates with humanity. Step two is the knowledge that Moshe Rabbeinu was the quintessential agent of transmission, capable of receiving Divine instruction with perfect clarity. That said, what did he do once he received the communication from Above? Did he add commentary or analysis? Did he then convey it along with his personal preferences?

Enter step three. Moshe Rabbeinu added absolutely nothing. Every single word of Torah was conveyed exactly as Hashem transmitted it. This is the Ikkar we have before us. As the Rambam writes, Moshe Rabbeinu filled the role of the court stenographer: transcription, and nothing but transcription. Read the Torah, and you won't see him at all — it is all Hashem's words, verbatim. He didn't redact or add commentary — he transcribed the Torah exactly as it was given. The gift of the Torah, then, is the gift of beholding *ratzon Hashem*, exactly as expressed. All that remains to affirm, then, is that the Torah we received is not just accurate, but still in effect. This will be expressed in the next Ikkar, with step four enshrining the immutability of the Torah for eternity.

One Long Electrical Circuit

*T*he Rambam further develops this idea of the Torah being an expression of Hashem's will by contrasting various *pesukim* in the Torah. Some we view as monumental, instructive, or informative, while others leave us furrowing our foreheads and wondering what significance they can possibly carry. The *pesukim* of the Aseres HaDibros we read with awe and trepidation: Picture the moment that turned us into a nation! Hear the powerful voice from Sinai echoing for all eternity! And then, we turn to *Sefer Bereishis*, where we find lengthy lists detailing the children of Esav and Yishmael. Is it of any interest that the wife of one of the Edomite kings was Mehetavel, daughter of Matred, daughter of Me-zahav? Instinctively, we begin to classify which *pesukim* carry weight and which are less momentous. But wait. The Torah contains no random historic notes. Every single word is the will of Hashem, and therefore carries immense significance. In terms of their nature, they truly are all uniform — each one is Divine, and with each one He is conveying a message to us.

This is not just a philosophical idea; it carries practical legal implications. A *sefer Torah* that is missing even one letter is rendered invalid. One cannot simply roll to another, undamaged section and read from there. A *sefer Torah* is akin to one long electrical circuit. Break the circuit at any point and you've lost all the powerful energy contained within. It doesn't matter which letter. Lose one letter from the name of Esav's third wife and you've lost the power in the portion of the Aseres HaDibros. It's all the word of Hashem.

And yet, while we can grasp this concept theoretically, it's difficult to apply it on a practical level. In some *pesukim* I can readily see significance, while in others, try as I may, I simply cannot. From some *pesukim* I can discern halachic principles and intricacies, while in others I can find no apparent lesson or ramification. Where does this leave me?

After emphasizing that "the sons of Cham: Cush, Mitzrayim, Put, and Canaan," are no less significant than "*Shema Yisrael*," the Rambam then offers an intriguing piece of advice. Follow in the footsteps of David HaMelech, he says, and turn to Hakadosh Baruch Hu in prayer, beseeching Him to open our eyes so we can perceive the Torah's wisdom. While *tefillah* is certainly a potent and vital element in comprehending Torah, the placement of this advice within the Ikkarim seems puzzling. The Rambam is focused, here, on delineating the parameters of our basic beliefs, not on imparting guidance or practical suggestions. Why insert this advice here?

The Rambam is not coming to offer advice at all. He's telling us a basic fact. What we are dealing with is way above our pay grade. Torah is not on our level; it's totally above us. Want to be able to step into this beautiful world? Ask Him. Beg Him. Because if you try accessing it on your own, you're bound for failure.

True, there are certain parts of Torah that we can grasp on some level. Ultimately, though, the nature of Torah is such that it is inherently beyond us, attainable only to the degree that He gifts us with comprehension. For this reason, we ask each morning: וְהָאֵר עֵינֵינוּ בְּתוֹרָתֶךָ — illuminate our eyes to be able to see the wisdom of Your Torah.

The Oral Torah Is Also Hashem's Word

T he belief that Moshe Rabbeinu transmitted the entire body of Torah to us exactly as Hakadosh Baruch Hu conveyed it to him is not limited to the Written Torah. While standing on Har Sinai, Moshe Rabbeinu also received the Torah Shebe'al Peh, the Oral Torah, which he then presented to Klal Yisrael. This body of Torah was taught to every Jew, but the responsibility of its transmission was entrusted to a select few who would serve as the Baalei Mesorah, the guarantors of the authenticity of our oral tradition. From Moshe Rabbeinu to Yehoshua, and on to Shimon HaTzaddik and R' Yehudah HaNasi, each generation was granted select individuals who mastered Torah Shebe'al Peh and ensured that the chain would continue unbroken.

Eventually, due to the difficulty of maintaining the authenticity of the oral tradition in the face of exile and horrific tribulations, the decision was made to commit this transmission to writing, first in the limited version that is the Mishnah, and eventually in a more expansive version that is the Talmud, or Gemara. The Gemara we have to this day is a living embodiment of the Mesorah, containing the unadulterated word of Hashem as transmitted through the generations until the time it was recorded. The pages of the Gemara are replete with spirited debate on every conceivable topic, and yet the opinions offered are never personal innovations. Each Tanna and Amora transmitted pieces of the Mesorah, fragments that were in need of clarification, and at times, reconciliation. The Amoraim discussed, debated, and argued over how to properly calibrate the details of the Mesorah. One Amora's piece of information is true but was said regarding one specific case; another's seemingly conflicting piece of the Mesorah must therefore be addressing a different scenario.

Just as Moshe Rabbeinu's role was that of a scribe in faithfully giving over the Torah exactly as is, the Baalei Mesorah, too, transmitted the Torah exactly as is. They did not inject opinions, concepts, or values as they saw fit. Consequently, the Oral Torah is strictly the word of Hashem. This is what is being conveyed in the Ikkar before us. Both the Torah Shebichsav and the Torah Shebe'al Peh that we received at Sinai were relayed by the Baalei Mesorah without any embellishment or adjustments, and remain the undiluted word of Hakadosh Baruch Hu.

No Impugning the Oral Tradition

*M*uch mention is made in the Mishnah and Gemara of two similarly aberrant sects within Jewry, known as the Tzedukim and Baysusim, who were disciples of individuals named Tzaddok and Baysus, respectively. This duo were originally students of Antignos Ish Socho, who was not only a Tanna but one of the select Baalei Mesorah. They, and their followers, notoriously rejected the Oral Torah, abiding only by what is explicitly stated in the Written Torah.

To us, their approach seems bizarre. Large swaths of the Written Torah can be understood only if accompanied by an oral interpretation. Yes, we must wear *totafos* on our arm and head each day, but who's to say what *totafos* are? Yes, we must take a certain beautiful fruit each Succos, but how are we to know which is the intended variety? With much of the basic wording of the Torah indecipherable without an oral tradition, the philosophy of these groups seems ridiculously untenable.

In truth, these groups did recognize the need for an Oral Torah, and actually conceded that there was one. Tzaddok and Baysus erred grievously in understanding a teaching of their rebbi, Antignos Ish Socho. Convinced that they had understood it correctly, they could not accept his teaching as legitimate Torah. Their conclusion, as the Rambam writes (*Hilchos Teshuvah* 3:8), and Chazal imply as well (*Avos d'Rabbi Nosson* 5:2), was that the Baalei Mesorah had, God forbid, not been true to their mission, and had inserted their own opinions into the oral tradition. In other words, they did not assail the concept of an Oral Torah; they impugned the credibility and reliability of those who transmitted it.

The Ikkar under discussion is precisely the one to which they failed to hearken. Eventually, this led them totally astray, and, tragically, caused an all-out campaign against both Torah leaders and those who followed the Torah path. It is in reference to the concept expressed in this Ikkar that the Rambam (ibid.) labels someone who denies the credibility of the Baalei Mesorah —

"makchish maggideha" — as an absolute heretic, noting the Tzedukim and Baysusim as examples.

Acknowledging the untainted transmission of Torah is of paramount importance in maintaining fealty to Torah beliefs and commandments. The moment one attempts to write off even a single concept or law of the Mesorah as having originated with the person who said it, he is effectively calling into question the authenticity of the entire Mesorah.

Why Korach Was Different

As Klal Yisrael traversed the Wilderness, en route from Mitzrayim to Eretz Yisrael, various individuals and groups challenged Moshe Rabbeinu's authority, repeatedly undermining his leadership. And yet, Moshe Rabbeinu remained unfazed, frequently beseeching Hakadosh Baruch Hu to refrain from judging his detractors harshly. Never did he ask that those who malign him be punished. There is one exception: his response to the challenge posed by Korach. There, Moshe asked that Korach and his followers die a spectacular death. Why did he depart from his usual conduct?

The answer lies in the nature of the affront. When the people campaigned to turn back to Mitzrayim, or complained about the food supply, or expressed irrational fear of entering Eretz Yisrael, Moshe was able to correct their course without calling for the destruction of the transgressors. The quintessential leader, he always found a way to move forward. Even when personally slandered with despicable falsehoods (see *Kiddushin* 33b and *Sanhedrin* 110a), Moshe did not counterattack. Korach, however, launched an attack on the veracity of Moshe Rabbeinu's transmission of the Torah, claiming that much of the guidance Moshe Rabbeinu had transmitted was invented by Moshe himself and did not originate with Hakadosh Baruch Hu.

This is where Moshe Rabbeinu drew the line. Personal attacks could be overlooked, but not an attack on the Torah itself. The claim that Moshe Rabbeinu had introduced his own thoughts into the Torah, even if only in regard to one or two specific matters, would immediately cast aspersions on the entire Torah. This could not be tolerated, and that is why Moshe Rabbeinu asked for the challengers to meet their end. Moreover, the death of Korach and his followers could not be a simple cessation of life, but had to be a dramatic, extraordinary event, one that offered a rare glimpse of direct Divine intervention. Such a death was not necessary for Korach's sake; it was a Heavenly repudiation of his claims for the benefit of everyone else, a Divine corroboration of the authenticity of the Torah, as conveyed by Moshe Rabbeinu.

The Role of Our Contemporary Chachamim

*T*he Mesorah was transmitted orally from teacher to student for generations, from Moshe Rabbeinu until the time of the writing of the Talmud. Although the oral transmission continued for some time even after the completion of the Talmud, it began to peter out; the tribulations of *galus* had taken their toll. *Semichah* — the formal transmission of Torah authority — ceased, and people's memories could no longer be relied upon as the exclusive repositories of the Oral Torah. From then on, Torah Shebe'al Peh would, for the most part, be encased in the Talmud.

Subsequently, a new process of transmitting Torah developed. When gaps appeared in the Mesorah, caused by lack of clarity and diminished erudition, it was often no longer possible to resolve these by locating individuals who had received this information as part of the chain of Mesorah. Left with no choice, students of Torah began to offer ideas born of their own scholarliness, intuition, and ingenuity, hoping to be on the right track. These ideas, however, often originated within the mind of each person. Were these ideas true? Were they Torah? Much of the time, yes. Other times not. From then on, we began turning to the giants of Torah in each generation in a new capacity — not primarily as bearers of specific information within the oral Mesorah, but rather as those who possess exceptional powers of discernment, and can help us differentiate between ideas that are true and those that should be discarded. They guide and educate us in how to properly interpret the Torah, and train us to develop our own abilities of discernment as well.

The Parameters of Torah

*L*et's return to the words of this Ikkar, in which we declare that the entire Torah that is in our possession is unimpeachably Divine. What exactly does this mean? Is every single Torah thought expressed inherently Divine? Over the generations, we have been blessed with a bounty of Torah literature, and today, more than ever, we are witness to the dissemination of Torah on a global scale, in written, audio, and video form. Must I regard every Torah thought I ever heard as an expression of the ultimate truth?

Some will respond by invoking the adage, "*Shivim panim laTorah* — there are seventy facets to the Torah" (*Bamidbar Rabbah* 13:15). Like a diamond that glistens, refracting a spectrum of colors, the Torah features many different angles, all of which are legitimate. This does not satisfactorily answer the question, though. The fact that the Torah has seventy facets does not automatically confer validity upon every notion a person might concoct in the name of Torah. While seventy different tracks may receive the stamp of approval, who's to say whether the thought being expressed is number seventy or seventy-one?

In line with what we have discussed above, however, the Ikkar comes into focus. We are not discussing what is or isn't legitimate

Torah. While that certainly requires parameters, those parameters are not the focus of the Ikkar under discussion. When we say the entire Torah that is currently in our possession is the one that was given to Moshe Rabbeinu, we are affirming the authenticity of the transmission of the Mesorah in its oral form. The Baalei Mesorah executed their mandate with absolute integrity, relaying the undiluted, unembellished Torah Shebe'al Peh, until it was ultimately codified in the Mishnah and Talmud, the form we still possess in our hands.

As we seek today to discern the Torah's position regarding the many issues that are not addressed by the Gemara, and have no clear precedent in the Mesorah, at times we succeed in developing true Torah concepts and applications that are truly worthy of inclusion in Torah Shebe'al Peh. Indeed, we are taught that every novel Torah thought ever expressed, even by those of us alive today, was shown on some level to Moshe Rabbeinu and effectively incorporated into the transmission of the Oral Torah (*Vayikra Rabbah* 22:1). On the other hand, there are thoughts and concepts that do not make the cut. After all, a basic feature of all genuine Torah study is careful scrutiny: analyzing, questioning, and challenging ideas that are proposed, and rejecting certain ideas as incongruent with established Torah precepts. We are seeking truth, and we will not accept any idea that lacks credibility. A half-baked notion that someone carelessly tosses out in the name of Torah hardly warrants inclusion under the umbrella of Torah Shebe'al Peh.

Ultimately, though, the concept enshrined in this Ikkar — our unwavering belief in the authenticity of the Mesorah — is not meant as an affirmation of our personal scholarliness. It's a statement of our confidence in the Baalei Mesorah, who faithfully carried out their mission of linking the past to the future by ensuring the integrity of the Torah they transmitted.

How Does This Affect My Daily Life?

*I*n the modern world, age-old values are being summarily discarded: the value of marriage and family, the value of belief in a Higher authority, and the value of personal responsibility and accountability for one's actions, to name a few.

In a sense, we live in the era of the end of vice. No longer do people commit immoral or indecent acts, because increasingly, those acts are no longer considered immoral. While deviant lifestyles are celebrated in the name of "tolerance," religious observance is somehow deemed less than tolerable. The Torah Jew finds himself continually on the defensive, cast as primitive, fanatical, and bigoted. These perceptions plague us not only in our dealings with the world outside the *beis midrash*, but on a more internal level as well, even among those who firmly adhere to the Torah's values and precepts. As we study the teachings of Chazal, we occasionally encounter ideas or pieces of information that seem out of sync with contemporary norms. Perhaps, on occasion, we, too, might hear a voice insinuating that today, these views or directives are no longer relevant.

We need to understand that the Torah we have received is not a human opinion. This is not a system created by "The Rabbis." Our Mesorah is the pure value system of Hakadosh Baruch Hu himself. The Torah, both written and oral, is His guidebook, and everything in it is true, accurate, and relevant. The Torah remains, in every generation, the authentic arbiter of what is right and what is wrong, what is laudable and what is repugnant, what is to be celebrated and what is to be castigated. One does not debate Hakadosh Baruch Hu. His Torah is something higher than all of us; it's our direct window to Him, and we submit our hearts and minds to it.

אֵלּוּ וָאֵלּוּ דִּבְרֵי אֱלֹהִים חַיִּים
Some Say This Way, Some Say That Way; Both Are the Word of Hashem

Torah is the word of Hashem. It's His personal journal. As such, we would expect Torah to be a list of clear, unambiguous facts and instructions. So why do we find so much machlokes throughout the Mishnah and Gemara? Why are there so many disputes? How can both sides be right?

In the last segment, we established that the Torah, both the Written Torah as well as the Oral Torah passed down from generation to generation and ultimately enshrined in the Talmud, is the unadulterated word of Hakadosh Baruch Hu Himself. The bearers of our Mesorah did not tamper with this legacy and did not insert opinions of their own. They served faithfully in their scribal role, transmitting the Torah exactly as they received it. This, however, sets the stage for a glaring question. If Torah Shebe'al Peh is not a set of personal opinions, but rather a record of pure *dvar Hashem*, how is it that it is not a monolithic work of information? The Oral Torah features numerous disagreements, many of which involve opposing and seemingly irreconcilable viewpoints. How can two divergent opinions both be considered the word of Hashem?

Before we can address this question, let's establish two vital points.

The first is that although Torah Shebe'al Peh contains many disagreements, they pale in comparison to the innumerable instances where no *machlokes* at all exists, with a clear understanding and halachah maintained. For instance, no one argues which day of the week is Shabbos, or whether a cow is kosher. Although more prominent and visible, *machlokes* actually represents a minute fraction of the sum total of the Torah in our possession.

Consider the design of the tefillin we don each day. Rashi and Rabbeinu Tam famously disagreed as to the correct placement of the *parshiyos*, the small scrolls within the tefillin. For this reason, many have the custom to don two pairs of tefillin daily, to satisfy both opinions. Yes, this does constitute a serious, practical *machlokes*. But let's take a step back and see what is not subject to debate at all. All agree that tefillin are boxes. All agree that they must be square, black, and fashioned from the hide of specific animals. All agree that these boxes must be hollow, and must contain specific portions of Torah, written in a specific manner, using specific materials. All agree that these boxes must be tied with leather straps and bound with unique knots.

The serious *machlokes* between Rashi and Rabbeinu Tam may obscure the fact that the vast majority of the halachos of tefillin have been passed down faithfully through the generations. Consider as well that this is the case with a mitzvah about which the Written Torah is astoundingly cryptic, giving only a mysterious word, *totafos*, to describe the item to be used. Enter a shul anywhere across the globe, from Jerusalem to Johannesburg, from Montreal to Montevideo, and the strength of our halachic accuracy becomes indisputably clear. The Jewish people have experienced thousands of years of exile, each family and community with its own story of trials and tribulations, and yet the tefillin utilized by Jews across the globe are all alike. This is a brilliant testimony to the durability of our Mesorah, which has remained intact, down to its intricate details, despite all we have gone through.

The second point: This Ikkar relates to the accuracy of the Torah's transmission from Moshe Rabbeinu down through the generations until this day. As we explained, both the Written Torah as well as its parallel oral tradition were given to Moshe and successfully transmitted to us. There is, however, one large body of Torah that stands outside this discussion, and that is the mitzvos, *takanos*, and *gezeiros* of Chazal, which were instituted long after the Torah was given to Moshe Rabbeinu. These include the mitzvos of reading the Megillah on Purim and lighting the menorah on Chanukah, for instance, as well as the various safeguards enacted over the generations to help people avoid transgression; examples include *muktzah*, *yayin nesech*, and *bishul akum*.

The Torah specifically charges the *chachamim* of each generation with the task of creating these safeguards as they see fit, and commands Klal Yisrael to adhere to whatever the *chachamim* will say. Effectively, the force behind these enactments is the power of the Torah itself. The specific directives, however, are prescribed by the *chachamim*. Within these topics, *machlokes* could arise regarding what exactly was instituted, and what exactly was the scope and range of the *takanah*. If we filter all these categories of Rabbinic laws out of our discussion and focus singularly on matters that were given to us by Hakadosh Baruch Hu Himself, we are left with relatively few areas of *machlokes*, with our Mesorah remaining remarkably intact and accurate.

The Beginnings of Machlokes

*L*et's take a step back into history, to where *machlokes* first crept into our Mesorah. For the first two thousand years after Moshe Rabbeinu received the Torah, we did a most extraordinary job of transmitting the Torah from generation to generation without any significant loss in the transfer. Just over two thousand years ago, Hillel and Shammai stood at the helm of Klal Yisrael. Hillel was the *nasi*, a scion of royalty, while Shammai served as the *av beis din*, the head of the judicial system. These two leaders interacted on every matter of Torah leadership, attending to the full spectrum of life's issues. And yet, after all was said and done, they had a grand total of four unresolved disputes. Four.

Just beyond this point, however, matters took a sharp turn. The students of these two giants, colloquially known as Beis Shammai and Beis Hillel, endured a period of tremendous upheaval. The country, and the Beis HaMikdash, teetered precariously on the abyss of destruction. Enemies circled from the outside, and internal divisiveness struck from within. It is not difficult to conjure the panic, uncertainty, and lack of stability they experienced. While we cannot know for certain what transpired in those days, we are told that the students of these yeshivos did not connect optimally with their rebbeim. Since they lacked the highest level of immersion in Torah and closeness to their rebbeim, their level of clarity suffered greatly, and fissures began to emerge. Whereas there had been a mere four disagreements a generation earlier, now there were dozens and dozens.

The first step toward *machlokes*, then, was this lack of clarity. Suddenly, pieces of information were lost. It might have been a full-fledged halachah or concept that went missing, or just a nuance or subtlety within a broader topic. What happened next? Even when dealing with the urgent need to fill in these gaps, Chazal did not, and could not, resort to offering their personal opinions to fill the void. As brilliant and scholarly as they were, inserting their own viewpoints was not the next best option; it was simply not an option at all. As detailed in the previous chapter, a basic tenet of our Mesorah is the unimpeachable integrity of those who transmitted it. They were committed to conveying the exact word of Hashem and nothing but. Inserting any man-made ideas would have run counter to their entire mission.

What, then, were Chazal's arguments all about? How did any side reach its conclusion? For a prototype of *machlokes* within Torah, we can look back to the time when Klal Yisrael was in the Wilderness, just after Moshe Rabbeinu passed away. With Klal

Yisrael utterly distraught by this loss, hundreds of halachos were forgotten. Ultimately, responding to a challenge laid down by Yehoshua, Osniel ben Kenaz was able to restore the missing halachos. He did this, we are told, *"b'pilpulo"* — by drawing upon his prodigious Torah knowledge. Apparently, even when missing information about one aspect of Torah, if one possesses enough knowledge about other, related topics, he can use that to recreate the missing piece.

Identifying the Missing Fragment

Suppose you sit down with your kids to do a 388-piece jigsaw puzzle, without the benefit of a picture of the full puzzle. Rifling through the contents of the puzzle box, you see that the puzzle seems to have only 387 pieces. One piece is missing. Hoping to locate it, you turn to your children, who have already done the puzzle, asking them to describe the missing piece. If they remember what the completed puzzle looked like, they might be able to help you. This would be akin to asking the Baalei Mesorah for a missing piece of Torah information. Chances are, though, that the kids will answer, "How should I know?" Indeed, how should they know? But suppose you went ahead and connected the other 387 pieces. The picture is now clearer. It's a countryside scene, with a barn. The barn, of course, is fire-truck red with white crossbeams. Smack in the middle of the barn is a small hole, where the missing piece belongs. Now you can see that the missing piece must be red with a touch of white on the edge. Can you describe it perfectly? No. The details can be suggested, not guaranteed, but a pretty good estimation can be made. Depending on the clarity of the surrounding details and intricacies, as well as the size of the missing piece, your estimation might even be provable. The key here, though, is that this determination is not being made based on your own opinion or preference. It's not a matter of what color you favor or what you want the piece to look like. Your opinion has value only insofar as it reflects the truth of the picture itself.

Our *chachamim*, from the time of Beis Shammai and Beis Hillel and onward, used nothing but the established word of Hashem as their tools. The only acceptable yardstick of proof was — and remains — the evidence presented by other pieces of Mesorah. Sometimes, parts of the picture indicate that a missing fragment looks a certain way, while other parts of the picture indicate otherwise. This is how they differed: They offered two reasonable versions that were both direct products of established Mesorah.

The Beauty of Debate

*T*he Mishnah (*Avos* 5:17) teaches us that any argument that is for the sake of Heaven will endure, while any argument that is not, will not.

What does this mean? If two people are engaged in a heated debate for purely altruistic reasons, we would assume the better outcome would be to reach a speedy and amicable agreement. Why would an everlasting argument be beneficial? The answer, in the case of Torah *machlokes*, is that both arguments contain truth. If each person is occupied with his own concerns and ambitions, and is proposing nothing more than his personal preferences or opinions, we would certainly hope that the two sides should arrive quickly at a fair resolution, ending the debate. But if the two are heavily engaged in an honest pursuit of truth, with each one sincerely analyzing and delving deeper into the will of Hashem, then we view everything they say with reverence. Even if ultimately, the halachah does not follow one person's opinion, the aspect and perspective he has uncovered is of eminent value and should be cherished. His opinion should endure eternally because it reveals one more brilliant ray of the diamond's refraction, another genuine aspect of Hakadosh Baruch Hu's will. The self-serving arguments of Korach and His followers were nothing but meaningless expressions of egotism, and as such, they evaporated with the fall of Korach. The arguments of Shammai and Hillel, on the other hand, contained not an iota of self. They were true assessments of the will of Hashem, and truly warrant endurance for posterity.

Furthermore, not only are their ideas treasured, but their passionate debate itself is to be admired. Picture a family in the aftermath of the passing of a mother. If the children did not enjoy a close relationship with their mother, her belongings won't mean much to them, and they might just dump them all unceremoniously, or hire a company to dispose of them in an estate sale. But if the children felt a close, loving bond with their deceased mother, then they will likely pore over her personal effects and even argue over who gets her candlesticks, her honey dish, her recipe box.

The fact that Klal Yisrael has argued, debated, and struggled mightily over even the most minuscule details of Torah is a glorious testament to the extreme value we place on Torah, and the importance we attach to discerning the truth. The loss that precipitated the *machlokes* is indeed dreadful — but the *machlokes* itself, the unwillingness to settle for anything less than the whole truth, is absolutely beautiful.

How Can Both Be Right?

*T*he question remains, however, how the chasm in interpreting Hashem's will can be so large. How can we have two conflicting opinions and still say that each is plausible? For instance, in the dispute over whether the Torah requires *shechitah* for fowl, one opinion says it is mandated, while the other says it is not. Which opinion reflects Hashem's will? There is a dispute over the status of Yerushalayim today. One opinion is that the city was sanctified for all eternity, while another holds that its elevated *kedushah* was limited to an earlier time. How can both these opinions be correct? Either the city today retains its full sanctified status, or it does not. How can the two opposing views both be the true word of Hashem?

In describing the intense debates and differences between Beis Shammai and Beis Hillel, the Gemara makes a remarkable statement (*Eruvin* 13b): "For three years, Beis Shammai and Beis Hillel debated each other. These said that the halachah follows their view, and these said that the halachah follows their view. A Heavenly Voice went forth and declared: '*Eilu v'eilu divrei Elokim chaim* — both these and those are the words of the living God. But the halachah in practice follows Beis Hillel.'"

Debates between Beis Shammai and Beis Hillel carried on for three years, unresolved, until a decisive voice rang out from Above. The verdict? Both Beis Shammai and Beis Hillel are expressing the actual views of Hakadosh Baruch Hu. The law, though, is expressed by Beis Hillel.

Until the point of halachah, both viewpoints are true and valid. How can this be?

The Ritva addresses this point, wondering how it is possible to say, "Both these and those are the words of the living God" when one prohibits something that the other permits. He answers, citing the Baalei HaTosafos, that when Moshe Rabbeinu ascended to Heaven to receive the Torah, he did not merely receive a package of facts. Certainly, every Torah precept was conveyed with clear instructions: Do this, don't do that; this is commendable, that is loathsome. Kashrus, Shabbos, monetary law, and all other areas of halachah were clearly delineated. Each of these laws, however, came not alone but with a full package of detailed background. What is the rationale behind this halachah? How is it affected when other laws are involved? Explaining the entire background to Moshe Rabbeinu served as an invaluable comprehension aid, for it enabled him to understand the exact parameters of where and when each law applied.

In presenting this full range of reasoning to Moshe Rabbeinu, Hakadosh Baruch Hu revealed both the logic supporting the halachah as well as the logic that would theoretically have dictated otherwise. In fact, says the Ritva, Moshe Rabbeinu was shown

98 different angles on each matter: 49 reasons to permit, and 49 reasons to prohibit. Practically speaking, this does not change the law an iota. If the Torah says that the bluefin marlin is kosher, or that the gecko lizard is *tamei*, these are incontrovertible facts. That there are logical reasons to argue that this fish ought to be *tamei*, or that this lizard ought to be deemed kosher, does not affect the halachah. Essentially, Moshe Rabbeinu was being told that despite the dozens of potential reasons to the contrary, the rationale for the final halachah is eminently superior to these considerations. It's not that the other lines of reasoning are untrue, it's just that they don't carry enough weight to sway the halachah.

By way of analogy, picture a judge deliberating the following case.

It's a smaller city, somewhere in the American Midwest. Recent growth and opportunities have led to a population surge, prompting the need to revamp the existing roads. One major project proposed by a group of private developers and approved by the municipal authorities would completely overhaul a major roadway and the surrounding neighborhood, creating the infrastructure to support the burgeoning population. One thing stands in the way of this massive project. Although most residents have agreed to sell out and relocate to accommodate the construction, one tenant refuses to move from her apartment, no matter what is offered to her. Her refusal is holding up the demolition of her apartment building and bringing the entire project to a standstill. With no further recourse, the developers invoke eminent domain laws, arranging for the municipality to force a buyout and eviction for the public good. The tenant challenges this action, and the matter ends up in court.

The city's lawyers argue that the tenant has been offered an outlandish sum, more than double the actual value of her apartment. They point out that she spends each winter in sunnier climates, leaving her residence empty many months of the year. Forcing her to move, they argue, will not cause her undue hardship, while her eviction will enable massive construction that will bring hundreds of new jobs to other residents in the area. Additionally, the new roadways will ease access to a nearby hospital, potentially saving many lives.

The tenant's lawyers present a series of counterarguments. The tenant suffers from medical issues that leave her partially disabled. A forced move, they maintain, *would* cause her undue hardship. They demonstrate that the proposed project can be rerouted in a manner that will obviate the need for her eviction, and they argue that the local eminent domain laws apply only to public projects, whereas this project, although designated for the public good, is being implemented by the private sector. Furthermore, permitting private developers to evict residents for their own benefit would set a dangerous precedent, in which developers could upend people's lives for any project they can portray as beneficial to the public.

Are these arguments all true? Let's assume that they are. After all, the tenant was offered money and the project is in fact important and the woman truly is impaired and there are indeed alternative solutions. There are many facets to this issue, and all of them may be valid. This does not mean, however, that all the considerations carry equal weight. In this scenario, the judge will ultimately have to decide upon the correct course of action. His decision will favor one side or the other, but this does not mean he is declaring any of the claims to be false. He's simply weighing all the arguments and deciding which carry the most validity.

This is *eilu v'eilu*. Both sides are expressing genuine truth, as both opinions are based on legitimate interpretations of Torah law. The two sides in a *machlokes* are not injecting their own opinions. They are discussing and weighing the applicability of different concepts transmitted to us by Moshe Rabbeinu. While the opinions may vary greatly, as long as they are both rooted in Mesorah, they are each valid.

In fact, throughout Shas, we find that the Gemara will record a dispute — between Rav and Shmuel, Abaye and Rava, or others — and then note that there are a number of scenarios where there was no disagreement: Rava conceded to Abaye in this case, Abaye agreed with Rava in another. This whittles down their disputes to a far more limited range. This, essentially, is the process we are describing. Both Rava and Abaye were expressing eminent truths. Divergent as their opinions were, both acknowledged that the opinion of the other was in fact credible and valid under certain conditions. The debate related to the exact line of demarcation: Until what point is this angle more compelling? Beyond which point would the other's opinion prevail?

A halachic ruling is the result of a qualified Torah scholar, who has knowledge and who studied under earlier authorities who transmitted to him the rules of how to determine the halachah, weighing all the legitimate angles, assessing which carries the most value in a specific circumstance, and giving that opinion the final imprimatur upon which we are to act. In every case of a halachic ruling, a true and binding assessment has been made. No individual can ever use the concept of *eilu v'eilu* to justify charting his own path in defiance of a ruled-upon halachah.

How Does This Affect My Daily Life?

When we encounter a halachic question, we turn to the Torah and our rabbanim for guidance. At times, the answers may not be clear-cut. Often, we are told that the matter is subject to *machlokes*: Some rule leniently, others are stringent. On the communal level as well, divergent halachic approaches abound, leading to significant divisions between various factions of frum Jewry. Construction of *mikvaos*, wearing tefillin on Chol HaMoed, building an *eiruv* in a major urban area — these are but a few topics that are subject to marked dispute.

The rift is further magnified by contemporary issues or innovations that require a halachically valid response. Does government supervision render milk kosher? Is human genetic engineering permitted? One rav rules this way, another rav says that way. Some communities follow this opinion, others take a drastically different approach. So much divide, so much disagreement.

And yet — these passionate debates reveal the beautiful facets of Hakadosh Baruch Hu's diamond. With the guidelines transmitted through the ages, we are all doing our utmost to discern Hakadosh Baruch Hu's will. There are many angles and many approaches, as unfortunately, we lack the authoritative body of Sanhedrin to issue an unequivocal ruling. Yes, the lack of clarity is distressing, but the full-throated, legitimate spirited debate it spawns is something of beauty. Because doing the will of Hashem matters to us, we won't settle for anything less.

If people attempt to justify entrenched dubious practices or to find sources in the Torah to validate in-vogue moral standards, we pay them no regard.

הָעִקָּר הַתְּשִׁיעִי
The Ninth Ikkar

אֲנִי מַאֲמִין בֶּאֱמוּנָה שְׁלֵמָה שֶׁזֹּאת הַתּוֹרָה לֹא
תְהֵא מְחְלֶפֶת וְלֹא תְהֵא תּוֹרָה אַחֶרֶת מֵאֵת
הַבּוֹרֵא יִתְבָּרַךְ שְׁמוֹ.

I am steadfast in my absolute belief that
this Torah [that we have received] will
never be exchanged for another, nor will
there be another Torah from the Creator,
blessed is His Name.

וְהַיְסוֹד הַתְּשִׁיעִי הוּא הַבִּטוּל וְהוּא שֶׁתּוֹרַת מֹשֶׁה הַזֹּאת לֹא
תִתְבַּטֵּל וְלֹא תָבוֹא תוֹרָה מֵאֵת ה' זוּלָתָהּ וְלֹא תִהְיֶה בּוֹ תוֹסֶפֶת
וְלֹא יִגָּרַע מִמֶּנָּה לֹא בִּכְתָב וְלֹא בְּפֵרוּשׁ אָמַר לֹא תֹסֵף עָלָיו וְלֹא
תִגְרַע מִמֶּנּוּ.

The ninth foundational belief is that of negation,
meaning that this Torah, which we received from Moshe,
will never be nullified, nor will there ever be another Torah
from Hashem. Furthermore, no additions or subtractions
will ever be made to the Torah, both the Written Torah and
the Oral Torah, as the verse states: *You shall not add to it
and you shall not subtract from it* (*Devarim* 13:1).

לֹא תֹסֵף עָלָיו וְלֹא תִגְרַע מִמֶּנּוּ
Absolute Perfection Does Not Change

The ninth Ani Maamin sets forth the absolute immutability of the Torah. The Torah is not subject to change at any point. Nothing will ever be added to the Torah, nor will the Torah or any fraction of it ever be annulled. No mitzvah or precept can ever be supplanted by a new one.

*P*erfection, by definition, cannot be improved. If something is good, great, or fantastic but short of the perfect mark, there is room for it to be enhanced. Features that are presently lacking can be added, while hindrances or unnecessary elements can be removed. Once the object achieves perfection, however, it is no longer subject to any improvement. Think of a key, carefully crafted to work in a specific lock. When the bittings have been cut to precision, the key functions flawlessly. At this point, if you cut away a piece of the key, it will no longer operate properly. Likewise, if you add a bit of metal to the key, it will merely jam in place, the appendage serving as nothing but a detriment. A perfect state means that any change, whether by addition or subtraction, will be for the worse.

A key's perfection is limited to a singular dimension: the ability to effectively operate in a specific lock. This idea, however, on an infinitely greater scale, is true regarding the Torah as well.

The Torah is not a random compilation of information. As the expression of Hashem's will — *daas Elyon* — and the definitive guide to every aspect of life and the world, it is complete and perfect, with nothing left to improve. Take away a part of the Torah, and it will be lacking. Add something to it, and you've damaged it. In other words, if someone wishes to add a mitzvah of his own volition, his error lies not merely in the presumptuousness of deeming a design of his own intellect to be a mitzvah, but more significantly, in his failure to realize that the Torah is perfect, and ergo, impossible to improve (Rambam, *Moreh Nevuchim* Vol. 2, Ch. 39).

We are expressing two points here. One is that the Torah is perfect and complete, and does not leave space for addition or subtraction. The second is that this state of perfection is so absolute that it encapsulates every time period and situation the world will ever experience. There will never be a time or place where one can say that although the Torah held true yesterday, that was based on yesterday's circumstances, whereas in today's reality things have changed. The truths of the Torah transcend any specific situation, and will hold true eternally.

Now, we could stop here and simply say that the reason the Torah is both perfect and eternal is just because that's the way it is. This, however, falls far short of the truth. In reality, Torah is, *of necessity*, both perfect and unchangeable, and any other option is an impossibility. Why is this?

Torah is not a freestanding book, or a random collection of halachos, *sugyos*, and *hashkafah*. It is a presentation of the very essence of Hakadosh Baruch Hu. In a sense, it is a depiction of His personality. Just as analyzing a person's actions and opinions can yield an understanding of the person himself, when I approach a topic in Torah, I'm coming face-to-face with a higher reality that helps me understand Hakadosh Baruch Hu Himself.

Human beings are fickle; our opinions and values are malleable. Today I like you, tomorrow I don't. Today I like this food, tomorrow I don't. Today I'm energized and excited, tomorrow I'm washed out. The child who was so attached to his candy might find it unappealing when he becomes an adult. The teenager who loved skiing, attacking the most challenging slopes, eventually ages and has no energy or drive to even ride the chairlift. Our moods vary, our roles in life change, and as we mature, our views evolve alongside our changing selves. It is quite normal for a person to have a different opinion on a matter than he had a few years earlier.

Hakadosh Baruch Hu, on the other hand, does not have mood swings. He does not become emotional. He doesn't go through phases. In short, He is utterly unchanging. Since the Torah is a direct manifestation of Hakadosh Baruch Hu's values, and Hakadosh Baruch Hu Himself never changes, the Torah itself can never change. Entertaining the possibility that even a minute detail of the Torah can change is much the same as entertaining the possibility that your reflection in the mirror will wink even as you stand perfectly still.

In truth, the bond between Hakadosh Baruch Hu and the Torah runs far deeper. A mirror is a perfect reflection of the person standing opposite it, but the mirror shares no integral connection with that person. Similarly, a diary might provide an accurate and insightful window into a person's experiences, opinions, and personality, but the diary itself is untethered to the writer. While it is true that Torah is a perfect representation of Hashem's unchanging will, it is far more than a simple write-up. When we received the Torah, the Midrash tells us (*Shemos Rabbah* 33), Hakadosh Baruch Hu informed us that this was a transaction like no other. Typically, after the seller transfers ownership of an item, he vanishes from the scene, as he is not bound to the item. Regarding the Torah, Hashem tells Klal Yisrael (*Shemos* 25:2): וְיִקְחוּ לִי — you're actually taking Me into your lives. I'm right here, communicating with you any time you connect to the Torah.

Hakadosh Baruch Hu cloaks Himself, so to speak, within the Torah. When a person engages in Torah, he is not merely absorbing information, but rather tapping into a live link, through which he actively bonds with Hakadosh Baruch Hu. Not only is he connecting with the words of Hashem, he is meeting Hashem directly, and coming face-to-face with ultimate perfection.

How Does This Affect My Daily Life?

*T*he idea that Torah is a detailed manifestation of Hakadosh Baruch Hu's will should completely reframe the way we sit down before a Chumash or Gemara. We're not studying abstract concepts; we're peering into another world, and encountering Hakadosh Baruch Hu. When we debate a point within Torah, it's not merely an academic exercise — it's a way to attain a deeper and higher truth, to grasp and clarify the will of Hakadosh Baruch Hu.

In this regard, the Baal HaTanya (*Likutei Amarim* Ch. 37) expresses a beautiful thought. He notes that a person engaged in Torah study is commonly described as a *korei baTorah*. This choice of terminology seems peculiar, as *korei* literally means to call out, such as when seeking to gain someone's attention. Wouldn't it be more appropriate to use a verb connoting learning or studying, as opposed to calling?

Says the Baal HaTanya:

עֵסֶק הַתּוֹרָה נִקְרֵאת בִּלְשׁוֹן קְרִיאָה קוֹרֵא בַּתּוֹרָה פֵּרוּשׁ שֶׁעַל יְדֵי עֵסֶק הַתּוֹרָה קוֹרֵא לְהקב"ה לָבוֹא אֵלָיו כִּבְיָכוֹל כְּאָדָם הַקּוֹרֵא לַחֲבֵרוֹ שֶׁיָּבֹא אֵלָיו וּכְבֵן קָטָן הַקּוֹרֵא לְאָבִיו לָבֹא אֵלָיו לִהְיוֹת עִמּוֹ בְּצַוְתָּא חֲדָא וְלֹא לִפָּרֵד מִמֶּנּוּ וְלִשָּׁאֵר יְחִידִי חַס וְשָׁלוֹם. וְזֶהוּ שֶׁאָמְרוּ קָרוֹב ה' לְכֹל קֹרְאָיו לְכֹל אֲשֶׁר יִקְרָאֻהוּ בֶאֱמֶת וְאֵין אֱמֶת אֶלָּא תּוֹרָה דְּהַיְינוּ שֶׁקּוֹרֵא לְהקב"ה עַל יְדֵי הַתּוֹרָה דַּוְקָא לְאַפּוּקֵי מִי שֶׁקּוֹרֵא אוֹתוֹ שֶׁלֹּא עַל יְדֵי עֵסֶק הַתּוֹרָה אֶלָּא צוֹעֵק כָּךְ אַבָּא אַבָּא.

When a person immerses himself in Torah, he calls out to Hakadosh Baruch Hu to draw close to him, as it were, just as a person would call over his friend, or as a small child would implore his father to come to him and not leave him all alone. This is implied in the verse: "Hashem is close to all who call upon Him, to all who call upon Him in truth" (Tehillim 145:18) — since there is no "truth" but Torah, this must be referring to one who calls out to Him specifically through Torah, as opposed to one who calls out to Him without engaging in Torah study, and simply implores, "Father, father!"

We all need Hakadosh Baruch Hu. We all crave a real relationship with our Father, and want to have Him close by, watching over us and caring for us. We need His help with our health, with raising our children, with our finances — we need Him at every turn. How can we communicate and connect with Him? Certainly, *tefillah* is a potent tool. Talk to Him, and He will always listen. But if you really want to draw close, to have Him right there beside you, then there's a stronger method. Jump into a *sugya*. Immerse your mind and heart in the debates of the Gemara. Challenge yourself to achieve a deeper understanding of halachah.

The Torah is your direct connection to Hakadosh Baruch Hu. Invest the effort to understand Him, and He'll draw close to you, watching over you and guiding you through life.

וְלֹא תְהֵא תּוֹרָה אַחֶרֶת
Utterly Immutable

If Torah is an expression of the unchanging will of Hashem,
then halachah, the practical application of these truths, will
transcend all of life's variables. The same halachah holds true
yesterday, today, and tomorrow.

n a sense, it is this precept more than any of the other Ikkarim that serves as the demarcation line between Judaism
and many other religions, most notably Christianity and Islam.[1] These, as well as some other, smaller, religions concede the
authenticity of Jewry being the *Am HaNivchar*, the Chosen Nation.
They concede as well the veracity of Torah and its transmission at
Har Sinai. What viable route to legitimacy does this leave them?
After all, once they agree that Torah is true, they are compelled to
admit that all Torah laws and precepts are binding, and any innovations or changes can be justified only if the Torah itself allows
for such flexibility. Their only viable route to deviating from the
dictates of the Torah and creating a new brand of religion is to
somehow claim that at some point there was a rule change, with
the old system no longer in effect.

---

1. See Rambam, *Hilchos Teshuvah* 3:8.

It is claims like these that are completely repudiated by this Ikkar. This Ikkar tells us that not only did the Torah never change, the Torah cannot change. With this in hand, all discussion, proofs, and debates as to the validity of these religions are utterly eviscerated. The discussion of other such religions can only begin if change is possible — and this Ikkar gives the firm response. The Torah itself guarantees that it will never change. End of debate.

Irrevocably Chosen

*L*et's consider the claim, espoused by other religions, that we have somehow been demoted from the chosen status that the Torah affords us. Hakadosh Baruch Hu selected the Jewish nation as His children. Was this limited to a specific situation? Is this special status dependent upon our doing His will properly? The Torah provides us with a clear answer. Amid a detailed listing of the horrific suffering Klal Yisrael will endure when they turn away from Hashem, the Torah gives a firm assurance: לֹא מְאַסְתִּים וְלֹא גְעַלְתִּים לְכַלֹּתָם לְהָפֵר בְּרִיתִי אִתָּם, *I will not have been revolted by them nor will I have rejected them to obliterate them, to annul My covenant with them* (*Vayikra* 26:44).

The same point is expressed by the *nevi'im* (see, for instance, *Malachi* 3:6), and is reiterated emphatically in *Iggeres Teiman*, the Rambam's epic letter to the bewildered communities of Yemen. We were chosen for all eternity, come what may.

Since the Torah is applicable to every time, place, and situation the world will ever experience, and the Torah itself proclaims our eternal chosen status, it is impossible for Klal Yisrael to ever be removed from this pedestal. The Torah's proclamation of our eternal status is a statement of Hakadosh Baruch Hu's personal position. His opinion does not change. Whether we are up or down, on the right path or the wrong one, we are His children forever.

Can a Navi Change the Halachah?

A navi has no halachic jurisdiction whatsoever. He cannot use his powers of *nevuah* to determine for us which halachos are binding or correct, to adjudicate monetary cases, or to rule what is permitted or prohibited. Although Klal Yisrael turned to *nevi'im* for guidance in many areas, in matters of halachah, *nevuah* confers no special power, and a *navi* may weigh in only by virtue of his Torah scholarship. Despite his status as a prophet, his opinion is no more influential than that of any other Torah authority, and ultimately the halachah will follow the majority opinion. The Torah provides an established system of halachic decision-making, and nobody, not even someone who possesses prophetic ability, has the power to override the system.

There is one situation that we believe a navi when he tells us to override halachah: to allow for an extremely limited, case-specific exception to halachah. If, for instance, a *navi* claims that he has received a direct message from Above that the prohibition of eating shellfish is no longer in effect, we pay him no heed. If, however, a qualified and proven *navi* says that although shellfish are absolutely forbidden by the Torah, in this specific circumstance an exception must be made to the rule, we do listen to him. The difference? A *navi*, or anyone else, cannot alter the Torah's rules one iota. The Torah's rules do not change. The *navi* can convey, by virtue of his *nevuah*, that the Torah's law does not apply to this specific situation.

Technically, even creating a limited carve-out constitutes a change to the law, insofar as the law was originally inclusive of all potential situations. The reason this is acceptable is that the Torah clearly instructs us to believe the *navi*, within certain parameters, as it says (*Devarim* 18:15): אֵלָיו תִּשְׁמָעוּן, *To him shall you hearken*.[2] Once the Torah gave us this instruction, his prophecy regarding a limited-time halachic exemption is not a deviation from

_____

2. See Rambam, *Sefer HaMitzvos*, Positive Mitzvah 172.

Torah law at all, but rather a fulfillment of his Torah-ordained mandate.[3]

The prototype exception is that of Eliyahu HaNavi offering a *korban* on Mount Carmel, even though the halachah is that no *korban* may be brought outside the Beis HaMikdash. Eliyahu HaNavi had no power to change that halachah. What he was able to do, by virtue of his status as a qualified and proven *navi*, was to recognize that the broader halachah was not warranted in the specific situation before him, and that he needed to take a drastic step to save the Jewish people, who were teetering on a dangerous abyss. The correct course of action, according to the Torah, in that circumstance, was to bring his offering on Mount Carmel.

Even Where There's a Rabbinic Will, There's Still No Halachic Way

What about the *chachamim*? Don't they have the power to introduce halachic innovations?

While addressing this matter comprehensively would require a lengthy case-by-case discussion, the short answer is: No. The sages throughout the generations, as great as they were, were never accorded the ability to change even the minutest detail of the Torah. Their ability lay specifically within the powers and responsibilities that the Torah itself conferred upon them. Take, for example, the rabbinic mandate to wait after consuming meat before consuming dairy, or the rabbinic injunction against moving *muktzah* items on Shabbos. These restrictions fall into a broad category known as *seyagim*, or fences, and are a fulfillment of the Torah's precept of וּשְׁמַרְתֶּם אֶת מִשְׁמַרְתִּי, *You shall safeguard my charge* (*Vayikra* 18:30), which the Gemara (*Yevamos* 21a) explains to mean: עֲשׂוּ מִשְׁמֶרֶת לְמִשְׁמַרְתִּי — enact safeguards for my Torah.

---

3. Abarbanel, *Rosh Amanah*, end of Ch. 13.

This classification spans the vast majority of rabbinic innovations, which represent nothing more than a fulfillment of the *chachamim's* express obligation to create fences to protect the laws and integrity of the Torah. When they saw potential for error, they imposed precautionary measures to safeguard against transgression of the Torah's commandments. The *chachamim* fulfilled this responsibility faithfully, but were never granted authority to institute new laws that fell outside the parameters of their Torah-mandated obligation. Furthermore, the *chachamim* made it abundantly clear that their enactments were not dictated by the Torah itself and did not have the status of Torah commandments. The intent of these rabbinic laws was not to add to, detract from, or modify existing halachah, but simply to build a wall of protection around the Torah itself and ensure its optimal fulfillment.

An additional realm of rabbinic innovation, though smaller in scope, is that of introducing new mitzvos, such as the recitation of Hallel or *netilas yadayim* prior to eating bread. The *chachamim* could not randomly institute any new mitzvah, no matter how meaningful or beautiful they may have deemed it. They could introduce a new mitzvah only when following the Torah's directives for this process. Indeed, each of the handful of mitzvos they innovated involved long, painstaking effort and research to ascertain that the mitzvah was warranted by the Torah's blueprint. The *Talmud Yerushalmi* (*Megillah* 6b) tells us that a gathering of eighty-five sages, including over thirty *nevi'im*, struggled over the decision to heed the call of Mordechai and Esther to institute a festival of Purim, acquiescing only when they concluded that there was adequate Torah grounds for this innovation.

Lastly, the area in which the *chachamim* were most visibly active was in the clarification of halachah, as they debated and fine-tuned the application of the Torah's laws, as handed down from Sinai, to various scenarios. This process is not one of innovation, but rather of analysis and winnowing of the existing information to determine the parameters of its applicability. This power of the sages is explicitly dictated by the Torah, as it states: וְעָשִׂיתָ כְּכֹל...

אֲשֶׁר יוֹרוּךָ, *You shall do… according to everything that they will teach you* (*Devarim* 17:10). The Torah invests the decisions of the *cha-chamim* with full legal authority, and mandates, on a *d'Oraysa* level, that we accept and follow these rulings.

In short, no one at all — not a *navi*, not a leader, not even the greatest *gadol hador* — has the power to make even the slightest change to the Torah. Torah is complete, perfect, and eternally unchanging. Adding new laws or restrictions is permitted only if and when the Torah itself calls for these actions.

How Does This Affect My Daily Life?

*T*orah applies at all times, in all situations. Applying this means constantly asking ourselves, no matter where we may find ourselves, what the Torah expects of us in that particular situation.

A practical scenario where this concept plays a role is in the questions that tend to arise when we are out of our usual routine or milieu. Imagine that a person is on vacation, or perhaps attending an out-of-town business convention. He is out of his zone, and questions keep popping up. Is what I am about to do halachically correct? Is this tantalizing food, or this appealing vacation spot, in line with Torah values? Will this gathering contravene my moral standards? Often, the answers are complex, with many aspects to consider. Arguments pro and con can be made, and the bottom line might be nebulous.

Know this: Times and situations change, but Torah, and halachah, never take a break. The fact that I'm alone in my hotel room with no one the wiser as to what I see or do doesn't grant me license to let my guard down. The fact that I only realized after arriving at my camping site that my grill wasn't *toiveled* doesn't mean I can use it just this once. The fact that it's way past midnight and I'm exhausted doesn't excuse me from saying Shema properly.

Yes, different rules apply to different situations. There is a time for standard routine and a time for a vacation, a time to enjoy the pleasures of this world and a time to refrain from those pleasures. What is correct in one situation is not necessarily correct in another, and what I am supposed to do today is not necessarily what I should do tomorrow.

Yet the rules themselves don't change. They never bend to me, and I never have a day off to just do what I want. Wherever I find myself, and whatever I want to do, my question must always be what the Torah expects of me in this specific situation.

הָעִקָּר הָעֲשִׂירִי
The Tenth Ikkar

אֲנִי מַאֲמִין בֶּאֱמוּנָה שְׁלֵמָה שֶׁהַבּוֹרֵא
יִתְבָּרַךְ שְׁמוֹ יוֹדֵעַ כָּל מַעֲשֵׂה בְּנֵי אָדָם וְכָל
מַחְשְׁבוֹתָם שֶׁנֶּאֱמַר הַיֹּצֵר יַחַד לִבָּם הַמֵּבִין
אֶל כָּל מַעֲשֵׂיהֶם.

I am steadfast in my absolute belief that
the Creator, blessed is His Name, knows all
the deeds of human beings and all of their
thoughts, as the verse states (*Tehillim* 33:15):
He Who fashions their hearts together,
Who comprehends all their deeds.

In the Rambam's Words

וְהַיְסוֹד הָעֲשִׂירִי שֶׁהוּא יִתְעַלֶּה יוֹדֵעַ מַעֲשֵׂה בְּנֵי אָדָם וְאֵינוֹ
מַעֲלִים עֵינוֹ מֵהֶם וְלֹא כְּדַעַת מִי שֶׁאָמַר עָזַב ה' אֶת הָאָרֶץ אֶלָּא
כְּמוֹ שֶׁאָמַר גְּדֹל הָעֵצָה וְרַב הָעֲלִילִיָּה אֲשֶׁר עֵינֶיךָ פְּקֻחוֹת עַל
כָּל דַּרְכֵי בְּנֵי אָדָם וְאָמַר וַיַּרְא ה' כִּי רַבָּה רָעַת הָאָדָם בָּאָרֶץ
וְאָמַר זַעֲקַת סְדֹם וַעֲמֹרָה כִּי רָבָּה הֲרֵי אֵלּוּ מוֹרִים עַל הַיְסוֹד
הָעֲשִׂירִי הַזֶּה.

**The tenth foundational belief is that He, the exalted
One, is aware of all the actions of mankind,** and does
not ignore them. This is as opposed to those who say
that Hashem abandoned the earth; rather, His conduct
is described in the verses: *Great in counsel and mighty
in deed, Your eyes are cognizant to all the ways of
mankind, [to grant each man according to his ways and
the consequences of his deeds]* (Yirmiyah 32:19); *Hashem
saw that the wickedness of Man was great upon the earth*
(Bereishis 6:5); *So Hashem said, "Because the outcry of
Sodom and Amorah has become great"* (ibid. 18:20). These
all attest to this tenth foundational belief.

יוֹדֵעַ כָּל מַעֲשֵׂה בְנֵי אָדָם וְכָל מַחְשְׁבוֹתָם
Hashem Is Aware of, and Attentive to, Every Single Thing We Do

I might be alone in the privacy of my home, or I might be just one of a vast crowd. I might be involved in something truly life-altering, an act of epic consequence, or I might simply be carrying out a run-of-the-mill, everyday action, boring and mundane. It makes no difference. Hashem is watching it all, everything I do and everything I think.

*T*his Ikkar and the next are closely linked. In this Ikkar, we highlight Hakadosh Baruch Hu's omniscient awareness of, and His focus on, all our thoughts and actions. In the next Ikkar, we stress that every one of our actions, major or minor, has consequences. Some of these consequences are beneficial, while others are detrimental, but every action creates a reaction. These two Ikkarim are bound together, as appropriating fair reward and retribution for our actions is possible only to the degree that the score is kept accurately. Hakadosh Baruch Hu does maintain a perfect tabulation, both of our actions as well as of our internal thought processes.

The Torah repeatedly emphasizes the concept of reward or

punishment for our actions. But on what basis are our thoughts evaluated? We are told that Hakadosh Baruch Hu generally does not mete out punishment for thoughts (*Kiddushin* 40a). This, however, likely refers to thoughts that remain in the domain of the mind. If the thought propels a person to act, it can be considered part of the action, and therefore punishable. This principle pertains to thoughts of committing a sinful act, such as eating veal parmesan, robbing a bank, or going harpoon-fishing on Shabbos. Since the *aveirah* has not actually been performed, the thought can be set aside. Some prohibitions, though, are transgressed by thought alone: belief in idols, hatred of another Jew, or thoughts of immorality, for instance. Envying your neighbor's gleaming vehicle or well-manicured lawn would likely qualify as well. Since the thoughts themselves constitute a full-fledged transgression, they warrant retribution. On the other hand, mere thoughts of doing a mitzvah are usually rewarded, even if the person ultimately could not perform the mitzvah due to circumstances beyond his control.

There is yet another dimension to Hashem's knowing our every thought. Many of our actions seem, on the surface, neutral or undefined. Watching a person exit his front door, we would not be able to label his departure positive or negative. After all, we have no idea where he is headed or what he intends to do. Similarly, when someone makes a comment before a crowd of people, his words can often be interpreted in more than one light. Was his comment intended to be hurtful, or was it just an innocent remark? Was another person's charitable gift an act of selflessness and concern, or was it really just a ploy to gain honor and recognition?

The only way to properly assess an action is to identify the thought process behind it. Knowing our thoughts is therefore critical to evaluating our actions. That seems to be the emphasis of this Ani Maamin. As proof that Hashem is aware of all our thoughts, the author of the Ani Maamin cites a verse that describes Hakadosh Baruch as knowing all the *actions* of mankind: הַמֵּבִין אֶל

כָּל מַעֲשֵׂיהֶם. Perhaps the operative phrase here is *el kol* — literally, *toward all* their actions. Not only is He aware of the actions themselves, He also knows toward where the action is headed, and which thought process spawned it.

Ultimately, His awareness of everything we do allows us to receive precisely what we deserve. By keeping an exact score, He can grant us our due compensation: the *schar* and *onesh* detailed in the next Ikkar.

And yet, this Ikkar and the next are divided into two distinct statements. Clearly, then, intertwined as they might be, each one must be conveying a unique, independent message. If we separate the reward-and-punishment element from this Ikkar, what are we left with? Aside from consequences, what significance lies in the knowledge that He is aware of what we do and think? The answer must be that this Ikkar is stressing the very fact that He is watching us.

Suppose you walk into a daycare center and begin to observe the toddlers in the room. Some are busy building block towers, while others are dressing dolls or engaged in various "art" projects. You sit down on the floor and watch one of these children in action. A block here, another block there. The tower of blocks goes up, the tower comes crashing down. How interesting do you find this? How long can you watch this without getting fidgety? Five minutes? Ten minutes?

The gap between small children and adults is infinitely smaller than the gap between ourselves and Hakadosh Baruch Hu. Yet He's watching us every moment of our lives, taking a keen interest in everything we do. That we are subjects of his attention is something incredible. Rightly understood, this recognition compels us to attach far greater importance to every detail of our lives. I am someone He wants to watch. My actions matter to Him. He considers my thoughts significant.

In the Presence of Royalty

*T*he *Shulchan Aruch*, which represents the sum total of the laws governing the life of a Jew, contains the following introductory words by the Rema, paraphrasing the Rambam (*Moreh Nevuchim* 3:52):

> "*Shivisi Hashem l'negdi samid — I place Hashem before me constantly*" *is a cardinal principle of Torah and among the virtues of the righteous, who walk before Hashem. For the way a person sits, moves, and behaves when alone in his house differs from the way he sits, moves, and behaves when in the presence of royalty. Likewise, his manner of speech and expression when among family and friends is not comparable to the way he speaks when seated with royalty. Certainly, when a person considers that the great King, Hakadosh Baruch Hu, Whose glory fills the universe, is standing over him and watching everything he does... he will immediately be filled with awe, humility, and fear of Hakadosh Baruch Hu, and will always be embarrassed [to do anything wrong].*

This precept is enshrined by the Rema as his introduction to the rules of life, setting the stage for everything that is to follow. *Shivisi Hashem* — the recognition that Hashem is right before me, constantly — is not about me seeing Him. It's about Him seeing me. He's always watching me, focused on everything I do.

This is not simply another halachah. This is the "preface to everything" halachah. If a person is expected to carefully calibrate all his actions and monitor even the tiniest details in each aspect of his life, then the first thing he must know is how enormously important his every action really is. Once a person realizes how much it matters, he can then be instructed how to get it all exactly right. You can tell me that I must tie my shoelaces in a specific manner if you first inform me that the way I tie my shoelaces matters. You can tell me to cut my nails in a specific order if you first inform me that the way I cut my nails matters. You can tell me to be careful to give exact change if you can first inform me that every penny of my financial dealings matters.

We are not meaningless individuals lost in a crowd. "A person is obligated to say, the world was created for my sake" (*Mishnah Sanhedrin* 4:5) The world was worth creating for the value that I alone bring to the table. I stand at the center of the universe, and everything I do is of eminent importance. I matter, and every one of my actions matters.

Several years ago, when I was learning in the Mir Yeshiva, I needed the rosh yeshivah, R' Nosson Tzvi Finkel, to sign a document for me. Upon inquiring when I could catch him, I was told to go to his apartment, directly across from the yeshivah, at the end of the afternoon *seder*. Once the rosh yeshivah would finish learning with his *chavrusa*, he was expected to have a moment to spare before heading to the yeshivah for Maariv. When I arrived at his home, I found that he was in incredible pain, due to his illness, to the extent that he could not even make it across the street for Maariv. Instead, we pulled together enough men to enable R' Nosson Tzvi to daven at home with a minyan. The person tending to him assured me that these episodes generally passed, and I could likely get the document signed after Maariv.

The rosh yeshivah was not able to stand, and he sat at the table for the entire davening, motionless, except for the occasional movement to turn a page. When Maariv was over, the crowd emptied out, and I approached the rosh yeshivah cautiously. As I drew near, his assistant came rushing over to intercept me. Apparently, although we had gone ahead and concluded Maariv, the rosh yeshivah was still in middle of *Shemoneh Esrei*. Due to his rigidity, I had simply assumed he was finished, when in fact he was still in mid-davening. I offered to come back later, but was told that it would be better to wait. The assistant motioned me out of the room and exited the room as well. I stood outside the door, in a spot where I could see whether R' Nosson Tzvi was done without him being able to see me. There was no one else in the room. As far as he knew, nobody was watching.

Here was a man who had every excuse in the world to rush

his *tefillah*. Indeed, his condition likely exempted him altogether. And yet, he sat there, unable to move but forging ahead nonetheless, word after word. His *Shemoneh Esrei* lasted, to the best of my calculations, about eighteen minutes. Eighteen minutes of superhuman perseverance, because each word mattered. To him, this was not "just another *tefillah*," but something priceless and everlasting.

How Does This Affect My Daily Life?

*M*any of us sorely lack appreciation for our own value and the significance of our actions. So much of what we do carries little meaning to us due to our failure to recognize how valuable even our most trivial actions are — and that results in a lot of apathy. To illustrate:

You wash *netilas yadayim* as you sit down to lunch. Glancing at your hands, you realize that although you splashed plenty of water, you missed a small area of your hand. Do it again properly? Does it really make a difference?

You've finished up your lunch, and you're reciting *Bircas HaMazon* before heading out for some errands. As you wrap up the final paragraphs, you stand up and begin putting on your coat or glancing at the phone. You only have a few words left... Does it really make a difference?

You emerge from the restroom, wash your hands, and begin reciting *Asher Yatzar*. Stop and focus, or mumble it hastily as you rush out? Does it really make a difference?

In our minds, these activities carry little significance, and so they often fall by the wayside. But wait. My actions are important enough for the *Melech Malchei HaMelachim*, the Creator and Ruler of the entire universe, to focus on. Whether I do this act properly or not is of eminent importance to Him. If that's the case, my every action matters. It's worth expending the effort to do it right.

הָעִקָּר הָאַחַד עָשָׂר
The Eleventh Ikkar

אֲנִי מַאֲמִין בֶּאֱמוּנָה שְׁלֵמָה שֶׁהַבּוֹרֵא יִתְבָּרַךְ שְׁמוֹ גּוֹמֵל טוֹב לְשׁוֹמְרֵי מִצְוֹתָיו וּמַעֲנִישׁ לְעוֹבְרֵי מִצְוֹתָיו.

I am steadfast in my absolute belief
that the Creator, blessed is His Name,
rewards with good those who observe His
commandments, and punishes those who
violate His commandments.

וְהַיְסוֹד הָאַחַד עָשָׂר הוּא שֶׁהוּא יִתְעַלֶּה נוֹתֵן שָׂכָר לְמִי שֶׁמְּקַיֵּם מִצְוֹת הַתּוֹרָה וּמַעֲנִישׁ מִי שֶׁעוֹבֵר עַל אַזְהָרוֹתֶיהָ וְכִי הַגָּדוֹל שֶׁבִּגְמוּלוֹ הוּא הָעוֹלָם הַבָּא וְהֶחָמוּר שֶׁבְּעָנְשׁוֹ הוּא הַכָּרֵת וּכְבָר אָמַרְנוּ בָּעִנְיָן הַזֶּה דֵּי הַצֹּרֶךְ וְהַכָּתוּב הַמּוֹרֶה עַל הַיְסוֹד הַזֶּה הוּא אָמְרוּ אִם תִּשָּׂא אֶת חַטָּאתָם וְאִם אַיִן מְחֵנִי נָא מִסִּפְרְךָ וְהֵשִׁיב לוֹ יִתְעַלֶּה מִי אֲשֶׁר חָטָא לִי רְאָיָה שֶׁיָּדוּעַ לוֹ הָעוֹבֵד וְהַחוֹטֵא לָתֵת שָׂכָר לָזֶה וּלְהַעֲנִישׁ אֶת זֶה.

The eleventh foundational belief is that He, the Exalted One, gives reward to those who fulfill the Torah's [positive] commandments and punishes those who transgress its prohibitions. Furthermore, His ultimate reward is the World to Come, and His harshest punishment is *kareis*, which we have already discussed [in other places] sufficiently. The verse that attests to this foundational belief is that which [Moshe Rabbeinu] said (*Shemos* 32:32): *And now if You would but forgive their sin! — but if not, erase me now from Your book that You have written*, to which Hashem replied: *Whoever has sinned against Me [I shall erase him from My book]*. This is proof that He knows who serves Him and who sins, so He can give reward to this one and punishment to that one.

שָׂכָר וָעֹנֶשׁ
Actions and Reactions

Hakadosh Baruch Hu placed us in this world with specific instructions of what to do and what to avoid. We fulfill His directives because they are His will, and we recognize that His positive commandments embody true goodness and moral virtuosity, and His prohibitions are the essence of wrongdoing. This alone should seemingly suffice to dictate our course in life: Do good because it's right, avoid bad because it's wrong. Yet Hakadosh Baruch Hu goes on to tell us that He is constantly keeping score, and we will be rewarded or punished for our actions. He is the perfect judge and the ultimate remunerator.

*I*magine that a person believes in the entire Torah, faithfully observes every mitzvah, and scrupulously refrains from transgressing. He wears tefillin every day, maintains exacting kashrus standards, and is meticulous about every detail of Shabbos — but he does not believe in future consequences. Why, then, would he live his life in such a manner? Presumably, the answer would be that he firmly believes in the absoluteness of right and wrong. He understands that Hakadosh Baruch Hu exists and created the world, and that He has presented us with the ultimate

value system. Forget the compensation; he does the mitzvos because he knows they are the intrinsically correct path in life, and
he avoids *aveiros* because he knows that they are fundamentally
wrong.

This individual sounds like a great person, truly altruistic. If
only more people were like him! Yet this Ikkar is telling us that
one who does not believe in future consequences is lacking in his
emunah. Why?

To compound this question, let's consider the following Mishnah (*Avos* 1:3), in which Antignos Ish Socho, a *nasi* and bearer of
the Mesorah, says, "Do not be like servants who serve the master
for the sake of receiving a reward. Rather, be like servants who
serve the master not for the sake of receiving a reward."

Apparently, performing mitzvos and refraining from *aveiros*
in order to score well and earn reward is frowned upon. Our
motivation should not be to receive compensation for what
we do.[1] How, then, are we to understand this Ikkar, which emphasizes the centrality of reward and punishment? Am I supposed to be focused on the prize, or am I supposed to ignore it
completely?

The key here, it seems, is to understand the divide between
awareness and motivation. It is critical to *know* that reward and
punishment exist. Ultimately, however, this should not be my *motivation* to act.

To illustrate, suppose it's a searingly hot day, and someone
hands you an ice-cold Coke. Why would you drink it? You're hot,
the Coke is cold, and drinking it feels great. Your motivation for
this action is clear. Somewhere in your mind, however, another
set of considerations is at play, one that involves calories and di-
ets and the effects of sugar. You certainly aren't choosing to drink
the soda based on the health factors. You're drinking it because it
tastes good. Yet this decision has consequences that you would be
well-advised to heed.

---

1. For a further discussion on the parameters of this concept, see Appendix A.

In other words, the motivation behind an action and the effects of that action occupy two entirely different spheres. As far as motive is concerned, the ideal we aim for is to observe the mitzvos simply for the inherent value of fulfilling His will, irrespective of any reward. On the other hand, we must be acutely aware that the consequences of our choices are real. They will occur whether I choose to acknowledge them, or whether I choose to stick my head in the sand and pretend they don't exist. Taking a breath of fresh air will supply your body with oxygen. Touching a hot stove will result in a burn. Some results and reactions are beneficial, some are detrimental; regardless, they will occur no matter my reason for performing that action.

Suppose you walk into a manufacturing plant, and while browsing around you come across an intriguing bottle containing a bright-colored chemical. The string of odd-sounding ingredients listed on the bottle does little to shed light on the nature of this colorful liquid. Your curiosity piqued, you contemplate taking a drink.

Ridiculous, right? You have no idea what this liquid is, and chances are that it can have quite a deleterious effect on your wellbeing. To say, "Well, I'm sure nothing will happen" is rather brainless.

The same holds true in the spiritual realm. Every mitzvah or *aveirah* act generates real consequences. In fact, these repercussions are far more intense and significant than any physical pain. The outcome of a spiritual choice resonates on a profound, cosmic level, and endures forever. The joy or pain one will ultimately experience due to his actions won't fade or lose potency with time, and choosing to ignore the consequences does not stop them from happening. Partaking of a food or beverage of unknown kashrus status with a dismissive, "Well, I don't think it really matters" is therefore as absurd as drinking from a bottle whose contents are possibly toxic.

This Ani Maamin establishes that Hakadosh Baruch Hu will accord due compensation for everything we do. The Rambam takes this a step further, adding that we are obligated to know what is the nature of this reward and punishment: Olam Haba and *kareis*, respectively.

It is not enough to believe in the concept generally; we must realize what the specific consequences are. In other words, if someone believes that Hashem will reward him for every good thing he's ever done, but he pictures his reward as some lavish all-you-can-eat buffet, his emunah is fatally flawed. But why does it matter if someone misunderstands the nature of reward and punishment?

From the standpoint of motivation, knowing what the big prize is going to be is admittedly inconsequential. If you promise your child a candy for good behavior, you will have many possible ways to fulfill your pledge. As long as he's duly incentivized, the specifics are irrelevant. The point of this Ikkar, however, is not to incentivize or disincentivize. It's to lay out reality: If you do A, then B will occur. This is not about receiving a prize for good behavior, or being penalized for poor performance. It's about recognizing that every action we do, no matter how big or small, generates automatic, intrinsic consequences. To appreciate what we are causing with our every decision, we must be cognizant of what these consequences are.

How Does This Affect My Daily Life?

*U*nderstanding that our actions have consequences is one thing. Internalizing this idea is far more difficult. Doing so, however, will reshape how we view our past behavior, how we approach our future actions, and how we relate to the behavior of others, as we will explain.

To illustrate how the awareness of reward and punishment impacts the way we view our past behavior, suppose you make a *berachah* on some potato chips, when you suddenly remember that you have already made the requisite *berachah* just a minute or two earlier. The realization that you have violated the laws of *berachos* may be fleeting and easy to dismiss, but although the action fades into the fog of the past, its effect is real and lasting. It's like a stain on a shirt — even long after the party is over, the stain doesn't disappear until you wash it out. Similarly, the knowledge that this seemingly minor misdeed has consequences for the future should spur you to take corrective action. Conversely, suppose you become inspired to be more careful regarding the laws of *lashon hara* or to maintain focus during *tefillah*. For a week, two weeks, a month, your commitment holds strong, but eventually, with the passage of time, you find yourself back where you started. Rather than viewing your efforts as an exercise in futility, realize that your actions have not been erased. Their effects are real, and have not dissipated.

Similarly, this awareness changes the way you approach your future actions. When you are deliberating whether to go out to the succah to have a snack, the realization that this mitzvah will put something priceless in the bank will give you the impetus to make the extra effort. Even when you have only one *berachah* left in *Shemoneh Esrei*, the knowledge that every word matters will spur you to squeeze in just a little more concentration. The same applies to avoiding negative behavior. Before tossing out a caustic line at an irritating neighbor, or before reaching for something on Shabbos that might be *muktzah*, the recognition that the resulting damage will be real and lasting will empower you to keep your lips or fingers closed.

Belief in future consequences also shifts our perspective as we interact with others. Say you've hired a handyman to install some shelving in your house. You figure it would be nice to offer him a coffee. But wait. He's a nonobservant Jew, and will in all likelihood fail to make a *berachah* on the proffered drink. Before you give a mental shrug, figuring there can't be any harm in being nice, stop and think: Are you really being kind to him? True, he'll appreciate the coffee, but drinking without a *berachah* can potentially do him real, lasting damage. While there are several halachically valid solutions to this dilemma, the starting point is to recognize that the potential spiritual harm of a missed *berachah* is just as real as the benefit of the physical drink.

Or perhaps you're sitting at your desk, finishing up your last data entries before heading home, and you hear a nonreligious coworker discussing his Saturday shopping plans. Does it pain you? Do you feel that a Jew who is ignorant of his religion is damaging himself eternally? If he were in physical danger, wouldn't you jump out of your seat to save him? Your conviction that Shabbos desecration puts him at real risk should motivate you to find a way to save him from spiritual ruin. Offer him an opportunity for some one-on-one learning. Invite his family over for Shabbos. Do something!

Once we understand the enormity of what mitzvos and *aveiros* cause, we can't just be passive or dismissive. Our approach to everything we do and every situation we encounter will be transformed by our awareness of the weighty consequences of every action and decision.

הַגָּדוֹל שֶׁבַּגְּמוּל וְהֶחָמוּר שֶׁבָּעֹנֶשׁ
The Ultimate Reward,
the Most Severe Punishment

It's not enough to merely know that there will be an ultimate reckoning, and that every action we do will be rewarded or punished. It is imperative, says the Rambam, to know what kind of reward and punishment to expect. So what are these consequences?

The ultimate reward is Olam Haba, an otherworldly existence that involves intense enjoyment beyond any degree of human comprehension. The ultimate punishment? *Kareis,* which literally means being cut off, or disconnected from that eternity. After death, when we get to *Shamayim,* our reward will not be a five-star mansion, billions in bitcoin, or endless culinary indulgences. Olam Haba is something beyond the physical, outside the realm of our concepts of enjoyment or pain. Can we gain some sort of appreciation for these esoteric ideas?

First, we must realize that not only are the ultimate consequences of our actions not physical, there is no way they could be. Our true self, our *neshamah,* is made of purely spiritual matter. As such, even the most phenomenal indulgences of this world are utterly meaningless to it, and the most excruciating physical pain affects it not a whit. Once we step out of our physical bodies and reenter a world of pure spirituality, all physical realities will not only lose their significance, but will no longer exist at all.

Since a *neshamah* is not physical and cannot be singed by physical fire, the fire of Gehinnom cannot be a physical one, nor can Gan Eden be a place of eating and drinking. Why, then, are the words of Chazal replete with physical descriptions of Gan Eden and Gehinnom? Simply to depict them in terms we can comprehend. We know that fire is painful, so we appreciate that Gehinnom is painful. It's the closest comparison we can give.

On a limited scale, however, even in our current state, we can understand that enjoyment and pain extend well beyond the physical. Think of how much people sacrifice for honor, and how far people will go to achieve a sense of accomplishment.

Imagine that an athlete trains for years to compete on the international stage. Finally, he succeeds in making the grade. Though ranked as an underdog, he pulls off a surprising first-place finish, setting a world record in the process. Think of the intense rush of emotion he experiences as he crosses the finish line. What is that feeling? Is it the physical sensation of crossing the line? Hardly. After all, every other athlete in the race, down to the last-place runner, will cross the line as well. It's the thrill of triumph, the joy of the culmination of years of training. How much is that emotion worth? Enough that people will throw years of their lives and vast sums of money into achieving it. They'll put aside their families, their social obligations, and their fortunes for the remote possibility of reaching this moment.

We all know the feeling of exhilaration that success brings with it, and the feeling of misery that accompanies failure. We bask in the glow of recognition, and cringe just at the memory of an embarrassing moment. People would give anything to exchange emotional suffering for mental health and peace of mind. Similarly, the value of *nachas* from children surpasses any dollar amount, and cannot be described in terms of simple physical enjoyment or pain.

We can understand, then, that there are forms of both joy and agony that speak to our inner selves far more deeply than anything our bodies alone can experience. While these feelings pale in comparison to what we will ultimately experience in the World to Come, they do provide a basic paradigm for raising the bar of our understanding of the ultimate pleasure and anguish that exist in that realm.

Pirkei Avos tells us (4:17) that a momentary whiff of Olam Haba is far more pleasurable than all the enjoyments of this world combined. The wafting aroma of a steak on the grill might be tantalizing, but it doesn't come close to the experience of eating that steak. Similarly, a mere whiff of Olam Haba doesn't yield even a faint idea of the true enjoyment of Olam Haba, yet it would still far exceed everything this world has to offer. Think of your greatest vacation ever, the greatest food you've ever eaten, the greatest everything, all rolled into one unbelievable occasion — and this fantasy won't even approach the pleasure of that momentary whiff.

Essentially, Chazal are telling us that Olam Haba is something unimaginably spectacular, beyond anything that can exist in a physical world. In our current state, we can't grasp this experience. Yet we do enjoy flickers and sparks of this experience at special moments, such as when we suddenly achieve a breathtaking new understanding of a difficult Gemara, or when we bask in the holiness of Shabbos. While we cannot fully grasp the nature of the pleasure of the World to Come at this point, we can discern the basic outline of a far greater experience than anything with which we are familiar. And, if we pay attention, every so often we can detect glimmers of otherworldly light shining through to this world.

The Reward for a Mitzvah is… a Mitzvah

So far, we've covered two key steps to understanding this Ikkar. The first is that the ultimate consequences of our actions are not, and cannot be, physical; they are of a completely different nature. The second is that these nonphysical consequences can be understood, to a certain degree, in the context of the joy and agony we experience in our lives that cannot be measured in physical terms or valued in dollars and cents. This Ikkar involves a third critical step, however, one that relates to the very fabric of the reward and punishment of the next world.

Chazal tell us (*Avos* 4:2) that "*schar mitzvah mitzvah* — the reward for performing a mitzvah is a mitzvah." What does that mean? Rav Chaim Volozhiner explains this in a way that sheds light on the true nature of ultimate reward and punishment.

There are actions that generate a consequence: Do a job and you'll get paid for it. Then there are other actions whose consequence is an outgrowth of the action itself. For example, suppose a child touches a hot stove and burns his finger. The burn is not a punishment for his misbehavior. It's a natural outcome of touching a scalding surface.

Or suppose it's midwinter vacation, and you're off to the mountains for a day of skiing. The hours fly by, and after a hard day on the slopes, you're exhausted and freezing. You head over to the lodge, in search of food, drink, and, most importantly, warmth. As you step inside, the oak door closes behind you, and you see the roaring fireplace at the other end of the large room. Would it be correct to say that if you move close to the fire, you'll receive a large dose of warmth as a reward? While you definitely will be warm, it's not exactly a reward. After all, the warmth and your proximity are not two independent properties. They are innately bound. The very act of drawing close will grant you warmth. Conversely, the farther you go from the fire, the less you will benefit from its heat.

Now we can better define what *schar* and *onesh* truly are.

The ultimate reward we are working toward is something called *kirvas Elokim*, closeness to Hashem. This concept may initially sound esoteric and intangible, but we can draw parallels from human relationships to help us grasp this concept.

Marriage represents the ultimate connection between two human beings. Yet sharing a life encompasses many diverse elements, some of them quite mundane. Tasks like paying the bills, washing dishes, or changing diapers don't seem particularly meaningful on their own, but in the context of marriage, these actions take on real value. Each act is an investment in the relationship and an affirmation of its importance. The greatest enjoyment that marriage provides is the feeling of enduring closeness and connection, something that completely transcends any fleeting physical pleasure. It's not about the groceries or the garbage, it's about building the marriage. And it is precisely these banal actions that cultivate the relationship. Now, as we described in the skiing example above, the relationship is not a prize for doing household chores. It's a reward, yes, but one that is inextricably linked to the effort of investing in the relationship. Conversely, the distance engendered in a marriage when the couple neglects their respective responsibilities is not a punishment, but a natural consequence.

On an infinitely greater scale, but in much the same way, we earn — or forfeit — the supreme reward of *kirvas Elokim*. The idea is not that if we do all the right things in life, we'll have that many points in our account to redeem for prizes. Rather, the reward is an outgrowth of the mitzvah itself. Do what Hakadosh Baruch Hu wants, and you're drawing closer to His warmth, building an incredible closeness with Him. Do the wrong thing, and you've taken a step away from that relationship and the pleasure it provides. Mitzvah acts, prosaic as they may seem, are precisely the way to build the relationship.

Each relationship between two people is unique, as the two of you have been through your own unique life experiences and have interacted in your own unique way. The same is true of your relationship with Hakadosh Baruch Hu. Only you have your specific life story, with your own triumphs and failures. Each mitzvah you've done has your unique imprint on it, and therefore, the relationship you've forged with Hakadosh Baruch Hu is unique to you alone. It's a relationship you can already feel here and now, as you consciously work to build the connection, but one that you will experience and appreciate fully only when you move on to Olam Haba.

Schar mitzvah mitzvah — the reward for performing a mitzvah is not something out there. It's the mitzvah itself.

This, in a nutshell, is the ultimate definition of reward and punishment: Closeness to Hakadosh Baruch Hu will bring the most unimaginable enjoyment. *Kareis*, on the other hand, means missing out on all that there is to enjoy. Put differently, if *kirvas Elokim* is akin to being close to the fireplace and warmth, *kareis* is akin to being locked out of the lodge. You're shivering in the subzero weather as you peer through the frosty window, seeing all your friends enjoying the warmth indoors, and realizing you could have been there.

How Does This Affect My Daily Life?

*T*he pot-of-gold-at-the-end-of-the-rainbow model might have been an effective motivator when we were children, as we conjured up all sorts of tantalizing treasures we hoped to one day receive as our reward. As we grow older, however, our physical growth and maturity must be matched by intellectual development as well, as we grow to understand what life is really all about and to appreciate the nature of the reward that awaits us. This reward is truly something incredible, but it requires us to raise ourselves higher and draw ever closer to Hashem. By choosing correctly and overcoming our challenges, we position ourselves to enjoy the ultimate enjoyment, that of a true bond with Hakadosh Baruch Hu.

Even in this world, where Hashem's Presence is concealed, we can experience the pleasure of a relationship with Him as we engage in the activities, both banal and sublime, that build this connection. Yet the day will come when we will be able to feel the joy of this relationship palpably. The stronger the bond we have cultivated, the more incredible the feeling of closeness we will experience.

The reward isn't hidden away in a treasure chest in the sky. The reward is created by you, down here, with each action you do.

וּבָחַרְתָּ בַּחַיִּים
The Power of Choice

In this Ikkar, we deal with the concept of reward and punishment, which are essentially the effects of our actions. Yet this entire edifice of schar v'onesh is built upon an unspoken underlying concept: that of bechirah. Experiencing consequences for our actions is possible only insofar as we bear responsibility for those actions. Robots don't receive rewards, nor do they get punished. Responsibility, and accountability, are squarely based on our ability to choose how to proceed, from the multiple options available. Each day of our lives, we encounter situations in which we must make a decision. We are not slaves to our nature or circumstances, and our actions are not predetermined. We have the power to choose.

Our lives revolve around one central challenge: being tugged in two directions, and having to choose the correct one. By triumphing in this battle, we earn eternal Olam Haba.

What are the mechanics of this battle? We have within us two sets of drives, referred to colloquially as the *yetzer tov* and the *yetzer hara*, the good and evil inclinations. From a young age, we tend to conceptualize these as "two little guys deep down inside me, each one trying to outshout the other." In truth, however, the *yetzer tov* and the *yetzer hara* represent a far more basic dichotomy, one that relates to the core composition of a human being.

What are we? What are we made of?

An angel, we know, is something completely non-physical, and is not bound by gravity, time, or any other property of our world. Angels don't eat or sleep. They exist in an entirely different realm, and have no bodily needs or functions. Animals, on the other hand, are the epitome of pure physicality. They have no aspirations, ambitions, or sense of holding themselves accountable to a higher moral code of conduct. They eat, drink, and reproduce, and are completely consumed with the physical and mundane. Let's say you were to take one angel and one animal and blend them into a brand-new hybrid creature. The result? A human being. On one hand, we humans have a physical body, much like any other creature. But we are also part angel, and possess an entirely different dimension: a Divine soul.

If we think about it, this union is utterly baffling. How can an angel be bound to an animal? How can something spiritual be harnessed to something physical? The body and the *neshamah* exist in completely different realms, with no point of intersection between them, and yet here we are, the nexus of these two worlds. To illustrate how bizarre this combination is, suppose I asked you to take your thoughts and place them in a bag on my desk. Suppose I told you to take your sense of pride and glue it to the wall. Could you possibly attach something metaphysical to a physical item? Yet the body-soul union is something we live with and consider eminently natural.

We recite the blessing of *Asher Yatzar*, thanking and praising Hakadosh Baruch Hu for the brilliant miracle that is our body. Immediately after reciting it the first time each morning, many have the custom to recite the blessing of *Elokai Neshamah*, which describes the Divine and pristine nature of the soul within us. Why couple the two? The Rema (*Darkei Moshe* O.C. 6) points to the final words of *Asher Yatzar: umafli laasos* — Hakadosh Baruch

Hu acts wondrously. These words serve as the bridge between the two blessings, whose juxtaposition draws our attention, and pays tribute, to the astounding interface of the physical world of *Asher Yatzar* and the spiritual dimension of *Elokai Neshamah*. That a Divine soul can be housed in a body of flesh and blood is truly a wonder.

Composed as we are of two completely disparate elements, we are drawn in two opposing directions. Our *neshamah* pulls us ever higher, to the ultimate logic and truth of what really matters, while our body pulls us toward the physical and mundane. The soul says, eat to provide yourself with energy to do what you are here to accomplish. Eat the foods that will best enable your body to function. The body says, eat to enjoy. Eat whatever tastes best or tickles your fancy. The body can be used by the *neshamah* as a tool to accomplish life's goals, or the body can run wild and take the *neshamah* along for the ride. You stand at the center of this tension, and you choose which side will triumph. Deciding between self-control and unbridled desire is in your hands.

Why the Need for a Tug-of-War?

On a simple level, the function of *bechirah* is to enable us to earn reward. If the challenges we faced were impossibly difficult, we wouldn't stand a chance. If the correct choices were obvious and easy, there would be no challenge, and we could not be credited for our decisions. After all, we would be reduced to angel-like beings, to whom Hashem's will is absolutely clear, and who therefore earn no compensation. The opportunity to proceed in either direction poses a challenge over which we can triumph, allowing us to stand proud of what we have accomplished and to bask in the reward we have earned.

The concept of *bechirah* runs deeper, though. The Ramchal points out that the reward and punishment of the World to Come are not some big prize up in the sky. As we have explained, the ultimate reward is *kirvas Elokim*, the intense enjoyment that arises from closeness to Hashem. Ultimate suffering results from distance from Hashem, and from the realization of how much better off a person could have been for eternity. In other words, reward and punishment are not external things that we will receive but rather the essence of who we have become and what we will be in the future. The closer I bring myself to Hashem during my life, the closer I will be when I move on to the next world. Each mitzvah act, then, is not a random way to put points onto my scoresheet, but rather a way to move myself closer to Hashem.

I am caught in a lifelong tug-of-war, with my animalistic and angelic elements each pulling me in their respective direction. Each decision moves me toward one side or the other.

Who I am, then, is not defined by my DNA, my personality, my abilities, or even my accomplishments. It is the choices I make that mold, define, and reveal who I truly am. For that reason, an innocent victim forced at gunpoint to commit a crime does not instantly become an evil person. Conversely, a felon who is compelled to perform community service is not automatically rehabilitated. It is the choice to perform certain actions, not just the actions themselves, that defines us. When we face an internal battle, when doing the right thing is difficult, when following the Torah is a real struggle — that is where we are forged. Exercising *bechirah* properly by choosing the right path and opting to fight the battle is what makes us special, and worthy of reward.

Life presents me with countless challenges each day, and every challenge gives me the opportunity to make a decision. With each decision I make, I am reformatting my essence, which makes me a changed person, either closer to or further away from Hakadosh Baruch Hu.

The Brackets of Bechirah

*M*uch as *bechirah* occupies center stage in our lives, we can wonder how much of our daily activity actually involves free choice. While in theory, everything we do is subject to free-will decision-making, on a practical level, due to our upbringing, circumstances, and religious background, many options are beyond the range of our ability to choose. Certain transgressions are simply not things we would ever consider. For the average person, avoiding a credit card transaction that might involve *ribbis* might be a challenge; stealing a million dollars off a friend's credit card would not be. Walking away from a conversation that might lead to speaking negatively about a neighbor could involve a tough choice; the option to murder said neighbor does not. Eating at a food establishment with an unfamiliar *kashrus* certification can pose a dilemma; eating a bacon sandwich does not.

The same holds true on the positive end of the mitzvah spectrum. Attending a Torah *shiur* is something most people can do. Learning for eight hours without interruption is something many cannot. Essentially, our range of opportunities to exercise free will lies within a certain bracket of limitations. To be sure, as we progress in life, this bracket continually evolves. With each good deed, we upgrade our free-will range, bringing ever-greater accomplishments within reach. With each wrongdoing, the bracket of limitation regresses. These upper and lower limits are constantly being adjusted, in various aspects of our lives, at every moment. Yet for all their flexibility, they do remain the bookends of our ability to choose, leaving certain options beyond our practical *bechirah* range.

While the battlefield of free choice is indeed limited and highly individual, *bechirah* involves another, intriguing dimension, one that encompasses everything we do. This is expressed in the following mitzvah in *Parashas Nitzavim*, which commands us to exercise *bechirah*: הַחַיִּים וְהַמָּוֶת נָתַתִּי לְפָנֶיךָ הַבְּרָכָה וְהַקְּלָלָה וּבָחַרְתָּ בַּחַיִּים

לְמַעַן תִּחְיֶה אַתָּה וְזַרְעֶךָ, *I have placed life and death before you, blessing and curse; and you shall choose life, so that you will live, you and your offspring.*

Hashem is informing us that the path of truth, of life itself, is the path of mitzvos, which has been charted for us throughout the entire Torah up to this point. Follow this path, and you will experience what life truly is. Abandon this path, and be doomed to devastation. The *pasuk* then concludes with an exhortation: Choose life!

Who is this addressing? If the target audience is those who heed the Torah's dictates, this additional mitzvah would seem superfluous. We've already been commanded to eat kosher, keep Shabbos, avoid *shaatnez*, and so on, so to the committed Jew, the commandments alone should suffice. And if the target audience is those who disregard the previous instructions, of what good is one more mitzvah? If the directive to keep Shabbos, clearly enshrined in Torah law and backed up with the threat of capital punishment, hasn't done the trick, why would a commandment to choose life suddenly change the dynamic?

Rav Shimon Alster explains that these words are indeed addressing those who are committed to keeping the Torah and abiding by everything they have been instructed previously. This new mitzvah is not merely a tacked-on reinforcement, but rather an entirely new instruction.

The basic demarcation of religious commitment is binary: Either you're committed or you're not. But even within the world of Torah observance, there is another great divide. Two possible motivations exist for fulfilling any mitzvah. One is that I love to do the mitzvah. The other is that I don't have a choice. Both motives are valid, and were, in fact, pivotal to our becoming the Chosen Nation at the base of Har Sinai. On one hand, we rose to this status by declaring *naaseh venishma*, we will do and we will hear. This proclamation constituted a moment of passionate devotion, an expression of unconditional agreement to anything Hashem would ask of us. On the other hand, at the very same moment in history, we were placed in utmost peril, with Hakadosh Baruch Hu raising the mountain over our heads and threatening that if we would refuse to accept the Torah we would be buried. Why was this dire warning necessary? Hadn't we already declared our allegiance? Rabbi Alster explains this was not a threat, nor was it a coercive measure. Rather, it was a way of impressing upon Klal Yisrael that there simply is no other choice. Your acceptance of the Torah is the linchpin of the existence of the entire universe. Say no, and the world will crumble.

These two facets of the giving of the Torah yield a key dichotomy. Acceptance of Torah involves both love and necessity. I do mitzvos because I love doing them. They're beautiful, meaningful, and invigorating. But I also do them because I understand how vital they are. They are the fabric of existence, and there simply is no other option but to perform them.

Both elements are imperative. Understandably, the optimal way to perform mitzvos is with passion, because you want to do it. But you're human, and some days you simply won't have that drive. You'll roll over in bed and wish you didn't have to go to Shacharis. At that point, when the track of enthusiasm is shuttered, you take the track of necessity, getting out of bed because that is the only option.

In a certain sense, free choice is an illusion. While technically we can choose whether to follow the Torah or close our eyes to the truth and do whatever we desire, in practice only one is a viable option. Every decision has consequences, and one who ignores the truth will eventually pay a steep price. One choice we do have, however. It's the choice of which of these two tracks to take as our primary path in life. We can follow the rules because we love this life, and the mitzvos are so meaningful to us. Or we can go through the motions, executing the mitzvos to perfection because we know there is no other choice. I don't love it, I don't appreciate it, but the rules are the rules.

This is where this new mitzvah enters the scene. Choose life! Don't just do it, choose it. Until now, you've heard the basic rules.

You've been shown what's right and what's wrong, what you must embrace and what you must avoid. Now, you're being told how to approach it all. Make it your choice!

What difference does this make? On a practical level, both the one who makes the choice to observe the Torah as well as the one who fulfills it by default check the boxes and get the job done. Yet there is one critical difference: לְמַעַן תִּחְיֶה אַתָּה וְזַרְעֶךָ, *so that you will live, you and your offspring.* Performing Hashem's will out of obligation creates a model citizen, but not one who exudes vitality. Do you want your Yiddishkeit to come alive? Do you want to radiate an enthusiasm that your children will appreciate, absorb, and incorporate into their own lives? *Uvacharta bachaim.* Don't just do the mitzvos because you have to; do them because you want to, and because nothing else is more valuable to you.

Admittedly, many options are beyond our range of free choice. I don't really entertain the possibility of eating lobster. But an element of *bechirah* does exist in every situation — my ability to choose to act the way the Torah tells me to.

How Does This Affect My Daily Life?

*B*echirah, the ability to choose, underpins the responsibility we bear for our actions. Yet the modern world increasingly favors the worldview of causal determinism, explaining both good and bad actions as nothing more than inevitable outgrowths of a person's upbringing or genetics. People cannot be criticized or taken to task for their way of life because that's simply "who they are," as if that were incontrovertible, and the individual utterly helpless.

The Torah tells us otherwise. We are accountable for our actions. This is not merely incidental; it is the very reason we are put into this world. The ability to make choices, to promote either half of our dual-natured selves, is what enables us to earn Olam Haba, the ultimate pleasure that Hakadosh Baruch Hu wants to grant us. The ticket to making ourselves "Olam Haba compatible" is to understand our responsibility and take charge of our lives. We are not automatons, nor are we enslaved to our genes, our acquired habits, or the dictates of society. We can take charge and rise up to the challenges, big and small, that we face each day. We can choose to do mitzvos, and we can choose how we do mitzvos.

We hold this decision-making power in our hands. By making the right choices, and choosing to choose, we develop ourselves into unique people, those that are truly close to Hakadosh Baruch Hu.

הָעִקָּר הַשְּׁנֵים עָשָׂר
The Twelfth Ikkar

אֲנִי מַאֲמִין בֶּאֱמוּנָה שְׁלֵמָה בְּבִיאַת הַמָּשִׁיחַ
וְאַף עַל פִּי שֶׁיִּתְמַהְמֵהַּ עִם כָּל זֶה אֲחַכֶּה לּוֹ
בְּכָל יוֹם שֶׁיָּבוֹא.

I am steadfast in my absolute belief
in the coming of Mashiach, and
even though he may delay, nevertheless
I await his arrival each day.

וְהָעִקָּר הַשְּׁנֵים עָשָׂר יְמוֹת הַמָּשִׁיחַ וְהוּא הָאֱמוּנָה וְהָאֱמוּת עַל
בּוֹאוֹ וְשֶׁאֵינוּ מִתְאַחֵר אִם יִתְמַהְמָהּ חַכֵּה לוֹ וְאֵין קוֹבְעִין לוֹ זְמָן
מֻסָּם וְלֹא מְבָאֲרִים אֶת הַכְּתוּבִים כְּדֵי לִדְרשׁ מֵהֶן אֶת זְמָן בּוֹאוֹ
חֲכָמִים אָמְרוּ תִּפּוּחַ דַּעְתָּן שֶׁל מְחַשְּׁבֵי קִצִּין וּלְהַאֲמִין שֶׁיִּהְיוּ בּוֹ
עָצְמָה וְאַהֲבָה וּדְרִישָׁה אֵלָיו כְּפִי מַה שֶׁנֶּאֱמַר עָלָיו עַל יְדֵי כָּל
נָבִיא מִמֹּשֶׁה עַד מַלְאָכִי וּמִי שֶׁהִסְתַּפֵּק בּוֹ אוֹ הֵקֵל רֹאשׁ בְּעִנְיָנוּ
הִכְחִישׁ אֶת הַתּוֹרָה שֶׁהִבְטִיחָה עָלֶיהָ בְּפֵרוּשׁ בְּפָרָשַׁת בִּלְעָם
וְאַתֶּם נִצָּבִים וּמִכְּלָל הַיְסוֹד הַזֶּה שֶׁאֵין לְיִשְׂרָאֵל מֶלֶךְ אֶלָּא מִדָּוִד
וּמִזֶּרַע שְׁלֹמֹה בִּלְבָד וְכָל הַחוֹלֵק עַל דְּבַר הַמִּשְׁפָּחָה הַזֹּאת כָּפַר
בַּה' וּבְדִבְרֵי נְבִיאָיו.

The twelfth foundational belief relates to the era of Mashiach, and that is the faith [in Mashiach's arrival], the acceptance of the veracity of his arrival, and the belief that he does not [needlessly] tarry: *Though he may tarry, await him* (Chavakuk 2:3). We do not designate a specific time for his arrival, nor do we attempt to expound the various [pertinent] verses in order to glean from them the time of his arrival. Of such attempts, the Sages said, "May the minds of those who calculate 'ends' suffer agony." We must believe that he will possess strength and love, and that he will be sought-after, in keeping with how he is described by all the prophets, from Moshe to Malachi. One who is skeptical or flippant about this concept has denied the Torah itself, which explicitly guaranteed this, both in *Parashas Balak* and in *Parashas Nitzavim.* Included in this foundational belief as well is that there will be no Jewish monarch other than those who descend from David and Shlomo. Whoever challenges this dynasty has repudiated Hashem and the words of His prophets.

בִּיאַת הַמָּשִׁיחַ
The Arrival of Mashiach

Surely, there is no more evocative Ani Maamin than this, the song of hope of Jews through the generations. This Ikkar expresses our yearning for a day when the glory of Hakadosh Baruch Hu will be restored, and Klal Yisrael will finally live in security and peace. Instead of living under the shadow of antisemitism, we will occupy a role of eminence in the world and will be revered by all, as they acknowledge our chosen status.

*A*sk someone, ask yourself, to describe in a few words what the era of Mashiach will be like. Most likely, the response will be worry-free tranquility, an end to all pain and suffering — no more sickness, no more wars, no more infighting, no more straining to make a living.

In short, then, we look forward to Mashiach as the ultimate panacea, the antidote to all our problems. His arrival, we imagine, will usher in a utopian period whose distinguishing feature will be the absence of the difficulties we currently experience.

If this is our vision of the benefit Mashiach will bring, however, we run up against some thorny questions.

1.   There is something unique about this Ikkar. Each of

the other Ikkarim conveys a basic principle to which we must subscribe, but this Ikkar contains an additional element: Even though it is taking an exceedingly long time for Mashiach to come, we keep awaiting and hoping for his arrival. Taking the words of the Ani Maamin alone, we might construe this simply as a description of Klal Yisrael's perseverance and faith. Yet the Rambam emphasizes that this is not merely a descriptive point, but rather a forceful directive, as he cites the exhortation of the prophet Chavakuk: אִם יִתְמַהְמָהּ חַכֵּה לוֹ, *Though he may tarry, await him!* We are *obligated* to eagerly await Mashiach. Indeed, Chazal state (*Shabbos* 31a) that when a person faces his Heavenly judgment after 120, one of the first questions he is asked is, "*Tzipisa l'yeshuah?*" Did you anxiously anticipate the redemption? Merely believing Mashiach will come is insufficient. We have to want it, and look forward to it.

Every other Ikkar is a matter of belief. If I accept the precept as truth, I'm on board. This Ikkar, however, mandates not only belief, but also yearning. Why is this anticipation so critical? If I don't feel that I'm suffering, and I don't consider Mashiach's arrival so pressing, why isn't it enough for me to simply acknowledge that he will come?

2.   The Ani Maamin version of the Ikkar focuses solely on the arrival of Mashiach, but the Rambam adds an astounding qualifier. Noting that Mashiach must descend directly from the royal dynasty of David HaMelech and the tribe of Yehudah, the Rambam stresses that a core feature of our belief in Mashiach is that with his arrival, leadership of the Jewish nation will revert to the monarchy of the House of David. Now, suppose a person believes fully that Mashiach will arrive imminently. He envisions him as a Torah scholar of unparalleled caliber who will bring Klal Yisrael together in glorious unity. He will be the quintessential *gadol hador*, and all of world Jewry will turn to him for guidance and abide by his instructions. The country will remain a democracy, however, with the political leadership chosen by popular vote. Mashiach's place will be in the *beis midrash*, where he will serve as the

address for all halachic matters, from the intricacies of the high-tech Shabbos kitchen to the ethics of medical interventions. Mashiach will preside over Torah decisions, while the political leaders will guide national affairs. This sounds like a reasonable vision — yet the Rambam is declaring that such a vision is patently flawed, and one who subscribes to it has disavowed a fundamental tenet of Judaism. What about this is so terrible? If the intent of this Ikkar is to depict an idyllic period of utopian existence, what difference does it make what the structure of the future government will be?

3.   Over the generations, the Jewish people have endured persecution, violence, and unspeakable atrocities. Banished from one country after another, we have been forced to live under humiliating and horrific conditions. Even in the best of times, we had to constantly be on guard, as the slightest trigger could set off the local populace or turn the leadership against us. A monarch's whim could instantly dissolve communities, destroying everything they struggled for years to build. Lacking basic safety and peace of mind, they nevertheless forged ahead. Compare the historical state of the Jewish people to our state today. While we still face serious problems, on both the communal and individual level, any comparison between our overall state and that of previous generations is utterly laughable. Our national strength, our communal infrastructure, and our individual development are light years ahead of any other Jewish community in the past two thousand years. We talk of educational crises and children falling out of the system — and yet, as tragic as each lost soul is, our school system is nevertheless a resounding success compared to that which existed in prewar Europe. Not only did pitifully few children receive a Jewish education at all, but even the greatest yeshivos hemorrhaged huge numbers of students who left the fold entirely. With all the illness and tragic deaths that we hear of today, life expectancy has practically doubled, and modern sanitation and medicine have reduced child and maternal mortality to a fraction of what they once were. Once, it was understood that on any random day, a marauding mob might burst through

town, leaving the helpless Jews to cower in hiding, and then to bury the dead once the pogrom had subsided. A Jew walking the street could be forcibly conscripted or kidnaped, never to be seen again.

Objectively speaking, we are living in a remarkable era. Yes, we endure plenty of pain, and suffer from lack of direction, but we have made stupendous strides on every front: Torah, *tefillah*, mitzvos, *chessed*, *chinuch*, and so on. If we're down to complaining about parking spots and the cost of weddings, our current *galus* can't be so horrendous.

All this begs the question of why anticipating Mashiach is so vital. While the Jews living through the Crusades, the Inquisition, the blood libels, the Cantonist decrees, and the concentration camps required passionate faith in Mashiach to carry them forward, is that intense yearning still necessary today? Surely, the many serious issues of our time need to be addressed, but overall our lives seem relatively stable. Why is it a basic tenet of our belief to look forward to a completely revamped world? Do we really need Mashiach so desperately?

4. Even if we assume that the function of Mashiach is to solve all our problems and turn our existence into bliss, the choice of Mashiach as the answer still seems puzzling. Why reshape the entire world order? As noted in the previous Ikkar, the place of ultimate enjoyment is Olam Haba, a realm beyond our world. Wouldn't it make sense to solve all our problems forever by bringing Klal Yisrael directly to this destination? In short, beneficial as it would be to have all our issues and problems obviated, why is belief in Mashiach a central tenet of our belief system?

These questions force us to reassess our concept of what the era of Mashiach will be.

The vision of Mashiach arriving simply to cure all our worries forever represents a self-centered approach. I am suffering. I need help. This will be my solution. My troubles create the need to await Mashiach, and alleviating my suffering is the justification for his arrival.

A true understanding of Mashiach, however, requires removing myself from the center of this picture and replacing my concerns with those of Hakadosh Baruch Hu Himself.

It's *His* Redemption

*I*magine that a new business enterprise is launched, after a huge initial investment. A large workforce is hired, and the business concept promises outstanding potential for growth. A few months later, however, the business seems to have soured. Not only isn't it thriving, it's struggling to survive. Most of the employees are apathetic, and many are failing to perform their jobs correctly. Some seem to have forgotten the concept of work altogether, and spend their days at the office drinking coffee, chatting, and playing with their phones. Worse, although all these employees, down to the cleaning crews working the nightshift, receive generous salaries and numerous perks, many of them busy themselves organizing vocal protests to voice their imaginary grievances against the investor backing this entire enterprise. The few truly dedicated employees, who understand the value of their jobs and their responsibility to their employers, labor on with difficulty, struggling to remain productive in a workplace where they are ridiculed for their views and ethics. The investor? He sees the madness, and yet, for some mysterious reason, continues pouring in money to keep the enterprise afloat.

This is an apt analogy to the world we live in.

Hakadosh Baruch Hu created this world of ours with a purpose. He wants something out of this enterprise. Yet what results is He getting? By the numbers, it would seem like a colossal failure. The overwhelming majority of the world's population does not even subscribe to the basic monotheistic belief that He is the sole source of existence. To put this into perspective, estimates place the world population of declared atheists and agnostics at seventy times greater than the number of Jews in the world. Picture this: For every minyan of Jews who could potentially declare *"Shema Yisrael,"* a crowd of seven hundred of Hashem's creations screams back, "No Creator exists!" But wait — that number includes only those who categorically deny Hakadosh Baruch Hu's existence. Billions more believe in various other misguided ideologies, whether polytheism, pantheism, or any mutation thereof. Going further, of the 15 million or so Jews alive today — less than 0.2% of the world's population — how many adhere on any level to halachah and Torah values? And if we really take this all the way to the top, how many fully observant Jews excel in all areas of Divine service? Are we, the minuscule fraction of the world populace that actually seek to do the job we were hired for, satisfied that our performance is up to par?

The world around us is not merely out of sync with Hakadosh Baruch Hu's will; it is increasingly belligerent and hostile toward any expression of the true values that should underpin this world's functioning. A person voicing the Torah view on issues such as morality or sanctity of life risks being tarred as a bigot and extremist. As society trumpets the value system of the day, the ideals we cherish are ridiculed as archaic and out-of-touch. And Hakadosh Baruch Hu? He keeps feeding us, providing for our needs, and sustaining the entire world, despite its being so overwhelmingly against Him.

For the Jew who knows better, who discerns right from wrong, this has to hurt. If someone slaps your father and you stand by silently, there's something seriously wrong. You're the child of the investor who is pouring all that money into the corporation. You know he is keeping all those employees on the payroll, supporting them and their families, and you watch as they sit around lambasting your father. You may not be able to do much, but you can cry.

There will, however, come a day.

On that day, right will be right and wrong will be wrong. On that day, every human being will recognize with astonishing simplicity that there is One Creator Who controls everything. On that day, everyone will realize that all that matters is His will, and the entire world will focus on doing exactly that. The drive for depravity will evaporate, dissipating like smoke in the wind, and the temptations that currently pull us so strongly will be but a relic of history. The idea of a person being drawn to inappropriate material online, sharing a tantalizing bit of gossip about a neighbor, or even carrying on a conversation during Chazaras HaShatz will seem as utterly ludicrous as bowing down to a cow. Much as we look back with bafflement at the ancients who worshiped idols, wondering how on earth they could have held such beliefs, we will look back at today's world with utter bewilderment, wondering how we ever could have been attracted even slightly to behavior reflecting a lack of financial integrity or moral debauchery. Klal Yisrael will be revered, and their rightful status as the chosen nation, the princes of Hakadosh Baruch Hu, will be universally recognized. We will live our Yiddishkeit with the proudest sense of fulfillment, finding meaning and connection in our every action. This is what the era of Mashiach will be, as Hakadosh Baruch Hu's enterprise functions in its full beauty.

With this perspective, we can now address the above questions. It's not enough for Mashiach to resolve our personal issues, end our suffering, and turn our existence blissful. The world requires a massive course correction, one that eclipses the specific needs of each individual. Where do I fit into this picture? What about my personal suffering? I will stand on the periphery, not at the center, but the picture I will be part of is a fantastic one. In a world gone right, our problems will disappear. With all of humanity driven by a common cause and unified under the leadership of Mashiach, war, hostility, and infighting will naturally disappear.

Other forms of suffering and anguish will be resolved as well. By way of analogy, a critically ill patient typically has a compromised immune system, which puts him at risk of contracting various other diseases that have no connection to his original ailment. Similarly, we today are functioning with limited strength, on a compromised system, which results in all sorts of suffering, hardship, and pain. With the arrival of Mashiach, Klal Yisrael will return to its full strength, and the side effects of *galus* will vanish.

Symptoms of a Far Worse Disease

*I*n his commentary to *Hilchos Tefillah*, the *Be'er Heitev* cites the Mahari Tzemach's advice that one who is experiencing a personal difficulty should have that difficulty in mind when reciting the words in *Shemoneh Esrei*: כִּי לִישׁוּעָתְךָ קִוִּינוּ כָּל הַיּוֹם, *For we hope for Your salvation all day long*. The Mahari Tzemach adds that on numerous occasions when hardships arose in his life, they were resolved after he had this intention. What connection is there between our problems and these particular words of davening? Why is this practice efficacious? The answer lies in reframing our personal problems as outgrowths of *galus*. Yes, we have difficulties, and they can be significant, but they are merely symptoms of a far worse disease, the malfunctioning of the world at large. Cure that disease, and all our personal issues will be resolved as well. This ability to think on a grander scale and view our personal suffering through the lens of Hakadosh Baruch Hu's distress with the state of the world empowers our *tefillos* and increases our likelihood of achieving the desired result. That small step of feeling His pain and asking for the world to reach its optimal state serves as a powerful mechanism in solving the side effects of the absence of that state.

The second question above dealt with the centrality of restoring the monarchy of the House of David. If Mashiach's function is to reshape the world, merely having a brilliant *talmid chacham* and *tzaddik* ensconced in a corner of the *beis midrash* is insufficient; it is essential that the entire nation and country follow his leadership, as per the will of Hashem. The style of governance at that time will reflect the Torah's laws and values in every realm, from taxation to healthcare to social welfare programs. Therefore, Mashiach — representing the authority of Hashem and His Torah — must preside not only over religious matters, but over civil matters as well.

What about the need to yearn for Mashiach? Why is it so critical to our belief system? Why isn't it enough to believe that he will one day arrive? The answer is that yearning for Mashiach is not merely about the future — it's a powerful statement about the present as well. If something hurts, you scream. If you have a toothache, all you can think about is the dentist. If you are dealing with a serious problem, you are consumed with finding a solution. And if the state of the world bothers you, you long for it to change. If you can look at the state of the world and simply shrug it off, that's a terrible indictment of your inner sentiments.

We express our yearning for a better existence repeatedly in davening. One example is in the *Aleinu* prayer, with which we conclude each *tefillah*. The first segment of this prayer extols the greatness of Hakadosh Baruch Hu and the magnitude of His creation. We declare that although we stand in complete submission before Him, at this point His Shechinah and resting place are up in the heavens. His radiance does not fully permeate the universe, as most of the world turns to other beliefs. We alone enjoy that special bond with Him, recognizing Him as the One Who created and runs the world, a belief reflected in the *tefillah* we have just concluded. The second paragraph begins with the words: וְעַל כֵּן נְקַוֶּה לְּךָ ה' אֱלֹהֵינוּ לִרְאוֹת מְהֵרָה בְּתִפְאֶרֶת עֻזֶּךְ, *And therefore we put our hope in You, Hashem, our God, that we may soon see Your mighty splendor*. We look forward to the time when we will no longer stand alone, when all of humanity will recognize Hakadosh Baruch Hu and turn to Him loyally. The key words here are וְעַל כֵּן, *and therefore*. The first paragraph is what feeds the second. I firmly see and know the truth — ergo, I anxiously await the time when I will see it bloom before my eyes. Our bond with Hakadosh Baruch Hu is glorious and beautiful, and I can't wait to share this experience with the entire universe.

It's possible that today will be the day we've long been awaiting. It's also possible that it will not. Regardless, I am standing and waiting, looking out my window for Mashiach, because I can't wait any longer. As far as I'm concerned, today *has* to be the day. Tomorrow is a day too late.

Back when I was growing up, a particular sports team was in the throes of an ignominious streak, having gone over eighty years without winning a championship. Nevertheless, tens of thousands of fans would faithfully pack into the stadium each spring to root for their team. Picture a fan who's already in his mid-seventies. He's been attending the games religiously ever since he was a teenager. Since then, he has been watching and hoping — sixty years of dashed dreams. And yet, if you ask him why he's back at it again this year, he will undoubtedly respond, "Because this year is the year." Last year wasn't the year. The year before wasn't the year. Why are you so confident that this year it will happen? What is happening now that didn't happen before? It doesn't really matter. Because if that's what you believe in, and that's what you're dreaming of, then this year has to be the year. It's a matter of passion. In the case of the sports fan, that passion is not backed by logic — but in the case of Mashiach, *lehavdil*, the passion is backed by Hashem's guarantee that Mashiach can come today, if we only heed His voice.

We need Mashiach desperately. We need the madness to stop. We need a strong, central Torah leadership to be restored, with Mashiach acting as a beacon of clarity as he guides us to perform Hashem's will. We've been wandering aimlessly long enough. It doesn't matter if I can show why now is the time. *Achakeh lo* — I keep waiting anxiously, confident that today is the day.

How Does This Affect My Daily Life?

The *Be'er Heitev* adds another meaningful directive, sourced in the Arizal. As you say the words, כִּי לִישׁוּעָתְךָ קִוִּינוּ כָּל הַיּוֹם, *For we hope for Your salvation all day long*, take a moment to actually feel a sense of longing for the *geulah*. At the very least, says the Arizal, when you move on to heaven and are asked if you yearned for the *geulah*, you'll be able to respond in the affirmative by pointing to these few moments each day.

There are other prime opportunities to await the *geulah* as well. From the tear-filled *kinnos* of Tishah B'Av to the joyous singing of *"L'shanah haba'ah b'Yerushalayim"* at the Pesach Seder, our anticipation of Mashiach is a constant theme in our lives.

On any given day, we encounter plenty of situations that should spur us to be *metzapeh l'yeshuah*. When you hear someone ridiculing a particular form of mitzvah observance. When you notice a Jew, your brother, using a phone on Shabbos. When you witness infighting and rancor between groups of Jews. When you see an observant Jew paying more attention to the pairing of his wine than to the questionable hands that poured that wine. Does this bother you? Do you long for something better?

Are you pained when you see how terrified believing Jews are to openly declare their convictions in many parts of the world? When you hear people proudly trumpeting their pride in moral decadence? When you observe how online popularity trends dictate the principles and platforms of society's leaders? Don't you think Hakadosh Baruch Hu deserves better?

And when you struggle with a difficult Gemara, or fail to appreciate the radiance of Shabbos — does the longing ache? When you taste the beauty of Yiddishkeit, but recognize that the experience could be so much more profound and more tangible, do you yearn for more? Do you wish you could feel the connection to Hakadosh Baruch Hu in every *tefillah* and mitzvah?

We are bombarded every day with so many disturbing occurrences. Tempted as you might be, don't shrug them off. Be pained. Turn to Hakadosh Baruch Hu and tell Him how you feel. *Achakeh lo b'chol yom* — long for Mashiach every day, at every turn.

צְפִּיתָ לִישׁוּעָה
Yearning for the Day

Yearning for Mashiach is fundamental to being a Jew, and this longing is the ultimate testimony to a person's inner-most beliefs. If a person truly values Hashem's Torah and mitzvos, he will look forward to the day when the entire world will recognize the truth and align themselves with Hashem's vision of perfection. Yet our longing for Mashiach is more than just a reflection of our value system. It actually serves as the catalyst for his coming.

I n *Parashas Re'eh*, when the Torah discusses the site of the future Beis HaMikdash, it stipulates that this sacred edifice may not be built in any random location, but must rather be situated in a specific place. Where is that place? The Torah does not say. Instead, it makes this enigmatic statement: כִּי אִם אֶל הַמָּקוֹם אֲשֶׁר יִבְחַר ה' אֱלֹהֵיכֶם מִכָּל שִׁבְטֵיכֶם לָשׂוּם אֶת שְׁמוֹ שָׁם לְשִׁכְנוֹ תִדְרְשׁוּ וּבָאתָ שָׁמָּה, *Rather, only at the place that Hashem, your God, will choose from among all your tribes to place His Name there shall you seek out His Presence and come there* (*Devarim* 12:5).

The words "at the place that Hashem, your God, will choose" indicate that we must obtain this information from a higher source — namely, a *navi*. We cannot rely on our own powers of reasoning to determine the correct location. Yet the *pasuk* then instructs us to "seek out His Presence," conveying that we can and should search for this location, and that we possess the ability to discover it. If we are capable of ascertaining the correct site of the Beis HaMikdash ourselves, why do we need a *navi* to tell us where it should be built? And if we do require a *navi*, why bother searching at all?

The Midrash (*Sifri, Re'eh*) provides the following resolution: דְּרֹשׁ וּמְצָא וְאַחַר כָּךְ יֹאמַר לְךָ נָבִיא — begin the quest on your own and you find it, and then the *navi* will tell you the correct location. But why is this two-step process necessary?

The Malbim offers a remarkable insight. Prophetic inspiration and guidance from Above are not supplied freely. A *navi* cannot simply lodge a request for whatever he wishes to know and receive the information. Hakadosh Baruch Hu decides when and where to transmit prophecy, as He deems warranted.

The *navi* can solicit Hakadosh Baruch Hu's assistance in determining the location of the Beis HaMikdash, but in the absence of a concerted national effort to locate that site, his request will go unanswered. Hakadosh Baruch Hu may proactively offer us certain things, but help with finding the designated spot of His home in this world is not one of them. In this realm, supply is linked to demand, and Divine guidance is provided only when people sincerely seek it.

The two steps detailed in the *pasuk* are inextricably bound. We cannot possibly create a Beis HaMikdash on our own; we need the guidance of a *navi*. Yet initially, the *navi* is incapable of providing that guidance, for he cannot access the relevant *nevuah*. Only when we invest the effort to search and strive to the best of our ability will the *nevuah* be released to the *navi*. *Derosh u'metzo* — do whatever you can, *v'achar kach yomar lecha navi* — and then, only then, will the *navi* be granted the ability to guide you.

Even today, Hashem's home is ready and waiting for those who seek it. Only if we truly want it, and strive to do whatever we can to bring it back, will it be given to us.

More Than Mere Commemoration

R'Yosef Elefant adds an incisive point. The concept of zecher l'churban is ubiquitous in our lives, and we perform numerous acts to remember the Beis HaMikdash: breaking a glass under the *chuppah*, placing ashes on the forehead of a *chassan*, leaving an unplastered space on the wall of our homes, and so on. Similarly, mitzvos such as Sefiras HaOmer and eating Korech at the Pesach Seder remind us of observances at the time of the Beis HaMikdash. We tend to think of these acts simply as a way to keep the Beis HaMikdash at the forefront of our consciousness.

Truthfully, though, these actions carry far more weight.

Yirmiyahu HaNavi bemoans how distanced we have become from the Beis HaMikdash, lamenting: צִיּוֹן הִיא דֹּרֵשׁ אֵין לָהּ, *She is Zion — no one seeks her (Yirmiyah* 30:17). The Beis HaMikdash lies abandoned, with no one searching for it. If we are being taken to task for this, then apparently, we are expected to actively seek it out. Chazal (*Succah* 41a) understand these words as a mandate to perform specific actions in commemoration of the Beis HaMikdash.

Yet this source is a call for דְּרִישָׁה, *seeking*, not זְכִירָה, *remembering*. As such, it echoes the same call for seeking expressed in the Torah's directive of לְשִׁכְנוֹ תִדְרְשׁוּ, *you shall seek out His Presence*. We are not looking for memorials. Rather, we are using concrete actions to express our very real yearning for the *geulah*. I don't eat Korech to remember the Beis HaMikdash; I eat Korech as a vivid expression of where I want to be. I don't leave my wall unplastered as a memorial; I leave it that way to demonstrate my feeling that this is not my real home. When we give a *machatzis hashekel* before Purim, count Sefirah each night until Shavuos, or shake lulav and esrog throughout the days of Succos, we are not reenacting ancient practices — we are expressing what we hope to very soon be doing.

Believing that the *geulah* will come is not enough. Even wanting the *geulah* is not enough. Our yearning needs to be woven into the very fabric of our lives, as expressed tangibly by our actions. We need to be in searching mode. Our mindset, and the structure of our lives, must be focused on bringing the *geulah*. The possibility of the Beis HaMikdash being restored hinges upon our looking for it. If our minds are constantly focused on the *geulah*, and we continually express, through our *tefillos* and actions, that we crave a better world — a world filled with knowledge of Hashem, in which we can once again serve Him properly and wholeheartedly — then Hakadosh Baruch Hu will restore the Beis HaMikdash and finally bring us home to Eretz Yisrael.

This concept resonates powerfully throughout the daily *Shemoneh Esrei* prayer, much of which hinges upon various aspects of the *geulah*. But the concept is particularly evident in the final *berachah* that relates to the redemption. Many of the requests we make in the main body of *Shemoneh Esrei* follow a pattern: Please provide us with health — because You are the true Healer. Please grant us financial security — because You are in control of all economics. Please answer our prayers — for You are the God Who hears prayers. This formulation reflects the purpose of *tefillah*, which is to articulate our recognition of Hashem's Omnipotence. Hakadosh Baruch Hu does not need our prayers, and can certainly provide for our needs regardless of whether we beseech Him. Withholding good from the world until humans ask for it is simply a method of bringing people to appreciate Who is really providing all their needs. Through *tefillah*, we express this realization: Please give me what I need, because I recognize that You alone can help me. With this acknowledgment, we fulfill the objective of *tefillah*, and make ourselves worthy of receiving what Hakadosh Baruch Hu wants to give us.

A notable deviation from this format appears in the *berachah* beginning: אֶת צֶמַח דָּוִד עַבְדְּךָ מְהֵרָה תַצְמִיחַ, *The offspring of Your servant David, may You speedily cause to flourish*. We ask for the return of *Malchus Beis David*, and the ultimate redemption, and then we give a reason that diverges from the pattern. Rather than emphasize that we turn to Hashem because only He can accomplish this, we declare: כִּי לִישׁוּעָתְךָ קִוִּינוּ כָּל הַיּוֹם, *for we hope for Your salvation all day long*. Apparently, for Mashiach to come, it's not enough for us to recognize that Hashem is in charge. We need to want the *geulah*, and ask for it. The key is to tell Hakadosh Baruch Hu how anxiously we're waiting.

Regarding this *berachah*, the Chofetz Chaim[1] explains that Hakadosh Baruch Hu granting us the *geulah* is akin to an employer paying his employee for his work. Unquestionably, the payment is owed; in fact, halachah mandates that a worker be paid immediately, on the day he completes his work. But there is one caveat — the employer is obligated to pay immediately only if the worker requests his pay. If he finishes the job and heads home, the boss has no obligation to chase him down to pay him, and may wait for a more opportune time. Similarly, says the Chofetz Chaim, Hashem is prepared to bring the *geulah*. But we need to ask for it. We need to come to Him and say that we don't want to continue in our current state, and that we badly need the *geulah*.

How Does This Affect My Daily Life?

*O*ne of the questions we will be asked when we reach the Heavenly Court is, *"Tzipisa l'yeshuah* — did you await the redemption? The requirement to yearn for the redemption is not fulfilled by merely thinking about Mashiach once a day, checking the box, and crossing it off the list. We owe it to ourselves to actively cultivate this yearning, because it's our ticket home.

When you pass the small, unplastered space on your wall, tell yourself, "My house may be nice, but I want to go home." As you go through your day, riding the rollercoaster of life, use the situations you encounter as a springboard for longing for Mashiach. When you see things that are wrong, wish for the day when they

---

1. Quoted in *Siddur Chofetz Chaim, siman* 168.

will be right. When you see things that are right, wish for the day they'll be even better. Then, gather all your aches, hopes, and aspirations, and turn to Hashem in prayer. Ask Him to bring the day of redemption, and tell Him how much you need it. He is waiting to hear that we want it, and then He will call us home.

לְחַשֵּׁב אֶת הַקֵּץ
Calculating the Date of Mashiach's Arrival

On his deathbed, Yaakov Avinu attempted to reveal to his children when Mashiach would arrive — but it was not to be. The information was withheld from him, and would remain hidden from Klal Yisrael throughout their lengthy sojourn in galus. Chazal (Sanhedrin 97b) followed this path and strongly discouraged us from seeking to determine the date of Mashiach's arrival.

The Rambam, quoting these words of Chazal, enshrines this perspective in halachah unequivocally. Our role is not to make calculations and attempt to ascertain the time when the *geulah* will occur. Rather, we are enjoined to constantly await and yearn for Mashiach, and do all that we can to bring him. The time of his actual arrival is beyond our purview. Cursed be those who engage in such efforts.

And yet, many of the greatest Torah giants have done precisely that. R' Saadiah Gaon (*Emunos V'Deios* 8:3) records a date for the *geulah*. Rashi (*Daniel* 8:14) notes that the date provided by R' Saadiah has already passed, and writes that many will continue on this path, fine-tuning the process as they identify additional dates. He seems to find no issue with these endeavors. Similarly, the Ramban (*Sefer HaGeulah* 4) offers what he considers the correct date. In attempting to explain the words of Daniel (ibid.), who alluded cryptically to the timing of Mashiach's arrival, many commentators, including the Malbim, offer calculations of Mashiach's anticipated arrival date.

In fact, on the very same page of the Gemara that cautions against engaging in calculations, an incident is recorded in which Amoraim discussed an ancient scroll, found in the archives of Rome, that detailed the anticipated period of Mashiach's arrival and the timing of the various phases of the *geulah*.

The stance of the Rambam himself is similarly intriguing. He writes, in *Iggeres Teiman*, that Mashiach's true arrival date is not only unknown, but is inherently undecipherable. After all, he says, a concrete timeframe of 400 years was given for the Egyptian exile, and yet we left Mitzrayim after only 210 years; the 400 years were redefined in a way that could be reconciled with this reality. Apparently, even absolute numbers can be interpreted in numerous ways. This is certainly the case, says the Rambam, with regard to a date that Hakadosh Baruch Hu specifically wishes to remain hidden.

Incredibly, however, the Rambam then goes on to write that he has a family tradition, from father to son all the way back to the time the Jewish people were exiled from Yerushalayim, that the end date is alluded to in Parashas Balak — and he then provides that date!

R' Saadiah Gaon. Rashi. Rambam. Ramban. Malbim. The list goes on.[2]

How did they justify this?

To uncover the answer, we must examine the statement of Chazal (ibid.) that warns against calculating the date of the redemption: "R' Shmuel Bar Nachmani said in the name of R' Yonasan: May the very essence of those who calculate 'Ends' suffer

---

2. For a comprehensive listing of the dozens of commentators over the generations who have offered dates for the *geulah*, see R' Reuven Margolies's footnotes to *Shailos U'Teshuvos Min HaShamayim, Teshuvah* 72.

agony! For they say: 'Since the date of the End that we calculated has arrived and [Mashiach] did not come, he will never come!'"

The Gemara is emphasizing that the ire directed at those who engage in calculations arises from the ensuing risk of potential fallout. If assorted dates are trumpeted as the true and absolute day of redemption, and then those dates pass with no sign of Mashiach's arrival, people are liable to lose faith, and delete the concept of Mashiach from their belief toolbox entirely. If these dates turned out to be false, they will reason, who's to say that the other statements made about Mashiach carry any more validity? We can extrapolate that an additional risk would be posed if the date provided was well into the future. Knowing that Mashiach's arrival is centuries away could plunge down-trodden people into despair and cause them to lose their tenuous grip on Yiddishkeit.

Both the *Zohar* (*Bereishis* 118) and the Ramban (*Sefer HaGeulah* ibid.) note that the prohibition to calculate these dates is limited to the time period when Mashiach's arrival is presumably distant. Once a point is reached when his arrival must be imminent, there would no longer be any restriction. Furthermore, the Ramban and Abarbanel (*Maayanei HaYeshuah* 1:2) maintain that the prohibition relates only to providing definitive dates; offering a date merely as a potential time of Mashiach's arrival would be allowed, as it would be unlikely to generate ill effects.

What emerges, then, is that while the actual calculation of dates might be forbidden in certain contexts, and is generally shunned, the concept itself is not inherently and categorically forbidden. Accordingly, the aforementioned Torah giants saw fit to make these computations and predictive statements, in situations and according to methods they determined permissible.

The question remains, though: What benefit was there in attempting to predict the time of Mashiach's arrival? Even if calculating these dates was permitted, what was the point of doing so?

To answer this, we need to understand the significance of

these dates. If we assume that Mashiach is destined to arrive on one fixed date, then almost all the calculations offered by the sources, spanning a wide range of dates in various centuries, would be fundamentally false. After all, he can't possibly arrive on more than one occasion. Conversely, if we assume that all these dates have validity, emanating as they do from credible sources, then how do we make sense of the existence of multiple options for Mashiach's arrival? How can more than one date be correct?

It must be that these are moments of opportunity, not guaranteed dates of Mashiach's arrival. As we know, not all days on the calendar are created equal. Shabbos and Yom Tov are uniquely sanctified days, with incredible potential for connecting to Hakadosh Baruch Hu. The month of Elul and the Aseres Yemei Teshuvah are a time when Hakadosh Baruch Hu is exceptionally close to us, coming near so that we need only reach out to feel His Presence. On these occasions, given His proximity, we can accomplish so much more, with relative ease. The same applies to our ability to trigger Mashiach's arrival. At times, he waits at a distance, so bringing him requires more intense effort. Other times, he stands just beyond our doorstep, so we need to do only that little bit to bring about the *geulah*.

The Rishonim were not engaged in needless prognostication, nor were they seeking to satisfy curiosity. Rather, they sought to apprise Klal Yisrael of the windows of opportunity that existed, in the hopes that we would seize the moment and do what was necessary to make the dream of redemption a reality. "He's at our doorstep," they were saying. "Get up and open the door."[3]

---

3. Even regarding predictions of the time of Mashiach's arrival that do not run afoul of the sharply worded prohibition cited above, and even considering the possible benefit of these predictions, the Rambam (*Hilchos Melachim* 12:2) strongly discourages expending time and effort on these calculations, warning that such involvement is not beneficial, and does not lead to either *ahavas Hashem* or *yiras Hashem*. The correct path for us is to wait anxiously for Mashiach, focusing on the more general knowledge that he will one day arrive.

How Does This Affect My Daily Life?

Though many of the dates in question have come and gone, every so often an additional date crops up as the purported day of Mashiach's impending arrival. Generally, these emanate from sources that are dubious, or are statements that have been misconstrued. Even if these dates are reliably sourced, and backed by people of integrity, they serve as no guarantee of Mashiach's arrival on a particular day. Only Hakadosh Baruch Hu determines when Mashiach will actually come. Our task is to recognize the opportunity we are being afforded and grab it.

Jump at the chance — today! — by maximizing your *avodas Hashem*. Daven with a bit more intensity and feeling. Put aside all distractions, and dive into Torah study. Look for *chessed* opportunities, and foster better relationships with your family and friends, as well as with those you consider distant or different.

In our time, specifically, we often feel that Mashiach's arrival must be imminent. Recent events have shaken the world, leading to many a hushed whisper expressing the hope that this would culminate in the ultimate salvation. In truth, we have no way of knowing whether this is the moment we've been waiting for. We have no *navi* to let us in on the secret. But suppose for a moment that we are indeed hearing the footsteps of the Redeemer's arrival. Is our response to sit at the back of our local shul and debate whether he's coming? To pontificate endlessly about medications and government policies? If this is the track we take, we are squandering a priceless opportunity.

We need to capitalize on this opportunity. Ask yourself: What should I be doing better? Which steps can I take to bring us over the finish line? Mashiach is so close — am I doing my part to make it happen? Let's discuss how to enhance our appreciation and *kavod* for our shuls. Let's debate the best way to invigorate our Shabbos table and our Shabbos afternoon. Let's contemplate how we can incorporate more immersive Torah learning into our lives. There are a plethora of options for improving our *avodas Hashem*, and we each have unique areas where we are primed for growth. We must, however, challenge ourselves to seize the moment. When Hakadosh Baruch Hu asks us what we did with His gift, we don't want to be left speechless.

הָעִקָר הַשְּׁלֹשָׁה עָשָׂר
The Thirteenth Ikkar

אֲנִי מַאֲמִין בֶּאֱמוּנָה שְׁלֵמָה שֶׁתִּהְיֶה תְּחִיַּת הַמֵּתִים בְּעֵת שֶׁיַּעֲלֶה רָצוֹן מֵאֵת הַבּוֹרֵא יִתְבָּרַךְ שְׁמוֹ וְיִתְעַלֶּה זִכְרוֹ לָעַד וּלְנֵצַח נְצָחִים.

I am steadfast in my absolute belief that there will be a resurrection of the dead at the time that such will be the will of the Creator, blessed is His Name.
[By doing so], His perception [in our world] will become exalted for all eternity.

וְהַיְסוֹד הַשְּׁלֹשָׁה עָשָׂר תְּחִיַּת הַמֵּתִים וּכְבָר בֵּאַרְנוּהָ.

**The thirteenth foundational belief is that of the
resurrection of the dead,** which we have explained
previously.

תְּחִיַּת הַמֵּתִים
Where Aspirations Come to Life

Techiyas HaMeisim. A time when generations of Jews will rise from their graves, joyously emerging to greet a new world. It's a scene we've attempted to conjure in our mind's eye ever since we were children. To once again greet the dear relatives whom we miss terribly. To meet the grandparents for whom we were named, and about whom we've heard so much. To see Avraham Avinu, Moshe Rabbeinu, and Eliyahu HaNavi! And yet — for this to qualify as an Ikkar, it must go beyond these powerful sentiments. Having people return to life, then, must play a key role in His master plan.

There will come a time, we are told, when the dead will come back to life, as all generations join together in a new world order. The details of this future period are hazy and subject to much debate. It will involve multiple stages, and various Rishonim envision the precise order and nature of each phase in dramatically different manners. The Rambam does not seem to include within this Ikkar the requirement to know these intricacies, however, which indicates that the Ikkar mandates only a belief that the dead will be resurrected at some future time. It is this core piece of information that is so pivotal.

Why is the fact that the dead will return to life so integral to our belief system? To be clear, we are not referring to the coming of Mashiach. That the world will eventually reach a state of perfection, with Torah dictating the way to conduct life on both a national and a personal level, is fundamental to the trajectory of our world. That, however, is the focus of the previous Ikkar, not the current one. Here, we are dealing with the resurrection. In the context of the world reaching perfection, resurrecting those who are no longer alive would seem unnecessary. For the departed individuals as well, the need for this is hard to understand. After all, they are presumably enjoying an experience beyond our comprehension, as they receive in Olam Haba the reward they earned throughout their life. What benefit is there in dragging them back into this world?

Over the centuries, many Kadmonim — among them the Rekanati, the Sefer HaIkkarim, the Mabit, the Maharal, and others — have grappled to understand the purpose of Techiyas HaMeisim.

They proposed various ideas. One is that although the *neshamah* derives the utmost enjoyment from the sublime experience of being in Hakadosh Baruch Hu's proximity, it is nevertheless necessary to grant reward to the physical body as well. After all, it was not the *neshamah* that overcame its nature to serve Hashem properly, but rather the body, which struggled throughout the person's life to avoid being pulled toward corporeal desires and pleasures. By doing so, the body morphed into something truly elevated, and is deserving of reward. Rising from the dead to live in a utopian world will enable the body to receive the physically pleasurable reward it deserves.

On the flip side, we are told that there will come a great and awesome day of judgment, when every human will receive his final verdict for eternity. This, too, requires a live body, as the soul alone is incapable of performing any actions, whether right or wrong, and the body, bereft of a soul, cannot be held accountable for anything. It is the synthesis of body and soul that gives rise to a human being, with potential and responsibilities, and it is this synthesis that will stand in judgment.

Looking to the words of the Rambam himself sheds precious little light on the nature of Techiyas HaMeisim. In delineating this Ikkar, the Rambam simply says that he has described this matter previously. No further information is provided. Fascinatingly, the Rambam penned a full letter, *Maamar Techiyas HaMeisim*, to emphasize the critical role of Techiyas HaMeisim in the belief system of a Jew. In it, he stresses the incontrovertible veracity of Techiyas HaMeisim, insofar as it is clearly documented in Tanach and the teachings of Chazal. And yet, in the entire work he does not devote one line to describing the purpose of Techiyas HaMeisim.[1]

Compounding the difficulty with understanding the Rambam is his assertion (ibid.) that the era of Techiyas HaMeisim is but a transient phase. At some point afterward, the world will transition to a more elevated, completely non-physical phase. This makes the intermediary Techiyas HaMeisim phase all the more difficult to understand. What purpose does it serve? Why pull all the *neshamos* from their resting place in Gan Eden just to come down to earth for a few years before reverting to an immaterial state? Inasmuch as the world of Techiyas HaMeisim is not our ultimate goal and endgame, it must be a stepping stone to something higher. How so?

The Ticket to an Enhanced Olam Haba

*T*he *Sefer HaIkkarim* suggests this approach,[2] which he believes is in fact the Rambam's view.

Hakadosh Baruch Hu created the world with a vision of perfection, in which man would possess no internal drive for

---

1. For further discussion of the Rambam's position in *Maamar Techiyas HaMeisim*, see Appendix A.

2. *Maamar* 4, Ch. 30. This idea also appears in the Rekanati (*Parashas Bereishis*). Although the *Sefer HaIkkarim* does not point to a source for this idea within the Rambam's writings, it would seem to fit quite well with the Rambam's words in *Hilchos Melachim* 12:4-5 and *Hilchos Teshuvah* 9:2.

anything but the service of Hashem. He would be challenged from the outside, to be sure, but innately he would seek only to perform Hashem's will. Adam HaRishon personified this vision on the first day of his existence, as he walked in Gan Eden on that fateful Erev Shabbos. But he and Chavah sinned, causing that utopian scene to come crashing down. Mankind was then reduced on many levels: Lifespans were shortened, the chores of daily living became far more difficult, and man's ability to live on an elevated spiritual plane was drastically curbed.

This is the world we live in. Every step is a challenge.

It is difficult to gain an appreciation for learning. It is hard to feel any enjoyment from a long *tefillah*. And it is most certainly not easy to raise our children with proper values and love of Hashem while besieged by a plethora of obstacles, both spiritual and material. We try so hard, yet at every turn we are confronted by another issue, be it paying a mortgage and tuition, finding a shidduch, or dealing with a struggling child. Besides the big challenges, such as life-threatening illnesses or national lockdowns, we are constantly bombarded by the frustrations of daily life, from dental appointments to flat tires. These minor challenges wear us down, so that we need to battle continuously to keep our internal flame burning and growing.

And yet these difficulties and impediments in our lives serve the greatest purpose, as it is precisely these struggles that make us into who we are. The ongoing daily battle is what helps me develop into a true *eved Hashem*, because the goal is not so much to win the battle, but to engage in it — every day. This is what draws people close to Hakadosh Baruch Hu and makes them deserving of Olam Haba.

That said, however, we are still lacking. Yes, Hakadosh Baruch Hu sees our struggles and recognizes our valiant attempts, but we still come to our final judgment without having performed certain mitzvos. I earn exceptional credit for attending night *seder* each evening, but I never managed to finish Shas. I earn abundant reward for allocating *maaser* money according to my limited means, but there was still so much *tzedakah* I could not give. I merit vast compensation for challenging my inborn weaknesses, but I did not succeed in gaining control over certain deep-rooted tendencies. This is no condemnation of us — we are judged only for the way we dealt with life relative to our individual abilities and limitations. Nevertheless, there's an entire level of reward that we have not accessed.

Enter the period of Mashiach. The Rambam writes in numerous places that the physical world will still look and function the same way, but what a world it will be! No more struggling. No more suffering. No more difficulties. Life's challenges will disappear, with everyone enjoying good health, financial security, and general tranquility. No more hospitals, no more foreclosures. The challenges from within will dissipate as well, as conquering our negative traits will pose no difficulty once the world has been filled with awareness of the truth and motivation to do what is right. Then, we will be able to realize all our dreams unhindered. The roadblocks will have been removed, and we will be able to accomplish all that we desire. By utilizing this special time, we will earn vastly greater reward, and a far more elevated level of Olam Haba.

Coming back down to this world, then, will enable us to return to Olam Haba in a far better position. Essentially, the world of Mashiach, and the gift of Techiyas HaMeisim, are one fantastic bonus round — a ticket to enjoying additional closeness to Hashem when we return to Olam Haba.

Reward Without Challenge

Our general understanding, however, is that reward is rendered possible only by the existence of a challenge, which enables a person to make a difficult decision and successfully overcome the *nisayon* before him. If the truth will be blindingly evident at the time of Techiyas HaMeisim, and nothing will stand in the way of our performing Hashem's will, from whence will come the *schar*?

R' Saadiah Gaon and others maintain that although we will no longer possess any internal drive to defy the will of Hashem, some level of external *yetzer hara* will still exist, albeit minimally. This inclination toward evil will be foreign to our natural instincts, but the possibility of temptation will continue to exist, akin to the serpent's enticement of Adam HaRishon in the hours after his creation. This possibility will enable those who resist temptation to be rewarded.

In line with our explanation of Techiyas HaMeisim, however, an additional possibility likely holds true. Elsewhere, the Beis Yosef (cited by *Mishnah Berurah* 622:19) asks how it is possible to bring merit to a departed individual by performing a mitzvah. Given that reward is granted based on one's choices and actions, how can the deceased receive a "freebie"? He answers that if the deceased was a person who strove to perform mitzvos, and surely would have wanted to do this very act had he still been alive, then considering that his death was very much not in his control, the mitzvah performed in his merit is regarded as if it were done on his behalf by *shlichus* — a mitzvah by proxy. What emerges then, is that a deceased person can accrue merit from a mitzvah only if he was a person who truly appreciated and would have wanted to do this very mitzvah. If, however, he showed blatant disregard for this type of mitzvah, the mitzvah could not be viewed as his action and he would receive no remuneration.[3]

We see, then, that a deceased person can accrue reward from mitzvos done on his behalf even though their performance poses no challenge to him. Apparently, these mitzvos are viewed as an extension of the challenges he overcame, and the difficult choices he made, during his lifetime, in regard to this mitzvah.

---

3. The exception would be mitzvos performed by one's children, as children are considered to be bound with their parents, like a single physical entity. They can therefore benefit a parent spiritually regardless of the parent's viewpoint or feelings.

The same would apply to the time of Techiyas HaMeisim as well. Even though challenges might not remain, the ability to perform mitzvos at this special time will be gifted to a person who yearned for opportunities to fulfill mitzvos during his lifetime. His performance of mitzvos at this time will be viewed as a continuation of that desire, and he will be able to receive reward and continue his growth.

Techiyas HaMeisim for Whom?

*T*he Rambam writes[4] that although practically every Jew will enjoy some form of Olam Haba, the concept of Techiyas HaMeisim is far more limited. Only *tzaddikim* will arise, while *reshaim* will not be granted this return to life. What is the reason for this distinction between Olam Haba and Techiyas HaMeisim?

In line with the above, the answer seems to be that Olam Haba reflects my personal bond with Hakadosh Baruch Hu. In this regard, every Jew has some connection. It might be hard to discern, it might be microscopic, but there's always some spark there, some point of connection where the person's *neshamah* meets Hakadosh Baruch Hu. Techiyas HaMeisim, however, is a gift. It's the chance to achieve all that you wish you could have accomplished. This gift is reserved for those who actually sought to refine themselves, to grow spiritually, and to accomplish more. For them, the impediments to growth will be removed, so that their aspirations can be realized. For the one who had no interest, on the other hand, there's no reason to return.

The Rambam mentions two extremes, the righteous versus the wicked. These poles are separated by a gaping chasm, which is where most of us find ourselves. Ultimately, a line has to be

---

4. *Peirush HaMishnayos*, introduction to *Perek Cheilek*, citing *Midrash Rabbah*; see also *Taanis* 7a.

drawn demarcating the *tzaddik* from the *rasha* — and our goal is to do our utmost to end up on the right side of the equation. What we're aiming for, then, is to be considered closer to the *tzaddikim* than to the *reshaim*. We need to ensure that wherever on the spectrum we're holding, we're pushing for more, constantly striving to be bigger and better.

In the teachings of Chazal, we find a number of more specific tickets to Techiyas HaMeisim. We are told (*Kesubos* 111b) that those who immerse themselves in Torah study will merit Techiyas HaMeisim. Furthermore, even those who play a supporting role, by helping to finance the world of Torah or otherwise attaching themselves to those who study Torah, will rise as well, as per the guarantee: עֵץ חַיִּים הִיא לַמַּחֲזִיקִים בָּהּ, *It is a tree of life to those who grasp it* (*Mishlei* 3:18). There are various ways to merit a share in this future world, but they hinge on being a person who strives to be an *eved Hashem* and cherishes that role, doing whatever he can to fulfill the will of Hashem.

How Does This Affect My Daily Life?

We've established that Techiyas HaMeisim is a limited privilege, granted only to those who qualify.

It goes further. Even among those who do make the cut, Techiyas HaMeisim is not a simple yes-or-no proposition.[5] Apparently, a person's abilities and potential come that day will reflect what he accomplished and aspired to while still alive. How strong was his ambition? How passionate was his drive? Did he aspire to fulfill all the mitzvos, or just some of them?

There will come a time when the world will be filled with

---

5. See *Sefer HaIkkarim* ibid. This concept also appears, in greater length, in *Derech Hashem* (*Chelek* 1, 3:10). Although the *Derech Hashem*'s approach to Techiyas HaMeisim is not identical to that of the Rambam, it would seem that they would concur on this point.

brilliant Divine wisdom, like an ocean filled to capacity with wa-ter: כִּי מָלְאָה הָאָרֶץ דֵּעָה אֶת ה' כַּמַּיִם לַיָּם מְכַסִּים, *For the earth will be as filled with knowledge of Hashem as water covering the seabed.* (*Ye-shayah* 11:9). The Chofetz Chaim explains (*Mishlei* 11:9)[6] that on the surface, the ocean seems rather uniform and even. We know, however, that the depth of the ocean varies greatly. At the coast-line, it's shallow enough to wet your toes and no more. Wade a few feet out, and suddenly the floor beneath you drops, giving you a lot more water in which to swim. At the beach, the water depth can be measured in feet or even inches. Head to the Mari-ana Trench, and the seabed lies seven miles down. This, says the Chofetz Chaim, is what we will experience in the future to come. Hakadosh Baruch Hu will fill the world with radiance, but that does not mean everyone will receive equal dosages. On the sur-face level, all will enjoy the clarity of perceiving Hakadosh Baruch Hu. The true amount of perception each of us will merit, however, will vary greatly, depending on how much we prepared ourselves to absorb and how much knowledge of Hashem we aspired to achieve. The greater our ambition, the greater the gift we will re-ceive when our dreams become reality.

The oft-quoted adage, אֵין דָּבָר הָעוֹמֵד בִּפְנֵי הָרָצוֹן — loosely, where there's a will there's a way — is generally understood as a testa-ment to the power of determination. Yet even willpower cannot propel a person past certain limitations. This gives rise to an alter-nate understanding of this saying, attributed to the Imrei Emes: True, you have limitations. True, there are obstacles that truly in-hibit you. True, the results are not always in your hands. But noth-ing prevents you from wanting something.

Techiyas HaMeisim, then, is not only about the future. It's about reshaping my view on life today. The purpose of life in this world is to land in Olam Haba in the best possible position, and getting there requires taking stock of where we're headed. It's not enough to focus on the tally of our good actions versus our bad

---

6. As elaborated upon by Rav Matisyahu Salomon at the Tenth Siyum HaShas (5757/1997).

actions. We need to focus on our very core, assessing who we are and where our ambitions lie. Our task in life is to mold ourselves into people who sincerely seek greater and greater levels. It's not easy, but much of the brilliance of our Techiyas HaMeisim, and our ultimate Olam Haba, depends on how I live my life right now, and what type of person I strive to be.

We all have challenges. We all have limitations and constraints. But by doing the very best we can to maximize our potential and utilize our abilities and strengths, we demonstrate our ambition for so much more. Even when we find ourselves unable to accomplish as much as we would like to, we can still do our utmost, and then hope for the day when we can do more. By doing so, we can earn ourselves the opportunity to come back for the bonus round, when we can propel ourselves to the next level.

In Closing — Living the Ikkarim

*T*he thirteen Ikkarim are thirteen key pieces that play a critical role in the life of every Jew. Not merely thirteen independent concepts, these thirteen come together to form the foundation upon which our conduct in life is built. Together, they provide one uniform system, the canvas upon which our *avodas Hashem* comes to life.

The Gemara (*Shabbos* 31a) lists six questions that a person will be asked after he passes away and ascends heavenward, one of which is: נָשָׂאתָ וְנָתַתָּ בֶּאֱמוּנָה — loosely translated as, "Did you conduct your life with emunah?" The *Pele Yoetz* (*Masa U'Matan*, see also Emunah) notes that Klal Yisrael is described as a nation of *maaminim bnei maaminim*, believers, descendants of believers. Emunah is our defining feature, embedded in the very DNA of every Jew. What, then, is the purpose of the question?

The *Pele Yoetz* explains that the question we will be asked is not whether we believed in Hashem, but whether our actions reflected that belief. When you went to work, did you remember that Hakadosh Baruch Hu controls the spigot of wealth? A person who understands that will ensure that all his dealings meet the standards required by halachah. He won't miss a *tefillah* to seal an extra deal. He won't speak *lashon hara* about a colleague or engage in predatory practices against a competitor. He will contribute readily to charitable causes, and set aside fixed times for Torah study.

He will act this way because he knows that Hakadosh Baruch Hu created everything, and is in control of every aspect of the world's functioning. He knows that the Torah's rules are eternally relevant and binding, not only with regard to cows and oxen but also to today's high-tech world. He knows that he is responsible for his every decision and action. He knows that eventually, the big payoff comes to those who truly deserve it, and those who don't will be filled with eternal regret, because the ultimate Judge is watching, keeping score, and remunerating.

What matters most is not emunah, concludes the *Pele Yoetz*. It's whether one's actions reflect emunah.

When a real-estate tycoon walks away from a multimillion-dollar deal due to *ribbis* concerns, he doesn't just believe. He radiates belief.

When an elderly Holocaust survivor wraps tefillin around an arm with a number on it, he doesn't just believe. He is a vivid testimonial to belief.

When a person, alone in the privacy of his home, is careful about what he sees, he doesn't just believe. He is affirming his passionate emunah.

Our actions, and our whole demeanor, are the true indicator of our emunah, and it is regarding this that we will be questioned.

The United States Navy boasts a fleet of mammoth aircraft-carriers, ships carrying squadrons of planes that can be launched on brief notice from a runway on the deck. Each of these ships is a virtual city unto itself. Nimitz-class aircraft carriers, for decades the largest ships in the Navy, carry approximately 6,000 personnel. Of these, 3,500 tend to the functioning of the ship itself, from the commanding officer and navigation crew down to the cooks and the laundry and cleaning crews. An additional 2,500 service the aircraft. At the heart of this billion-dollar enterprise is a singular purpose: To launch warplanes from points across the globe at short notice. And yet, of this entire marine city of 6,000 individuals, a grand total of 200 are pilots. Imagine the feeling of a pilot strolling down the flight deck. What goes through his mind? All this exists to serve me. All those people manning the engines, streamlining supply systems, ensuring quality of armaments, are here just for me. An entire universe has been built for me, and for the fellow members of my elite club. I have a mission to fulfill, and everything on this immense ship has been carefully placed to allow me to perform my task optimally.

How does this awareness affect the pilot's life? It gives rise to a feeling of responsibility that permeates every moment of his day. When dinner is served, he will refrain from eating something that he suspects will make him nauseous in flight. If the sailors are sitting around drinking beer, he will demur, knowing that the alcohol might impair his judgment. Others on the ship may be up late at night, but he retires early, to ensure that his mind will be sharp. He's up and on deck early, always ready to spring into action, because he is a man with a mission. Dedicated as he is to serving his country, he will not allow himself to be distracted from this goal, nor will his privileged ranking cause him to become haughty and self-absorbed.

We, too, have been placed on this planet with a mission. The billions of people populating the world, engaged in every imaginable profession, serve as the support crew. While their contribution is valuable, and sometimes indispensable, they are not the focus of creation. We are.

My mission is all-encompassing. It affects how I get up, when I go to sleep, what I eat, and how I manage my time. I walk down the street with a deep sense of pride, but also humbly, ever-focused on my mission. Being selected for this mission is the source of my pride — and the basis of the profound responsibility I carry.

Let's return for a moment to our fighter pilot. Suppose he fell down a flight of stairs, hit his head, and suffered a bout of amnesia. Physically, he feels fine, but he looks around the ship uncomprehendingly, wondering where he is and what he's doing here.

The ship's physician tries to jog his memory. "You see, you're a fighter pilot, with top aviation skills. And there's this war going on, with nasty enemies that we're battling, so you're playing a key role."

The pilot blinks. "Role? What role? Who gave me this role? Who says there is a war?"

"Well, how do you think you ended up on this massive hunk of floating metal, a thousand miles from anywhere? Obviously, you're here for a reason."

Slowly but surely, matters are explained to him.

> There's a commander-in-chief back home who ordered this mission. You can't see him, and you've never spoken to him, but he is quite real and definitely exists.
>
> This commander is the ultimate decision-maker, and no one can overrule his battle plan. You receive specific orders regarding which targets to attack at which time, and you may not challenge those orders. If the orders are not clear, you may consult with a higher-ranking officer. Then, you must execute these plans with exquisite precision.

You occupy an elite position, and you must carry out your role faithfully. Your every move is observed by your superiors, and your success or failure in obeying commands will have repercussions for your future.

If you succeed, then not only will you become known as a star pilot, but you'll be a national hero, credited with a critical role in the country's ultimate triumph. Every sailor and airman on board is convinced that victory will be ours. It's only a matter of time before we make it happen.

We were not dropped onto this spinning, hurtling mass in the middle of billions of miles of outer space without a battle plan. The specifics of this plan are presented in detail throughout the

Torah, while the backdrop and general parameters of the battle are delineated in the thirteen Ikkarim.

> There's a Commander-in-Chief Who created us and fashioned everything about us for the purpose of this mission. We can't describe Him, and we haven't met Him personally, but He is most definitely there.
>
> No one can challenge His authority, and we obey His orders alone.
>
> He communicates with us through the Torah and the prophets, and has transmitted a set of clear, inviolable, and unchanging orders to us. No static blurred the transmission, and He has declared these orders to be permanently in force.
>
> Our choices to follow or disregard the Commander's orders directly impacts our standing and relationship with Him.
>
> There will come a day when the battle will be won, and the purpose for which He fashioned this world will be realized.

So when you walk down the street, stand proud. You're a member of the *Am HaNivchar*, one of the select group of pilots on this massive, teeming ship. Billions of people fill an assortment of roles, but yours stands at the pinnacle of Creation, and will ultimately determine the success of the entire enterprise. You have been equipped with the abilities to overcome the unique challenges you will face, and you are eminently qualified to carry out your mission. You understand the nature of the battle, and the high stakes involved.

Now, your mission begins.

Appendices

Appendix A
Additional Insights, Ikkar by Ikkar

Ikkar 1 — The Rambam's View of Constant Creation

*T*he concept that the universe is constantly being recreated is well documented, most famously by the *Nefesh HaChaim* (1:2) and *Tanya* (*Shaar HaYichud VeHa'Emunah*), among others. Even when not stated explicitly, this idea follows as a natural corollary of the principle expressed by the Rambam and others that only Hakadosh Baruch Hu has true staying power, whereas all other matter would instantly cease to exist were it not for His input.

Some claim that a passage of the Rambam (*Moreh Nevuchim* 1:73) may imply that the Rambam may not agree with the above view. In the passage in *Moreh Nevuchim*, Rambam discusses the philosophy of a group known as "Ashari," whose adherents claim that man bears no liability whatsoever for his actions. After all, since the world is constantly recreated, the action in one "frame" is independent of that in the next one. The fact that the next moment happens to be created in a way that follows the previous one is Hashem's decision alone, not man's. As such, one who pulled the trigger did only that; the movement of the bullet and the subsequent murder have nothing to do with him, and thus he should not be assigned any culpability. The Rambam ridicules this view as the epitome of foolishness. How, then, can constant recreation be woven into the fabric of the Rambam's Ikkarim?

Upon closer examination, it becomes clear that this passage poses no difficulty at all.

Let's take a step back for a moment. Regardless of the Rambam's position, there are others, such as the Nefesh HaChaim mentioned above, who certainly subscribe to an understanding of some form of constant creation. How do these adherents explain why man is culpable for his actions if in fact the world is created anew each moment? The answer, quite simply, is that Hakadosh Baruch Hu refreshes the world's existence within the pattern we call *teva*, nature, which is designed to obscure Him from our view. Therefore, we can count on certain results following certain actions. Theoretically, the bullet does not have to continue its trajectory, but Hakadosh Baruch Hu tells me in advance that if I choose to pull the trigger, the next frame following my action will be in sync with that action, as per the system of *teva*. Knowing this, I am liable for my decision. To shrug off responsibility and negate the possibility of reward and punishment by blaming Hakadosh Baruch Hu is not only ludicrous, but flies in the face of everything He tells us about the purpose of our lives. With this in mind, we can return to the Rambam's utter rejection of the Ashari philosophy. The Ashari maintained that man could not possibly be liable for any actions he would take, due to the disconnect between action and result. Such a position, absolving mankind of responsibility for their actions, is anathema to the very basics of our beliefs, and certainly deserves to be utterly rejected, even by those who clearly endorse constant recreation. As such, that which the Rambam dismisses the Ashari view is most understandable, and would seemingly bear no indication of the Rambam's stance on constant recreation. It is the absurd notion that man bears no responsibility that is rejected, not the concept of constant recreation itself.

In truth, however, a careful reading of the passage in *Moreh*

Nevuchim reveals that the Rambam is not addressing the concept of constant recreation at all, but is, rather, condemning the adherents of the Ashari philosophy because of their renunciation of *bechirah*. They believe in determinism, thinking that Hashem alone decides which actions will happen, and man is therefore utterly incapable of anything, even pulling the trigger. According to this worldview, we are essentially no more than puppets acting out Hashem's decisions, and have no free will at all. Understandably, these ideas are antithetical to Judaism, for they negate the possibility of mankind having any real purpose or accountability. This is a more fundamental issue than constant creation and goes well beyond attempting to disconnect the final result from the initial step. It is this heresy that the Rambam rails against, not constant recreation.

Ikkar 2 —
The Words of Shema Yisrael

*A*lthough Hashem is in charge of all world events, we nevertheless refer to Him as *Elokeinu*, **our** God, in recognition of His enhanced Hashgachah over the Jewish people, as opposed to humanity at large (see Rabbeinu Bechaye and other Rishonim). The Name יְ-הֹ-וָ-ה, on the other hand, is not unique to Hashem's relationship with the Jewish people, as this Name refers to His role as the absolute and eternal Master of the world, which pertains equally to Jew and non-Jew alike, as well as to every particle in the universe.

❧

The concept of Hashem's absolute *yichud*, meaning that there is no force in existence except Him, is reflected in the *Shulchan Aruch's* statement (*Orach Chaim* 61:6) that when reciting the word *echad* in *Shema*, one should bear in mind that Hashem is the absolute ruler of heaven and earth and that His rule extends to all *four* "corners" of the earth.

Ikkar 4 — First Existence, and Creation With a Purpose

This Ikkar is a bit of an enigma. At face value, the concept of Kadmus — that Hashem existed prior to our universe or any other matter — would seem to follow logically from the first Ikkar, which establishes Him as the Creator and Supervisor of the world. After all, creations necessarily postdate their creator. Why, then, is there a need for an additional Ikkar establishing Hashem as being the original existence?

Our presentation of this Ikkar provided a possible answer in line with the paradigm we followed throughout this book, as discussed in the introduction. In short, it appears that the Rambam's intention in delineating these Ikkarim was not to present theological arguments to convince those in doubt, but rather to establish basic tenets for those who already accept the truth of the Torah. Consequently, although Ikkarim may overlap to some extent, each one contains a separate and unique emphasis and yields a specific concept that we must incorporate into our lives.

One can ask, however, why the concept we have focused on in Ikkar 4 — that of our being created with a purpose — emanates from this Ikkar more than from the first Ikkar. Do we serve Him because He was here first, or because He is the Creator?

A careful reading of the Rambam's words provides the answer. Unlike the standard Ani Maamin abbreviated version, the Rambam's version of the first Ikkar does not focus on His creation of the world or relationship with others, but rather seeks to describe His personal essence, identifying Him as completely independent and untethered. Unlike Him, we are completely dependent upon myriad external factors; we humans and our habitat are

mentioned only as a vivid contrast to His existence. Ikkar 4, however, describes the sequence of existence. Sequence is necessarily
a function of relationship: this came first, that came second. Therefore, we understand this Ikkar as a depiction of our relationship
vis-a-vis Him, whereas the first Ikkar is a statement about Him
only.

This understanding appears to be corroborated by a statement
of the Rambam in *Hilchos Teshuvah* (3:7), where he uses these
words to describe a person who rejects this fourth Ikkar: הָאוֹמֵר
שֶׁאֵינוֹ לְבַדּוֹ רִאשׁוֹן וְצוּר לַכֹּל, *one who denies that He alone was originally
extant and fashioned everything*. Clearly, integral to this Ikkar is
the concept that He created our universe and maintains a relationship with it. It is here, then, that His role as our Creator is
emphasized.

Ikkar 7 — Clear Prophecy

*I*n this Ikkar, the focus is on the disparity between the prophetic abilities of Moshe Rabbeinu and those of other *nevi'im*. Moshe Rabbeinu's perfect clarity of prophetic vision
yielded a comprehensive *nevuah*, whereas the other *nevi'im* perceived far less detail. We likened this to the difference between a
black-and-white photo and one with crisp, vivid color.

This gives rise to the question of whether the visions of the other *nevi'im* left room for error or misinterpretation. Was their vision
unmistakably clear, just less vivid than Moshe's, or did their view
of these prophetic communications through an *aspaklaria she'einah me'irah* — a translucent lens — require them to interpret the
nevuah according to their own powers of reasoning?

The Rambam states emphatically (*Moreh Nevuchim* 3:24) that
the *nevi'im* perceived their visions with utmost clarity, leaving
absolutely no room for error. Otherwise, says the Rambam, Avraham Avinu would not have been able to heed the command of the
Akeidah, as he would have had to assume that such a mission,

which ran diametrically counter to the Divine values he had previously understood and adhered to, was simply a misinterpretation on his part. Avraham Avinu was able to proceed only due to the absolutely clear and unmistakable nature of the *nevuah* he received. This position seems to be echoed as well by the Ramchal (*Derech Hashem chelek* 3, 4:1), although, as Ramchal explains, there may be more than one element in a prophecy, not all of which are specified in the prophecy. Thus, Yonah knew that Nineveh would be "overturned," but did not know that it would be overturned spiritually, not physically.

For more on this subject, see *Avi Ezri, Hilchos Yesodei HaTorah* 7:6, based on *Teshuvos Maharil Diskin*.

Ikkar 7 — Can Parity With Moshe's Nevuah Ever Be Achieved?

*T*his Ikkar, as we described, establishes that the level of Moshe Rabbeinu's prophecy can never be exceeded. It does not, however, address the question of whether that level could be matched. For the purposes of this Ikkar, the fact that Moshe Rabbeinu's clarity of vision could not be exceeded is sufficient, for it precludes the possibility that a later individual could ever uproot the Torah by claiming to possess clearer vision. Even if someone of equal stature were to subsequently come on the scene, he would be unable to challenge Toras Moshe, insofar as the clarity of Moshe's transmission of the Torah is unimpeachable.

Yet the Torah does in fact guarantee that no other *navi* on par with Moshe will ever arise, as it states, in one of its final verses (*Devarim* 34:10): וְלֹא קָם נָבִיא עוֹד בְּיִשְׂרָאֵל כְּמשֶׁה אֲשֶׁר יְדָעוֹ ה' פָּנִים אֶל פָּנִים, *Never again has there arisen in Israel a prophet like Moshe, whom Hashem had known face to face.* This does not seem to be an outgrowth of the need to ensure the Torah's unimpeachability, but is, rather, an axiom established by the Torah, much like any other truth the Torah sets forth.

Interestingly, Chazal note that the above verse says that no *Jewish navi* ever achieved Moshe's level of prophecy, which implies that an exception arose in the non-Jewish world, in the form of Bilam. Understanding this statement at face value raises numerous difficulties. Consequently, some opine that the level Moshe Rabbeinu attained was integral, whereas Bilam was gifted with this level as a temporary phenomenon, akin to the phenomenon of even lowly individuals perceiving some level of prophetic vision during the splitting of the Yam Suf. Others say that Bilam's prophetic visions featured one or more specific qualities that were otherwise unique to Moshe, but his overall *nevuah* bore no resemblance to Moshe's.

Regardless of how one understands the nature of Bilam's prophecy, it poses no challenge to the Ikkar at hand. As we explained, the existence of a *navi* equal to Moshe Rabbeinu would not undermine the Torah's integrity, and the possibility of such a *navi* arising is proscribed only by the above statement of the Torah itself. Since that verse specifically alludes to the exception that was Bilam, by stipulating that no prophet like Moshe has ever arisen *in Israel*, the fact that a non-Jewish prophet did achieve some parity with Moshe presents no difficulty.

Why, in fact, does the Torah rule out, at least generally, the possibility of any other *navi* attaining Moshe Rabbeinu's level of prophetic clarity? The answer is that for a person to receive prophecy, he must first work to reach a lofty spiritual level, and then he is granted special Divine assistance, which propels him to a higher plateau of *nevuah* and closeness to Hakadosh Baruch Hu (see, for example, *Seforno, Devarim* 34:10). Moshe Rabbeinu received a unique measure of this Divine assistance in order to facilitate his perfect transmission of the Torah to us for all time (see *Sefer HaIkkarim* 3:12). This was a one-time, specific need, and once the need was met, there was no longer a reason for Hakadosh Baruch Hu to communicate with any *navi* this way, even if a person would theoretically attain a spiritual level identical to that of Moshe Rabbeinu. (See *Derashos HaRan, Derush* 4; Rambam, *Moreh Nevuchim* 2:39; and *Ohr Hashem*, by Rav Chisdai Crescas, *Maamar* 2, *Klal* 4, Ch. 3.)

Ikkar 11 — Reward as a Motivation

*A*s discussed within the main work, we are told in *Maseches Avos* that we are not to serve Hakadosh Baruch Hu in order to receive reward. The widely accepted understanding is that reward should not be part of our calculation: Ideally we are to perform mitzvos and avoid *aveiros* because it is Hakadosh Baruch Hu's will. Compensation, though it will assuredly be doled out, is not on our agenda. Anything less than altruistic mitzvah observance constitutes a flaw in our Divine service.

This approach is not universal, however. The Baalei HaTosafos write (*Pesachim* 8b s.v. *Sheyizkeh, Rosh Hashanah* 4a s.v. *Bishvil*; see also Rema, *Yoreh Deah* 220:15 and *Biur HaGra* §20) that the Mishnah's intent is simply to urge people not to do mitzvos solely for the sake of reward. If a person performs mitzvos only because he knows a prize awaits him, then his actions are flawed. If, however, he serves Hashem with a hybrid intention — at heart, he wants to serve Hashem, but he is also aiming to receive reward — then he is, in fact, a model citizen, even a *tzaddik gamur*.

Regardless, the exact parameters of the Mishnah's directive do not impact our understanding of this Ikkar. As discussed, the focus of the Ikkar is the awareness that our actions generate reward or punishment. It is this reality, not the motivation behind our actions, that is being discussed.

Ikkar 13 — The Rambam's View of Techiyas HaMeisim

*A*s mentioned within the discussion of this Ikkar, the Rambam penned a lengthy letter, *Maamar Techiyas Ha-Meisim*, on this topic, elaborating on the sources for Techiyas HaMeisim within the words of Torah, and demonstrating that the Torah considers the acceptance of this idea to be of critical importance. Apparently, there were those who sought to spread malicious rumors about the Rambam, alleging that he in fact did not believe in the veracity of Techiyas HaMeisim. The Rambam responded by dismissing those who attacked him, providing numerous sources to illustrate that not only was he of firm belief in Techiyas HaMeisim, there would be no possibility of any believing Jew to say otherwise, as Techiyas HaMeisim is a well established concept enshrined in the Torah.

The surest way to do this would be to limit the discussion, and simply say that since the *chachamim* clearly identified this concept as one well-sourced in the Torah, challenging this concept is as unacceptable as challenging any other fundamental Torah precept. Regardless of the Rambam's intent, however, we are still left in the dark as to the function of Techiyas HaMeisim.

There are those (e.g., a letter writer to Rav Yitzchak Hutner, *Pachad Yitzchak*, *Igros* 50) who understand the Rambam's words to mean that the problem with not believing in Techiyas HaMeisim is that this will cause one to undermine additional parts of the Torah, and will therefore result in *kefirah*. Yet a careful reading of the Rambam shows that he was not explaining the severity of rejecting this concept at all. He simply wrote that there are those who cannot accept the possibility of Techiyas HaMeisim, as it runs counter to the natural rules of the world as we know it. To this, the Rambam responds that attempting to refute the concept of Techiyas HaMeisim on account of its supernatural nature is illogical, as there are countless other instances in the Torah of nature-defying events, such as Moshe's stick turning into a snake. Anyone bothered by the miraculous nature of Techiyas HaMeisim has a much bigger issue on his hands — the entire concept of *nissim*. Techiyas HaMeisim is no more of a novelty than the miracles recorded by the Torah, and believing in it is therefore perfectly reasonable.

Appendix B
The Daas Imperative

Over the generations, much has been said in the context of the debate over what is the correct path to attaining emunah. Should one take the path of intense philosophical debate, engaging in proofs and counterproofs to clarify our beliefs through strenuous logical exercise, or should one opt for the route of *emunah peshutah*, taking a simple, unquestioning approach by relying on the great people before us and accepting with unwavering trust the tradition they passed down to us? Is one obligated to question, or is questioning forbidden?

It is quite possible that the correct approach is a confluence of the two paths (see, for example, *Sichos Mussar* by Rav Chaim Shmuelevitz, *Maamar* 52). Aside from the theoretical question of which is right, there is also the matter of practical *chinuch*, and ascertaining the ideal path is likely dependent on the specific needs and background of each particular audience. It is said that Rav Yerucham Levovitz, *mashgiach* of the Mir Yeshiva in Poland, would engage in intense philosophical discussion with the *bachurim* who came to the yeshivah from Germany, but would shut down the conversation when in proximity to *bachurim* from Eastern Europe.

Although wading into this larger debate is beyond the purview of this work, in the context of the Ikkarim it is worthwhile to clarify the Rambam's perspective.

While the Rambam himself engaged in extensive logical

analysis and certainly deemed this beneficial, the question remains: Did he view this analysis as obligatory? Does he maintain that the mitzvah of emunah mandates that a person engage in such pursuit? Is a person required to challenge his beliefs until he can prove them incontrovertibly?

The Rambam in several places delineates our obligation to believe in Hashem, using similar language. He expresses this concept just prior to his discussion of the Thirteen Ikkarim, and in his *Yad HaChazakah* (*Hilchos Yesodei HaTorah* 1:1), where he states: יְסוֹד הַיְסוֹדוֹת וְעַמּוּד הַחָכְמוֹת לֵידַע שֶׁיֵּשׁ שָׁם מָצוּי רִאשׁוֹן, *The foundation of all foundations, and the pillar of all wisdom, is to know that there is a First Being*. The word he uses is *leida*, connoting knowledge (*daas*), as opposed to *lehaamin*, which means to believe. Is the Rambam mandating logical pursuit of the grounds for emunah?[1]

What exactly is *daas*? We suggest the following. The Torah's first reference to *daas* is in the context of Adam HaRishon's relationship with Chavah: וְהָאָדָם יָדַע אֶת חַוָּה אִשְׁתּוֹ, *Now the man had known his wife Chavah* (*Bereishis* 4:1). Looking to the next words, which describe how Chavah bore children, it becomes clear that *daas* here refers to engaging in marital relations. Why would a physical act be referred to as one of *daas*, knowledge, something far removed from the physical?

Another interesting use of the term *daas* is in reference to a child's coming of age, at which point he is described as a *bar daas*. While a child's intellect certainly develops during his formative years, why do we use this specific term to denote adulthood? Even if the focus here is on the person's intellectual maturity, why employ the term *daas* as opposed to, say, *chochmah* or *binah*?

Knowledge, we recognize, is the domain of the brain. It is there that we store all the information we have amassed, and it is there that we calculate and assess possible courses of action, weighing

---

1. Adding to the intrigue, in *Sefer HaMitzvos* (Positive Mitzvah 1) the Rambam writes that we are commanded *lehaamin*, as opposed to *leida*. Inasmuch as *Sefer HaMitzvos* is a translation from Arabic, however, the literary subtleties and nuances in this work are less significant; see glosses to Frankel edition.

our choices based on the data we have accumulated. There are, however, different forms of knowledge.

To illustrate: Suppose terrorists strike in a remote town in Afghanistan, causing hundreds of casualties. You hear the news, feel sobered momentarily, and move on. Then, you hear about a terrorist attack that occurred near the Kosel, in which a young man was killed on his way to Shacharis. You recognize the name — it's someone you know. He wasn't necessarily your friend, but you've met him a few times over the years. Suddenly, the news is hitting you hard. Your heart goes out to his family, and you feel a stab of pain. What is the difference between these two stories? Is it that one is true and the other is not? Hardly. Both are backed up by credible reports, and you have no reason to doubt either one. From a factual viewpoint, both are accurate and tragic. And yet one remains squarely in your mind, an unemotional piece of data to be filed away, while the other permeates your being, traveling from your brain to your heart. It moves you emotionally, and it spurs you to action. This type of knowledge is called *daas*.[2]

Yirmiyahu HaNavi bemoans the terrible state to which Klal Yisrael has fallen, exhorting the nation to return to the way of Hashem to stave off disaster. Among other iniquities, he lists this (*Yirmiyah* 2:8): וְתֹפְשֵׂי הַתּוֹרָה לֹא יְדָעוּנִי, *Those charged with teaching the Torah did not know Me*. The notion of a Torah scholar lacking *daas* appears in other places as well (see, for example, *Vayikra Rabbah* 1:15), but this seems difficult to understand. If these were the teachers of Torah, how could they lack knowledge? With the above understanding, this *pasuk* is readily understood. These scholars certainly possessed knowledge of Torah, and were eminently well-versed in its intricacies. The problem was that their knowledge stopped right there. They should have been the standard-bearers for Klal Yisrael, with their actions reflecting the Torah they represented. Instead, their Torah remained theoretical, as their actions, tragically, did not follow suit.

---

2. See, for instance, Ramban, *Bereishis* 2:9; Ibn Ezra, *Bereishis* 31:20; and *Shiurei Daas*, R' Yosef Leib Bloch, "*Chochmah Binah V'Deiah*," p. 158.

Adam HaRishon recognized that Chavah was his destined partner, but that knowledge didn't remain in his brain. It was tangible enough to move him to action.

A young child lacks self-control, and typically expresses his desires by crying, screaming, or making demands. Even as he grows older and his intellect develops, a gap remains between what he knows and the way he behaves. As he matures, he can be expected to control his impulses, placing his mind in charge of his actions. At that point, he crosses a threshold, and his mitzvos and *aveiros* begin to carry legal significance. Now, he is a *bar daas*.

We can suggest, then, that when the Rambam states that we are obligated to know — *leida* — that there is a Creator, he is referring not to a philosophical pursuit, but rather to the inculcation of our emunah to the point that it reaches our heart. A person must know that there is one God, that the Torah is His word, and that He rewards those who fulfill the Torah and punishes those who do not. Yet this knowledge must not be restricted to the intellectual sphere. It must permeate a person's heart, and propel him to action.

Chochmah is not enough — we need *daas*, to ensure that the way we live reflects our ideals. The more we work on building *daas* and enhancing our mind-heart-action connection, the more natural our mitzvah observance will become, and the more intrinsic our emunah will become.

Appendix C
Comparing the Words of the Rambam, Ani Maamin, and Yigdal

*T*he focus of this work has been the thirteen Ikkarim, as enumerated in the Rambam's introduction to the last *perek* of *Maseches Sanhedrin*, as well as in the thirteen Ani Maamins found in the siddur, which are based on the Rambam's words. The siddur actually contains another expression of these thirteen principles, in the Yigdal prayer recited by many Ashkenazim before Shacharis, and by many Sefardim at the conclusion of the Friday evening *tefillah*. Yigdal contains thirteen stanzas, each one a poetic rendition of the corresponding Ikkar. Comparing these three versions and noting the divergences between them sheds additional light on their meaning.

Authorship:

*T*he **Rambam** wrote these Ikkarim in Arabic. They appear in his commentary to the Mishnah, which the Rambam completed at the age of thirty, in the year 1168.

The **Ani Maamin** version was not written by him; it was based on the Rambam's principles. It first appeared in siddurim beginning in the later part of the 16th century, over 300 years after the Rambam's demise. Astoundingly, the vast acceptance of these words notwithstanding, we have no inkling as to who authored them. Interestingly, numerous Sephardic *siddurim* feature wording that varies greatly.

It is unclear who authored **Yigdal**. The *Siddur Yaavetz* states that the author was none other than the Rambam himself, though at a later point he suggests a different author. Others also name the Rambam as the author (Maharashdam in *Sefer Ben Shmuel*; the author of *Sefer Amudei Avodah* writes that he came upon an old handwritten Roman *machzor*, which bore an inscription above the words of Yigdal stating that this hymn was composed by the Rambam). Ascribing Yigdal to the Rambam fits remarkably well, considering that the nuances of Yigdal generally align perfectly with the Rambam's words, as demonstrated below (with the exception of the later Ikkarim, where minor divergences appear). Others, however, ascribe authorship of Yigdal to a Rav Daniel Bar Dovid HaDayan of Italy (see *Siddur Avodas Yisrael*) or to a poet named Emanuel of Rome. For elaboration on these and other possibilities, see *Mekorei HaTefillah* pp. 9-10.

First Ikkar

*T*he **Ani Maamin** version emphasizes Hashem's creation of the world (*Borei*) as well as His constant *hashgachah* and management of what goes on (*Manhig*).

The **Rambam**'s first Ikkar, however, discusses the absolute nature of Hakadosh Baruch Hu. He mentions creation only as a comparison to the essence of Hakadosh Baruch Hu: We are finite creations, while He is infinite and unlimited in every way. His nature is utterly independent, while we are entirely dependent. His creation of our world is only incidental to this Ikkar, and the concept of *Manhig* does not appear at all.

The **Yigdal** version follows the Rambam, simply stating: נִמְצָא

וְאֵין עֵת אֶל מְצִיאוּתוֹ — He exists, and His existence is not subject to constraints of time or space.

Second Ikkar

*T*he **Ani Maamin** version presents the concept of Yichud — the oneness and unity of Hakadosh Baruch Hu — emphasizing that no other power exists. The line concludes with the words: הָיָה הֹוֶה וְיִהְיֶה, declaring that He is not bound by time, having always existed, and He will be in existence forever. It is not clear why these words have any relevance to this particular Ikkar, as the Ikkar discusses the negation of any other power, not matters of time.

The **Rambam**'s version makes no mention of time.

The **Yigdal** version, as well, speaks only of His infinite oneness, with no reference to time. (Perhaps the author of Ani Maamin wished to stress that just as Hashem's absolute unity fills all of space, it also fills all of time, leaving no void. This, then, would be included in the words אֵין סוֹף לְאַחְדּוּתוֹ in Yigdal.)

Fourth Ikkar

*T*he **Ani Maamin** version refers to Hakadosh Baruch Hu as the first and the last to exist (*Rishon* and *Acharon*), meaning that He is above any concept of time, and is not tethered to our world's existence.

The **Rambam**, though, as noted within the main work, refers only to His being the absolute first existence, with no mention of His being last to exist as well. The emphasis is clearly on negating the notion that the universe has existed forever (*Olam Kadmon*).

Yigdal again reflects the Rambam's words perfectly: רִאשׁוֹן וְאֵין רֵאשִׁית לְרֵאשִׁיתוֹ — He is first, and nothing could possibly have predated Him. No mention is made of *Acharon*.

Fifth Ikkar

*T*he focus of the **Ani Maamin** version is on *tefillah*, emphasizing that we turn to Him alone in prayer.

The **Rambam** does not stress the matter of *tefillah* specifically, but rather deals with the overarching concept of *avodah*, Divine service. The emphasis is on the negation of any hybrid system that allows for *avodah zarah* to complement our belief in Hashem.

Yigdal makes no mention of *tefillah*, referring only to the absolute sovereignty and grandeur of Hakadosh Baruch Hu.

Sixth and Seventh Ikkarim

*T*he **Ani Maamin** version expresses that the words of the prophets are true, and that the prophecy of Moshe Rabbeinu is true, as if to remove any doubt as to whether their claim of having received *nevuah* was false. The glaring issue here is that insofar as Moshe Rabbeinu was one of the prophets, why is the seventh Ikkar necessary? It would seem to be a detail within the sixth.

The **Rambam**'s version of the sixth Ikkar, however, does not affirm the integrity of the prophets themselves, but attests to the veracity of the concept of *nevuah*, establishing that Hakadosh Baruch Hu does in fact communicate with man. The next Ikkar, as well, does not pertain to Moshe Rabbeinu's truthfulness, but rather establishes that his prophetic visions were of utmost clarity, so no prophet can ever undermine the Torah by claiming clearer vision. [In this vein, even the closing words of the Ani Maamin stating that "he was the father of all other *nevi'im*" is not a full expression of the Rambam's principle; the Rambam was not discussing Moshe's relative superiority as ranked against others. He spoke of the absolute nature of Moshe Rabbeinu's prophecy being fundamentally unsurpassable].

The words of **Yigdal** once again align with the Rambam: The sixth Ikkar states: שֶׁפַע נְבוּאָתוֹ נְתָנוֹ אֶל אַנְשֵׁי סְגֻלָּתוֹ וְתִפְאַרְתּוֹ — He granted *nevuah* to select individuals; prophecy exists. The seventh Ikkar is expressed as: לֹא קָם בְּיִשְׂרָאֵל כְּמֹשֶׁה עוֹד — Moshe's prophetic ability is unrivaled. Neither of these two mention the concept of truthfulness.

Tenth Ikkar

*T*he **Ani Maamin** version emphasizes that Hakadosh Baruch Hu knows not only our actions but our thoughts as well.

The **Rambam** discusses only knowledge of our actions, not our thoughts. It would seem likely, though, that His understanding of our thoughts would be implicit as well, given that this would constitute an integral aspect of knowing our actions, insofar as an action cannot be fully grasped and/or assessed without understanding the thought process and motivations that generated it.

The **Yigdal** version does not explicitly refer to thoughts or actions, but rather to סְתָרֵינוּ, our secrets, or things that are hidden. This term often refers to actions committed in private, in which case this version follows the Rambam in speaking of actions. [It is possible, however, that the intention is to that which is hidden within us, referring to our thoughts. If so, however, it would create a peculiarity insofar as reference is made only to thoughts, whereas reference to actions is left out entirely.]

Eleventh Ikkar

*T*he **Ani Maamin** version describes the concept of reward and punishment for our actions.

Besides delineating the core concept of reward and punishment, the **Rambam** adds that necessarily included in this Ikkar is a basic awareness of the nature of these consequences, namely, Olam Haba and *kareis*, respectively.

Yigdal does not mention Olam Haba and *kareis* specifically, referring only to the ultimate meting out of reward and punishment.

Twelfth Ikkar

*T*he **Ani Maamin** version speaks of belief in the coming of Mashiach, and the obligation to anxiously await him.

The **Rambam**, in addition to these concepts, mandates a belief in the restoration of the monarchy to the Davidic dynasty.

Yigdal does not mention the restoration of monarchy.

An Additional Note:

*T*he Ani Maamin version stresses that even if Mashiach takes interminably long to arrive, אֲחַכֶּה לוֹ בְּכָל יוֹם שֶׁיָבוֹא — I nevertheless anxiously await his arrival every day. These words have sparked much discussion. Are we to believe every single day that he will arrive that day? If so, this would seem to conflict with Chazal's enumeration of various days when Mashiach cannot arrive. A suggested resolution would be to insert a comma before the word שֶׁיָבוֹא, rendering the phrase to mean: "Every day, I await his arrival." In other words, every day of my life I anxiously await him, whenever he will come.

Regardless, this conundrum relates only to the Ani Maamin version. The Rambam, while emphasizing the imperative to await him — חַכֶּה לוֹ — makes no mention of the בְּכָל יוֹם שֶׁיָבוֹא angle.

Opposition to Yigdal

*H*istorically, some have voiced opposition to Yigdal, based on two possible objections. The first, more fundamental, objection relates to the issue of promoting specific Torah concepts to a primary role, beyond other portions of the Torah (Arizal, cited in *Pri Etz Chaim* and by R' Yaakov Emden in *Siddur Yaavetz*). The second objection relates to a practical concern: that highlighting certain elements of the Torah may cause unlearned individuals to see these Ikkarim as the sum total of what they need to know, and develop a disregard for other parts of Torah (Maharil, *Likutim, siman* 59 s.v. *Amar*). This objection echoes the halachic prohibition on reciting the Aseres HaDibros in a public setting,[3] for the very same reason.

Neither objection relates to Yigdal specifically; they reject the concept of Ikkarim in toto. Remarkably, some will steadfastly avoid reciting Yigdal, citing the opposition of the Arizal, while having no compunctions about the institution that is Ani Maamin. Since the objections to Yigdal were based not on its actual wording, but on the underlying concept of Ikkarim, the objections apply equally, if not more, to Ani Maamin, leaving no logical room to reject one and embrace the other.

Although the Arizal did in fact have an additional reservation about Yigdal, this again was not specific to Yigdal, but was, rather, part of an overarching opposition to the recitation of any *tefillos* not originating in ancient times. The Arizal, as cited by R' Chaim Vital in *Pri Etz Chaim*, felt that only earlier authors, such as the Anshei Knesses HaGedolah or R' Elazar HaKalir, knew how to properly structure the kabbalistic angle of the *tefillos*. Insofar as the widespread custom in Klal Yisrael today is to recite all sorts of *tefillos* composed at far later dates, such as those of the Chida and the Shelah, there should be no grounds for singling out Yigdal in particular for omission.

---

3. See *Berachos* 12a and Rashi there, as well as Rambam, *Peirush HaMishnayos, Tamid* 5:1. This view is the accepted halachah, restricting any group recital of the Aseres HaDibros; see Rema OC 1:5 and *Mishnah Berurah* 16.

    Some go as far as to object even to standing during the reading of the Aseres HaDibros during the standard Torah reading, for fear that doing so would incorrectly attribute greater significance to this specific portion of the Torah; see Rambam, *Teshuvos* 263. To avoid such a misunderstanding, some begin standing a verse or two before the Aseres HaDibros.

Appendix D
Miracles vs. Free Will (Ikkar 1)

*W*hen was the last time you saw an open miracle? Most likely, experiencing a moment of remarkable serendipity, or a miraculous return from the jaws of death, is the closest any of us ever came to that. Aside from these rare glimpses, however, most of the time we must summon focus, patience, and perspective to recognize Hashem's hand in what is happening and to appreciate what He does for us. We can perceive His Presence, and even feel it, but it certainly isn't blatantly obvious, as He is not performing visible miracles at every turn. On the contrary, the developments we witness often seem to raise question marks regarding His conduct, and His plan for the world can be difficult to decipher. Indeed, Hakadosh Baruch Hu is described as *"Keil Mistater"* — the hidden God (*Yeshayah* 45:15), operating from behind a screen.

Perusing the *parshiyos* of the Torah, we encounter a vastly different form of Divine conduct, in which miracles abound and the hand of Hashem is most evident. The ten nature-defying plagues in Egypt showcased the power of Hakadosh Baruch Hu, as did the subsequent miracles at the Sea and in the desert. The *mahn*, a wondrous superfood, fell with exquisite precision, while water flowed from a rock, sustaining millions of people. When people defied Hashem's wishes, Hakadosh Baruch Hu's control was on full display as the earth swallowed Korach and his followers, or as Bilam's donkey opened its mouth to mock him.

What changed? Why did the people of those eras merit clarity and visibility, while we remain clouded by the fog of nature? Furthermore, long after the Jews left the Wilderness, the miracles kept happening, albeit no longer on a national scale. The Gemara recounts numerous stories of Tannaim and Amoraim who experienced miracles as a part of their daily routine. R' Daniel bar Katina would walk through his garden, noting which areas needed rain, and rain would then fall on those precise spots. R' Chanina ben Dosa's wife once went to get oven mitts to remove loaves of bread baking in her oven, even though her abject poverty left her with no ingredients to bake. Her confidence was not unfounded; bread appeared in the oven.

The Ramban famously addresses this point at the end of *Parashas Bo*, explaining that Hakadosh Baruch Hu's general modus operandi is to avoid open miracles entirely. He doesn't want to show His hand openly, and rather hides behind the cloak of obscurity, making it our job to come find Him. The open miracles described throughout the Torah were unique exceptions, to prove to the world that He exists and demonstrate how He operates. Once we've witnessed those exceptions, we are to use them as prototypes to understand all the rest of the world's operation.

The question remains, however, why many Amoraim did experience miraculous occurrences. Additionally, why would Hakadosh Baruch Hu have an aversion to miracles in the first place?

A miracle is no more a direct manifestation of Hashem than is nature. Everything, wondrous or banal, emanates directly from Him. The difference between miracle and nature is simply a matter of operating styles. There is a way to style events to appear constant, as if in a self-perpetuating system, and there is a way to style events to clearly show that they are not following rules, but are being actively manipulated. Each style evinces a different impression, but it is the same artist drawing the picture.

The Beis HaLevi (*Maamar HaBitachon*), among others, explains that Hakadosh Baruch Hu favors the operating style of obscurity because He wishes to maximize the purpose of creating this world, which is to bestow reward upon humanity. A key element of the ability to earn reward is *bechirah*, the possibility of exercising free will in choosing right from wrong. Only when people have the ability to make tough decisions are they truly able to earn reward for their actions.

Suppose that the moment a person shook his lulav and esrog, gold coins would come raining down from the sky. Or suppose that the moment a person spoke *lashon hara*, he would suddenly turn mute. Would we still have free choice? If the consequences of each of our decisions were immediately evident, we would be rendered completely choiceless. Likewise, if Hakadosh Baruch Hu were to keep intervening openly in world events, any argument for agnosticism would evaporate, making it impossible to perform any *aveirah* at all. In other words, it is the facade of nature and constancy that obscures Him to the degree that facilitates free choice. Since the focus of our lives is the struggle to fulfill Hashem's will in the face of challenge, a system that routinely allowed for miracles, thereby negating the element of challenge, would contradict our very raison d'être.

With this in mind, we can explain why select individuals of distinction experienced miracles on a regular basis. If a person understands with total clarity that everything that occurs in life, including the most mundane aspects of *teva*, are functions of the transparent hand of Hashem, then he will be no more impressed if his bowl of cereal suddenly levitates off the table than he is by the force of gravity that usually holds his bowl in place. To him, there is no difference between the miraculous and the natural; it's just a matter of which way Hashem prefers. Once he has achieved such clarity of emunah, his *bechirah* will not be affected by a nature-defying act, as he views all of nature itself as Divine. A routine rainfall, then, is just as wondrous as a crop-specific one. Bread appearing effortlessly in the oven is no less a gift from Above than bread that was baked from ingredients kneaded into dough. No concern exists that this person's free choice will be negated, as he has already surmounted this battlefront.

To employ a popular analogy: Suppose it's Purim afternoon, and a person in disguise enters your home. At first, you have no idea who he is, but after a few minutes, you suddenly realize whose face is behind the mask. With his cover blown, the person removes his mask, revealing himself. After all, once you know who he is, there's no longer any point in his pretending.

Indeed, Purim itself is a prime illustration of this point. We are told that *"Esther sof kol hanissim"* — the story of Esther is the last of the miracles. Rather than interpreting this as a statement of loss, the Midrash compares this phenomenon to the radiance of the dawn appearing over the horizon, heralding a bright day ahead. This can be understood in line with the above.

The story of Esther involved no earth-shattering miracles. Haman's edict of annihilation was followed by the intense lobbying of an "insider" and her family, resulting in the reversal of said edict. These things happen. Lobbyists have clout. Last-minute salvation? Certainly, but without any jaw-dropping wonders. The entire saga constituted a series of natural events.

Klal Yisrael, we know, merited salvation by recognizing the error of their ways and repenting for having partaken of the banquet of Achashveirosh. Yet several years had passed between that event and the decree of annihilation. Rather than being spurred to repentance after witnessing open and immediate retribution, they did *teshuvah* via a process of deep introspection. Was their salvation a miracle? Technically yes, but its occurrence within a "natural" setting created implications far greater than any supernatural miracle. Klal Yisrael learned from this to delve into natural events — events that could easily be explained away — and realize that these, too, are direct interventions by Hashem, a means of calling for *teshuvah*.

This recognition is the end of all miracles. After all, what is a miracle? Generally, this distinction is reserved for a remarkable aberration from the standard course of nature. Naturally, water flows evenly. A body of water parting spontaneously is a miracle insofar as it defies the paradigm we accept as a given. If, however, we wean ourselves off the concept that nature's rules govern the behavior of the universe, and view nature as well as His hand at work, then any aberrations lose significance, as both miracle and nature are essentially equal. In a sense, no rules were truly broken when miracles occurred; Hakadosh Baruch Hu simply opted, at those moments, to employ a different style. Once a person reaches this recognition, miracles, in a sense, no longer exist. You've seen the magician's handbook, so the tricks no longer carry any allure.

This idea holds major significance for our own lives. We need Hakadosh Baruch Hu's help in so many ways, and we know He's there, watching over us and caring for us as only He can — yet He's operating under cover. If we're seeking His intervention in our lives, we can look to the prototype of the great individuals for whom miracles were commonplace. True, none of us come anywhere near their elevated levels of belief. We can, however, follow their model. The more ironclad we consider the rules of nature, the less likely it is that He will create even minimal aberrations to help us. After all, His goal is to maintain our *bechirah*. But if we realize that the reins have never left His hands, and see His hand in even the most mundane events, we rise to the point where wondrous solutions no longer seem shocking, and open the door to far greater possibilities of salvation.